'The chapters in this collection comprise a thoughtful and thought-provoking analysis of Melvin Burgess's innovative, yet often controversial, fiction. It's a must-read for any serious scholar, teacher or student of young adult literature.' – **Janet Alsup**, *Purdue University, USA*

Melvin Burgess has made a powerful name for himself in the world of children's and young adult literature, emerging in the 1990s as the author of over twenty critically acclaimed novels.

This collection of original essays by a team of established and new scholars introduces readers to the key debates surrounding Burgess's most challenging work, including controversial young adult novels *Junk* and *Doing It*. Covering a variety of critical and theoretical perspectives, the volume also presents exciting new readings of some of his less familiar fiction for children, and features an interview with the author.

Alison Waller is Senior Lecturer in Children's Literature at The University of Roehampton, UK.

This latest series of *New Casebooks* consists of brand new critical essays specially commissioned to provide students with fresh thinking about key texts and writers. Like the original series, the volumes embrace a range of approaches designed to illuminate the rich interchange between critical theory and critical practice.

New Casebooks
Collections of all new critical essays

CHILDREN'S LITERATURE

MELVIN BURGESS
Edited by Alison Waller

ROBERT CORMIER
Edited by Adrienne E. Gavin

ROALD DAHL
Edited by Ann Alston & Catherine Butler

C. S. LEWIS: *THE CHRONICLES OF NARNIA*
Edited by Michelle Ann Abate & Lance Weldy

J. K. ROWLING: *HARRY POTTER*
Edited by Cynthia J. Hallett & Peggy J. Huey

J. R. R. TOLKIEN: *THE HOBBIT & THE LORD OF THE RINGS*
Edited by Peter Hunt

NOVELS AND PROSE

JOHN FOWLES
Edited by James Acheson

FURTHER TITLES ARE IN PREPARATION

For a full list of published titles in the past format of the New Casebooks series, visit the series page at www.palgrave.com

---

New Casebooks Series

Series Standing Order
ISBN 978–0–333–71702–8 hardcover
ISBN 978–0–333–69345–2 paperback
(Outside North America only)

You can receive future titles in this series as they are published by placing a standing order. Please contact your bookseller or, in the case of difficulty, write to us at the address below with your name and address, the title of the series and the ISBN quoted above.
Customer Services Department, Macmillan Distribution Ltd, Houndmills, Basingstoke, Hampshire, RG21 6XS, UK

New Casebooks

MELVIN BURGESS

Edited by

ALISON WALLER

palgrave
macmillan

First published 2013 by
PALGRAVE MACMILLAN

Palgrave Macmillan in the UK is an imprint of Macmillan Publishers Limited, registered in England, company number 785998, of Houndmills, Basingstoke, Hampshire RG21 6XS.

Palgrave Macmillan in the US is a division of St Martin's Press LLC, 175 Fifth Avenue, New York, NY 10010.

Palgrave Macmillan is the global academic imprint of the above companies and has companies and representatives throughout the world.

Palgrave® and Macmillan® are registered trademarks in the United States, the United Kingdom, Europe and other countries.

ISBN 978–1–137–26280–6 hardback
ISBN 978–1–137–26279–0 paperback

This book is printed on paper suitable for recycling and made from fully managed and sustained forest sources. Logging, pulping and manufacturing processes are expected to conform to the environmental regulations of the country of origin.

A catalogue record for this book is available from the British Library.

A catalog record for this book is available from the Library of Congress.

Typeset by MPS Limited, Chennai

Contents

Series Editor's Preface

Welcome to the latest series of New Casebooks.

Each volume now presents brand new essays specially written for university and other students. Like the original series, the new-look New Casebooks embrace a range of recent critical approaches to the debates and issues that characterize the current discussion of literature.

Each editor has been asked to commission a sequence of original essays which will introduce the reader to the innovative critical approaches to the text or texts being discussed in the collection. The intention is to illuminate the rich interchange between critical theory and critical practice that today underpins so much writing about literature.

Editors have also been asked to supply an introduction to each volume that sets the scene for the essays that follow, together with a list of further reading which will enable readers to follow up issues raised by the essays in the collection.

The purpose of this new-look series, then, is to provide students with fresh thinking about key texts and writers while encouraging them to extend their own ideas and responses to the texts they are studying.

Martin Coyle

Notes on Contributors

Mel Gibson is a researcher, lecturer, comics scholar and consultant. She is currently a Senior Lecturer at Northumbria University specializing in teaching and research relating to children and young people. She has also taught modules on children's literature and picturebooks. Her National Teaching Fellowship Award was used to develop a UK network of scholars researching comics, manga and graphic novels and her doctoral thesis was on British women's memories of their girlhood comics reading, tying in to her training work and continuing research. Mel has supported libraries, schools and other organizations since 1993 in developing their understanding of picturebooks, children's fiction, comics, manga and graphic novels.

Michele Gill works for The Open University in London where she teaches Children's Literature and Childhood and Youth Studies. She completed her PhD in Children's Literature at Newcastle University with a research project into contemporary representations of boyhoods in Young Adult fictions. Since completing her thesis, Michele has continued to develop her research into boyhood with current projects including a study of the ways in which teenage male prostitution is mediated in Western cultures and a monograph which explores the portrayals of boyhood in award winning children's literature since the 1930s in Britain, adding a historical perspective to the research begun in her PhD thesis. She has published a number of papers and book chapters relating to her research field. Michele is a member of the IBBY UK committee and one of the three co-founders of The Child and the Book, now an annual postgraduate conference which has been held in a number of European countries and North America.

Joel Gwynne is Assistant Professor of English at the National Institute of Education, Nanyang Technological University, Singapore. His research interests lie in the fields of contemporary literature, film and popular culture, especially their intersection with postcolonial, gender and sexuality studies. He is the author of two monographs, *The Secular Visionaries: Aestheticism and New Zealand Short Fiction in the Twentieth Century* (Rodopi, 2010) and *Erotic Memoirs and Postfeminism* (Palgrave Macmillan, 2013), and co-editor of two collections, *Sexuality and Contemporary Literature* (Cambria Press, 2012) and *Postfeminism and Contemporary Hollywood Cinema* (Palgrave Macmillan, 2013). He has published articles in the *Journal of Postcolonial Writing*, the *Journal of Gender Studies* and the *Journal of Contemporary Asia*.

Peter Hollindale, now retired, was Reader in English and Educational Studies at the University of York, where he established a highly successful undergraduate course on children's literature. His many publications in the field include editions of J. M. Barrie's 'Peter Pan' texts, and of Anna Sewell's *Black Beauty*, for Oxford World's Classics. His most recent book, *The Hidden Teacher: Ideology and Children's Reading* (Thimble Press, 2011) includes two chapters which explore children's literature's treatment of relationships between humankind, animals and the environment. This book includes the essay 'Ideology and the Children's Book', which received the United States Children's Literature Association award for the best article published in the field of children's literature studies in its year.

Robyn McCallum is a Lecturer in English Literature at Macquarie University, Australia, and a member of the advisory board for International Research in Children's Literature. Her research deals with the impact of cultural forms on children's texts, with a particular focus on adolescent fiction, and visual media, especially film. Her publications include *Retelling Stories, Framing Culture* (1998), with John Stephens, and *New World Orders in Contemporary Children's Fiction* (2008), with Clare Bradford, Kerry Mallan and John Stephens. Her book, *Ideologies of Identity in Adolescent Fiction* (1999), was the 2001 IRSCL Honour book.

Pat Pinsent has worked at the University of Roehampton for many years, previously as a Principal Lecturer in the English Department, and currently as Senior Research Fellow in the National Centre for Research in Children's literature. She was co-founder of the MA in Children's Literature and was responsible for the production of the initial Distance Learning materials for it. Her fifteen published books include *The Power of the Page: Children's Books and their Readers* (1993), *Children's Literature and the Politics of Equality* (1997), and a collection of studies of neglected twentieth-century children's authors (2006), together with many edited compilations of the proceedings of the annual conference of the International Board on Books for Young People (IBBY). She has had published numerous articles on both children's literature and her other main research interest, seventeenth-century poetry. Her main current preoccupations are the diverse ways in which children's literature is currently developing, and the relationship between it and spirituality/religion. Until recently she edited *The Journal of Children's Literature Studies*, and still edits *IBBYLink*, the journal of the British Section of IBBY, and *Network*, a journal for all women interested in spirituality, theology, ministry and liturgy.

Chris Richards is a Senior Lecturer in Media Arts Education at the Institute of Education, London, where he currently leads the MA Media, Culture and Education programme. He is the author of three books, *Young People, Popular Culture and Education* (Continuum, 2011), *Forever Young: Essays on Young Adult Fictions* (Peter Lang, 2008) and *Teen Spirits: Music and Identity in Media Education* (UCL Press, 1998). He is the co-editor of, and a contributor to, *Children's Games in the New Media Age: Childlore, Media and the Playground* (Ashgate, in press) and he is a co-author of *Children, Media and Playground Cultures: Ethnographic Studies of School Playtimes* (Palgrave Macmillan, in press). He majored in American literature at Sussex University in the 1970s, taught in London schools and colleges through the 1980s, and has taught Media, Cultural and Education Studies in higher education since 1989.

Kay Sambell is Professor of Teaching and Learning at Northumbria University, UK, and a national teaching fellow. She helped to establish one of the country's first Childhood Studies degrees and led the development of a range of undergraduate modules on children's and YA literature, which she continues to teach. She has also directed a number of initiatives aimed at improving student learning in higher education, such as the MEDAL project (http://hces-online.net/websites/medal/index.htm), which brought together a consortium of lecturers who teach about childhood to share and develop their approaches. Kay specializes in constructions of childhood and youth in literature for young people and is widely known for her research on dystopian and futuristic fiction for young readers. Her doctoral thesis, undertaken at the University of York in the early 1990s, was on the use of future fictional time in novels for young people.

John Stephens is Emeritus Professor in English at Macquarie University. He is author of *Language and Ideology in Children's Fiction*; co-author of *Retelling Stories, Framing Culture* and *New World Orders in Contemporary Children's Literature*; editor of *Ways of Being Male*; and author of about a hundred articles and two other books. He is a former President of the International Research Society for Children's Literature, and currently Editor of *International Research in Children's Literature*.

In 2007 he received the eleventh International Brothers Grimm Award, in recognition of his contribution to research in children's literature.

Alison Waller is Senior Lecturer at The University of Roehampton, London, where she convenes the MA in Children's Literature by distance learning. She is the author of *Constructing Adolescence in Fantastic Realism* (Routledge, 2009) and has published extensively on young adult writers, including Robert Cormier, Margaret Mahy, Philip Pullman and J. D. Salinger. She is co-organizer of an interdisciplinary Memory Network and her research interests include ideas of consciousness, memory and science in young adult literature, as well as the practice of adults rereading childhood books.

Karen Williams studied English Literature at Somerville College, Oxford, before completing her MA at Roehampton's National Centre for Children's Literature. She is currently undertaking her PhD at the NCRCL, investigating humour in nineteenth-century children's literature. Her particular research interests include the comic poet Thomas Hood, satire in children's literature and ecocritical approaches to children's texts.

Acknowledgements

With thanks to Melvin for his time and humour. And to the NCRCL.

Introduction

Alison Waller

Burgess the 'controversialist'

Variations on the word 'controversial' are most often used by critics and commentators to describe Melvin Burgess's fiction. '[U]ncompromising', claims *The Oxford Encyclopedia of Children's Literature*;[1] 'edgy, honest, provocative' is how *The Continuum Encyclopedia of Young Adult Literature* puts it.[2] Burgess himself is widely known as the 'godfather' of young adult fiction and 'a reluctant, if consistent, controversialist'.[3] This high-profile reputation stems from the publication of what was in fact his eighth novel for young people, *Junk* (1996), a multiple first-person narrative which details the adventures of two teenagers encountering street life and drugs culture in 1980s Bristol. The popular British newspaper *The Daily Mail* reported on *Junk*'s success in winning the 1996 Carnegie Medal in sensationalist style: 'Heroin addiction, brutality and prostitution [...] Teachers outraged by librarians' choice.'[4] However, Burgess himself claims that much of the controversy surrounding the novel was a 'paper tiger'.[5] Indeed, the scandalized tone of *The Daily Mail* was relatively isolated, and many more educationalists, librarians and reviewers have preferred to take a liberal stance towards *Junk* and Burgess's other contentious titles. *The Times*' response to his Carnegie success ('It's not books that corrupt'[6]) was perhaps more representative of the attitudes of such adult gatekeepers towards what young people might be exposed to and digest.

A significant exception is the infamous 'hatchet-job' carried out on *Doing It* (2003) by author Anne Fine, who was British Children's Laureate at the time.[7] She created a media, publishing and critical storm by reviewing the novel for British broadsheet newspaper, *The Guardian*, and describing it as '[f]ilth, whichever way you look at it'.[8] She also created her own controversy by suggesting that Burgess's portrayal of adolescent boys and their crude discussion of girls and sex was as damaging as representing the views of 'deluded' racists or anti-Semites might be. A number of other reviewers raced to the novel's defence, notably the children's literature scholar and child psychologist, Nicholas Tucker, who gently rebutted Fine's attack in *The Independent*.[9]

The 'debate' rumbles on in academic discussion of Burgess's young adult fiction, with Clare Walsh and, most recently, Kimberley Reynolds, attempting to lift *Doing It* clear of Fine's assault by focusing on its sympathetic characterization of the male protagonists, its comic plotting and wordplay, and its shift from 'guilt and unease to *jouissance*' in writing about sex for teenagers.[10] Elsewhere in this Casebook, Chris Richards and Michele Gill continue the critical dialogue.

Not surprisingly then, scholarly work on Burgess has tended to cluster around his YA (young adult) novels rather than his fiction for younger readers, often focusing on the most controversial ingredients of drugs (*Junk*), sex (*Doing It*; *Lady: My Life as a Bitch*, 2001) and violence (*Bloodtide*, 1999; *Bloodsong*, 2005; *Nicholas Dane*, 2009). This tendency has helped foreground his status as part of a tradition of pioneering or challenging writers for teenagers. For example, useful comparisons have been made with Robert Cormier and Judy Blume from the United States, and Aidan Chambers and Robert Swindells from the UK, with Burgess acknowledging his debt to Cormier and Chambers in particular.[11] However, the focus on social issues and taboos has also resulted in a slight shortage of analysis drawing attention to the literary qualities of his work, as well as his innovative style. As a highly vocal commentator on his own work, Burgess both feeds and contests this trend. His default persona in the public arenas of the blogosphere, online interviews, literary festivals and book signings matches a general perception of his fiction: 'edgy, honest, provocative'. Note, for example, his stance in an article called 'Sympathy for the Devil', written for the academic journal *Children's Literature in Education*:

> There's so much written about doing the right thing for young people, and really very little about taking risks [...] Teenagers are in a better position than most people to say yes to some of the more risky things life has to offer. That might be a bit scary, but it is life they're saying yes to, and when some blobhead turns up and tries to force them to say no instead—well, it makes me want to write a book for them.[12]

The impression given is of an author driven by social forces to write for and on behalf of a disadvantaged readership about specific social issues, but Burgess admits in the same article, 'although I am best known for my two attempts at social realism, *Junk* and *Doing It*, they are not typical of my work'.[13] Indeed, since his literary debut in 1990, Burgess has produced more than twenty novel-length works for young readers and his oeuvre includes fantastic tales of time-travel, metamorphosis and spectral projection, as well as animal stories, historical tales, horror, stories for reluctant readers, myth, fable, picturebook, short stories, Twittertales, radio and stage plays, cross-media game, fictionalization and metafiction.

This volume of new essays on Burgess firstly acknowledges the central position held by those controversial novels for teenagers within his own writing, and the significance they have for the development of young adult literature more generally: it presents critical debates about what defines YA, what is suitable fare for an adolescent readership, and what ideological messages are being offered to teenagers through novels such as *Junk*, *Bloodtide* and *Bloodsong*, *Lady: My Life as a Bitch*, *Doing It*, and *Kill All Enemies* (2011). It also encourages examination of Burgess's less obviously controversial work in order to familiarize the reader with what is a full and diverse career of writing for a youthful audience in a variety of modes and genres. To this end, it has been important to give space to his picturebook and some of his novels for younger readers alongside his YA fiction. In addition, the essays included in this collection introduce readers to aspects of style and theme in Burgess's work, as well as offering critical and theoretical approaches—such as masculinity studies, postfeminism, ethical criticism and ecocriticism—that can help illuminate some of these texts by decoding their complex meanings and systems of representation. The Casebook thus offers an initial reassessment of Burgess's literary output as valuable and interesting for more than just its controversial qualities. The rest of this introduction offers some commentary on key points of Burgess's career and themes in his work, and pays particular attention to some texts that have not yet been subject to scholarly analysis, before outlining the shape of the collection and presenting the critical chapters.

Animal adventures

Burgess's initial entry into the world of children's literature was relatively low key: his first novel, *The Cry of the Wolf*, was published in 1990 by Klaus Flugge at Andersen Press who, according to Burgess, claimed he could not put the book down.[14] It is a 'neo-fable'[15] about the mythical last wolves of England, who are pursued to the death by a man identified only as 'The Hunter'. Just one male cub escapes with the help of young Ben. The novel was shortlisted for the prestigious British Carnegie Medal in 1990 and was highly commended. It is somewhat ironic that it missed out on the award to Gillian Cross's *Wolf*, since both are ambiguous texts sympathetic to the complexities of wild animals and the violence of humanity, and both refigure the wolf as more than mere symbol of fear and threat.

When *The Cry of the Wolf* was published in the United States in 1993, a reviewer declared that '[a] kids' novel about animals is a tough road to travel if you want to get me to like it'[16] and although Aisling Foster in the British newspaper *The Independent* called it a 'ripping yarn',[17] American education and publishing industry magazines were more circumspect. Susan Oliver in *The School Library Journal* described it as 'an ecological thriller' which 'may be too violent for some children',[18] while the writer for *Kircus Reviews* suggested '[t]here's more food for confusion than for thought in this savage hunt and its ambiguous outcome'.[19] The difficulties cited by these reviewers might relate to issues of audience, especially since Burgess had been told by Andersen Press that he was unwittingly writing for teenagers in this first novel.[20] *The Cry of the Wolf* clearly falls within a convention of fiction for young people that pits children and animals against a cruel adult world—think of E. B. White's *Charlotte's Web* (1952), or Michael Morpurgo's *War Horse* (1982)—but it also has much in common with older animal writing that might appeal to young readers *and* adults, and which might be identified as 'crossover' fiction in more recent critical terminology.[21] Jack London's *The Call of the Wild* (1903, for which Burgess wrote an introduction in the new Puffin reissue in 2008) and A. J. Dawson's *Finn the Wolfhound* (1908, which Burgess claims as an influence in writing *The Cry of the Wolf*) provide useful context for this novel and its somewhat ambivalent position in the field of children's literature.

Alongside *The Cry of the Wolf*, much of Burgess's earlier fiction demonstrates a general concern with the contrasts and conflicts between human and natural worlds, an interest nurtured in his youth when he collected butterflies and enjoyed the autobiographical tales of naturalist Gerald Durrell. His other animal narratives include *Tiger, Tiger* (1996), *Kite* (1997), *The Birdman* (2000), *Lady*, and arguably *Bloodsong*, although these later works turn away from nature writing and serious debates about animal rights towards fairy-tale horror, allegory and posthuman dystopia. In the interview included in this Casebook, Burgess states that he has nothing now left to say about animals; but he names *The Cry of the Wolf* as one of the novels of which he is most proud. This pride is evident in correspondence he had with established author Robert Westall soon after the Carnegie Prize was announced, in which he wrote 'I've had a lot of praise for that book but it means something more coming from you [...]. Thanks especially for your appreciation of my style—that was the thing I've worked hardest for.'[22]

Indeed, the key strength of this narrative is its control of character and fictional space, as well as its pacy plotting. Unlike some later novels where multiple voices and complex social worlds produce a satisfying muddle for the reader to navigate, *The Cry of the Wolf* pursues its theme—and young Ben's growing understanding of the needs of the last wolf—with admirable single-mindedness.

As Peter Hollindale and Karen Williams both stress in their chapters in this collection, Burgess often questions the concept of human exceptionalism in what he sees as a biodiverse world, but a tension can also be identified between his strongly non-anthropocentric animal fiction and novels where people are not only central but also celebrated in all their flawed variety. Where his animal world is most often represented as 'completely devoid of sentimentality but far from heartless',[23] Burgess's humans are usually redeemed by the power of love and are sometimes rather romanticized. Taking a cue from literary criticism on eighteenth-century sentimental fiction, it is possible to argue that his work has its emphasis 'not on the subtleties of a particular emotional state but on the communication of common feeling from sufferer or watcher to reader or audience'.[24] The author himself explains, 'I do think that everyone really has to have those relationships and closeness with one another, and that's the redeeming thing: that we all actually want to be in one another's hearts'.[25]

Human heart

Two of Burgess's children's books, *An Angel for May* (1992) and *The Ghost behind the Wall* (2000), nicely illustrate this portrayal of redemption through human feeling (and are explored in more detail in Pat Pinsent's chapter in this collection). Both short novels are focalized through boy protagonists who are initially unsympathetic. In *Angel*, Tam's sullen attitude towards his mother can be explained by the fact that he is trying to cope with the difficult circumstances of his parents' divorce. In the time-travel adventure that forms the core of this narrative, Tam meets another awkward child, May, and through wanting to help her overcome her own traumas he learns the value of all human beings, even the strange old woman, Rosey Rubbish, who turns out to be a grown-up May and who Tam is therefore willing to love. In *Ghost*, David also comes to understand and appreciate an older character. His reluctant friendship with his elderly neighbour, Mr Alveston, develops through a series of violent episodes in which the young boy is haunted by the old man's childhood self. David has to recognize that even someone suffering from dementia as Mr Alveston does has a history worth hearing about, and the two characters work together to exorcize the past through memory and storytelling.

While these two novels lead readers to recognize the importance of human relationships through plot development, a number of Burgess's YA novels—*Junk*, *Bloodtide* and *Bloodsong*, *Doing It* and *Kill All Enemies*—take a different literary tack in approaching the broad concept of love and redemption. In these works, Burgess uses multiple narrators to provide alternative perspectives, a strategy that can simultaneously distance readers from individual characters *and* help to show these characters in a new light that might highlight their more human qualities. For example, in discussing *Junk*, John Stephens has pointed out that multiple first-person narrators can have the effect of creating a 'relativist perspective and moral indeterminism',[26] a point also made by David Rudd and Maria Lassen-Segar,[27] and which Robyn McCallum and Stephens pick up later in this volume in exploring the ethical possibilities of Burgess's Volson sagas, *Bloodtide* and *Bloodsong*. But giving voice to characters who seem initially unattractive or immoral ultimately also humanizes them, makes them seem vulnerable, and therefore provokes sympathy, as Michele Gill points out in her analysis of *Doing It* and *Kill All Enemies* in the first part of this collection.[28]

This critical reputation for heart may at first seem incongruous, but in some cases there is a clear affinity between Burgess's social realism and a certain measure of sentiment. In an early article on *Junk* for the academic journal *The Lion and the Unicorn*, Stephen Thomson explores the character of Tar, teenage runaway and sidekick to the more vibrant heroine, Gemma. Thomson notes that, unlike the majority of characters in YA novels, Tar seems most authentic when he is being described by other people, rather than when he is allowed his own voice:

> So, for instance, we see him sitting crying in the rain next to an extinguished bonfire, being watched through the window by Rob and Lily. ' "Isn't he lovely?" she said. I put my arm around her. "Isn't he lovely?" she said again' ([Rob] 121). Tar's performance here is for no one; it is spontaneous, unmediated even by speech, taken unawares. In this lies the guarantee of its utter truthfulness. Tar must be characterized not by a desire to be truthful but by an absolute inability to dissemble. His reasons for leaving home are 'painted on his face .... His upper lip swelled over his teeth like a fat plum. His left eye was black, blue, yellow and red' (2). So, again, when another character asks why he left: 'He just glanced up and touched the side of his face. I hadn't noticed the bruises. He didn't have to say any more' ([Skolly] 26).[29]

Thomson identifies a moment, not just of spontaneity, but of sensibility. Tar is literally sensitive to the blows his father has dealt him, but the implication is also that he feels emotions more strongly than the average young man or woman: there is also an invitation for the reader to experience vicariously his sensations of physical and psychological pain or pleasure.

Burgess returns to a sentimental vein in his more recent novel, *Nicholas Dane*, which tells the traumatic story of a young boy passing through a heartless social welfare system. The author's own ideas about the importance of love in this context are voiced by the third-person narrator, who comments on Nick's eventual self-belief and successful romantic relationship as a form of salvation: 'Love comes to us all, if only we can recognise it and hold on to it'.[30] The novel also features a character called Oliver who, in an image reminiscent of Tar's pet name 'Dandelion', is 'more like a dandelion seed than a boy' (90) and who suffers rape as an infant at the hand of his mother's boyfriend and repeated abuse throughout his young life. Burgess employs a classic realist narrative voice, directly addressing the reader with the intention of reflecting Oliver's reality in the mirror of fiction: 'By the time Nick came to make friends with him he had turned into the broken little blond rag we know, with nothing to get him through other than the ability to acquiesce to anything that was asked of him' (172). There is, of course, something Dickensian in this portrayal of an attractive but sensitive young boy trapped in the workhouse-like institutions of 1980s social care, and Burgess admits he wanted to create a homage to Dickens in *Nicholas Dane*. The connections to the plot of *Oliver Twist* are obvious. There are also stylistic debts (not always successful), from comic set-pieces—like the disastrous dinner party Nick's well-meaning neighbour Jenny throws to convince the social worker Mrs Batts that she can look after him after he is orphaned—to grotesque characters such as Michael Moberley, the pie-factory owner, and Tony Creal, the dastardly deputy head of Meadow Hill Children's Home. Ironically, Mrs Batts argues, in her broad Yorkshire accent, that 'some of the Children's Homes are very good these days. Times have changed a lot since Oliver Twist' (21). Burgess's point is, of course, that in many ways times have not changed much at all. Critic Grahame Smith's commentary on Dickens' social realism as 'an indictment of a society as a whole that is parentless'[31] can be applied as easily to *Nicholas Dane*: and if disadvantaged orphans in 1980s England could still face mistreatment as foul (if not fouler) than those Dickens wrote about in the nineteenth century, then readers might be encouraged to question the world they live in today.

It is also notable that Burgess has a general interest in the experiences of what he describes as the 'underdogs' of society[32] that extends beyond his fiction, sharing Dickens' belief that literature has utility in social activism. To form the plot of *Nicholas Dane* Burgess drew on his own interviews with victims of abuse who had been housed at children's homes in Manchester between the 1960s and late 1980s and who had finally brought successful cases to court; and for his most recent novel at the time of writing, *Kill All Enemies*, he spoke to young men and women excluded from schools and sent to Pupil Referral Units (PRUs) around the North West and asked them for stories. Although he does not necessarily match Dickens in actively campaigning for the rights of the poor, Burgess is nonetheless keen to pin his political views about disadvantaged young people to the mast. Following his research for *Kill All Enemies*, he wrote a piece for *The Times* that could have easily appeared in Dickens' weekly magazine, *Household Words*, arguing that the 2011 London riots were caused by youth responding in a violent and ineffective manner to the general greed and sense of entitlement they observed in adults around them.[33] Moreover, Burgess has become increasingly interested in global storytelling and youth rights, taking part in the British Council's India Lit Sutra programme in 2010 and visiting the Democratic Republic of Congo with Save the Children in 2011 to tell and gather stories about the child witches in Kinshasa.

Kill All Enemies skilfully melds together ideological outrage at the difficulties faced by some disadvantaged teenagers with an affectionate portrayal of those individuals and a gentle incitement to rebel against institutionalization. Despite this potentially radical message, critical reception of the novel has been mostly positive, even from those who work within the institutions being attacked. On the other hand, initial responses to *Nicholas Dane* were mixed, and although Nicholas Tucker felt that Burgess was 'the ideal author to recount these travails',[34] many reviewers worried about explicit content as well as structural and stylistic problems. The topics of paedophilia, child sexual abuse and institutional culpability that surface in *Nicholas Dane* remain taboo for YA authors—for any authors perhaps—in a way that drug taking, consensual sexual encounters, and casual violence no longer always are. Burgess may argue that debates about *Junk*, *Lady* and *Doing It* were media hype and a 'paper tiger' but he recognizes that 'there is obviously a great deal more anxiety on all sides that institutional abuse is not a suitable subject for teenagers to engage with'.[35] It is worth briefly exploring some of Burgess's novels that deal with different sexual appetites to revisit the idea of controversy in the context of

Nicholas Dane, since issues of sexual control, power and normativity are dealt with most dramatically in this novel.

Sexual taboos

As I noted earlier, Reynolds argues that Burgess celebrates adolescent sexuality in a number of his YA novels. She points to his portrayal of canine lust in the playful novel *Lady*, in which Sandra Francy metamorphoses from a highly sexed teenage girl into a highly sexed mongrel dog and encounters the world in a newly direct and sensual manner.[36] Sex in *Doing It* is celebrated viscerally too, often to comic effect. Burgess claims to have set out to create a 'knobby book for boys' in which young male attitudes towards sex would be presented alongside other discourses of desire in ways that might appeal to an audience of young men.[37] The novel relates the romantic and sexual frustrations and adventures of three adolescent boys, and as a number of critics have pointed out, its balance of coarseness and linguistic wit go some way to realizing such an ambition. For instance, Jonathan's first attempt at describing his 'snog' with his almost-girlfriend Deborah suggests it is 'like drinking Fine Old Wine'[38] but he immediately recognizes that he has not yet developed such adult tastes and that the simile is false and pretentious. His solution is to extend and develop the image so that kissing becomes not just an oral experience but a complete bodily one. He also comes up with another simile, based on his own tastes and knowledge rather than on literary convention: Deborah smells like 'a piece of fruit cake' and later in the novel she tastes like 'spices and winegums' (125) and is a 'lovely big banquet' (259). It is significant, of course, that Deborah is linked to foods in this way, since the story thread dealing with Jonathan's feelings towards her questions attitudes towards 'fat girls' and issues of body image in general. It is also pertinent that Burgess mixes sophisticated tastes (fine wine and spices) with more homely and childish tastes (fruit cake and winegums), indicating the underlying innocence of all the boys' sexual adventures in this novel, despite the explicitness of the narrative content.[39]

Jonathan's boyish enthusiasm and Sandra/Lady's unbounded joy can be read as reflecting Burgess's official stance on teenagers and sex: 'When they reach puberty, rather than lecturing them about disease and biology, let's throw them a party. There should be a cake, fireworks, the lot. Sex! Oh, boy, you're really going to enjoy this.'[40] Nevertheless, he is also keen to point out that '[s]ex doesn't have to mean sleeping with someone at the start. Young people should be encouraged to progress slowly, but with pleasure':[41] a relatively conservative ideology that would most likely find relatively few opponents amongst modern parents, educators and commentators. In her article on 'deviant desire' in Burgess's work, Lydia Kokkola observes evidence of this more moderate approach to sex in both *Lady* and *Tiger, Tiger* (in which the prepubescent boy Steve is metamorphosed into animal form to mate and impregnate the spirit tiger, Lila). Regarding the former, she argues that by turning Sandra into an animal that only desires sex when on heat, Burgess simultaneously curtails her sexual power and 'underlines the value of societal regulations', particularly those regulations that dictate age-appropriate exploration of physical intimacy.[42] In other words, as a bitch Sandra explicitly displays the desires she was supposed to keep hidden as a girl, but she also welcomes the external controls of seasonal mating to restrict her sexual activity. Kokkola's interpretation provides valuable nuance, negotiating a critical line between Reynolds' reading of *jouissance* and the verdict of one of the original reviewers of *Lady* who described the novel as a 'middle-aged man's fantasy of a teenage girl'.[43]

Other novels in Burgess's YA canon provide more serious constraints to young sexuality, clearly demonstrating the dangers of precocious sex, or sex that has power rather than pleasure at its core. Several commentators have explored the implications of the teacher-student relationship between Ben and Miss Young in *Doing It*, which begins as a teenage dream but soon becomes an uncomfortable display of the manipulative power an older, more experienced lover can wield over a relatively vulnerable young man: in her chapter in this volume, for example, Gill notes the surprising reversal of conventional ideas about masculinity inherent in this plot development.[44] Just as disturbing are the sexual dynamics in Burgess's lesser-known *Loving April* (which may have gained a bigger readership, jokes Burgess, if he had titled it *Shagging April*[45]). Set in the 1920s, this unusual novel has as its heroine an adolescent girl called April, who is mocked and mistreated by other villagers because she is an outsider. She is deaf mute, and due to her impairment everyone thinks she is also mentally deficient. Because she has been kept separate from her peers and left to 'run wild', she is socially unrefined and sexually vulnerable: as the newcomer to the village, Barbara, puts it, '"April's rather backward in some ways but very forward in others."'[46] The outcome of her unconventional status is destructive. Local boys, as well as a number of adult men, both fear her and think she is fair game for their physical desires, and while April's promiscuous reputation is unfair, it ultimately results in her rape. In this morally ambiguous scenario, readers have to work hard to untangle the text's message: is April being punished for not caring if she attracts male attention through her sensual appearance, or is there an implication that the underdog will always face abuse from those who are socially powerful and sexually controlling, as Pinsent argues in her contribution to this Casebook? In contrast, the altogether more private and gentle love affair that develops between April and Barbara's son, Tony, is age-appropriate and celebratory, described in terms that are both scintillating and innocent, sexualized and romantic:

> the golden days, the idyllic weeks [...] brought to life [...] by April suddenly leaning up and breathing in his ear, by the smell of dusky liquorice on her breath, by him sliding his hands under her clothes, by lying hidden in the grass, watching the little fishing boats sailing up and down the water, and kissing and exposing her skin to the sun. (117)

Burgess throws April and Tony a kind of pastoral party to celebrate their discovery of sex in this description, and like the 'spices and winegums' in *Doing It*, April's 'dusky liquorice' breath maintains elements of childlike pleasure amongst more mature desire.

The party is spoiled irrevocably in *Nicholas Dane*, however. It is not only age-inappropriateness and social inequality that shapes Tony Creal's abhorrent relationships with the boys he grooms at Meadow Hill, but also the novel's fierce adherence to heterosexual normativity. Burgess describes Creal as 'an absolute baddie',[47] and clearly this judgement is founded upon the character's crimes of child rape and abuse of trust; but a further plausible, if inconclusive, interpretation of Creal's monstrousness might be reached based on the fact that he desires boys rather than girls. While the novel is very clear in portraying homophobia as unacceptable, it mirrors other works by Burgess in explicitly valuing healthy heterosexual relationships, and it is pertinent that Nicholas finally finds love with the loyal Maggie. Contributors to this collection note that Burgess does not necessarily 'pursue the implications of "otherness"' in *Doing It* (Gill), presenting instead 'a monolithic, undifferentiated view of [...] male culture' (Richards) and their points are significant; although conversely, McCallum and Stephens argue that 'respect for the otherness of the other' is a key theme in the Volson novels.

History and stories

The reader's acceptance of certain types of otherness is also important in Burgess's historical fiction, especially if we take Jerome de Groot's point that this genre 'entails an engagement on the part of the reader [...] with a set of tropes, settings and ideas that are particular, alien and strange'.[48] In the Preface to *Burning Issy* (1992), which is set during the seventeenth-century Pendle witch trials, the author/narrator notes that the narrative is not 'an attempt to show things as they really were, because that would deny the world as [the historical characters] saw it and believed it'.[49] Thus, a number of magical and quasi-religious happenings that might challenge contemporary secularism and open up ideas of otherness are related in this novel. For instance, the reader witnesses the young orphan protagonist, Issy, knocking the Witch-finder general off his horse by the force of her mind; and in a final scene, the horned god who the witches worship appears in super-natural form to free her from prison. Nonetheless, Burgess keeps his narrative grounded in historical reality in a manner that also invites the reader to make connections with their everyday experience and to question where exactly difference lies. Underlying the superstition and supernatural elements in this narrative are a series of economic references that tie Issy's tale more closely to material facts than mysti-cism. Her long-lost aunt, Iohen, is well known as a wise woman with special powers, but her strongest characteristic is her fierce business sense and the trade she does as a cloth-merchant is as important as her undertakings as a community 'witch'. At each point of crisis or resolution in Issy's story, an exchange of money, goods or labour takes place: Iohen pays Old Demdyke the Pendle witch a farthing for some wax to create a new manikin to replace the one Demdyke has made to torture Issy's brother Ghyll; the pack-horse driver who rescues Issy on her flight from Iohen's supposed devil worship remarks that it doesn't matter to him if she is 'a saint, a witch, a beggar, a queen or a thief—so long as I have your silver in my pocket' (136); and even Issy's very origins are bound up with a kind of bargaining, as Iohen swaps her for a loaf of bread when she is a baby. Burgess reveals a seventeenth-century world that exists within a tangible system of exchange, exposing economic realities of the past and therefore avoid-ing a simple exoticism of history.

In interview, Burgess reflects on this process of telling stories about the past and notes that '[e]xploring people and their worlds imaginatively can, oddly enough, arrive at some surprising truths',[50] a premise that has also shaped his project of creating 'found fiction' that tells narratives of real people who seem at first glance to have nothing to say (like children in care in the UK or those accused of witchcraft in the Democratic Republic of Congo). Although it is possible to employ the precepts of literary realism to deconstruct the very concept of reality and the fragile nature of 'truth', as Stephens does in his stylistic analysis of *Junk*, for example, the importance of stories in providing meaning underlies much of Burgess's fiction. This is made clear in the Author's Note to *Junk*, in which he states, '[t]he book isn't fact; it isn't even faction. But it's all true.' In *Burning Issy*, the central puzzle and task for both protagonist and reader is to recover Issy's own story and storytelling provides a central motif for the whole novel. From Demdyke's imagined curse to the arrested witches' fictional confessions, narratives are key; and Iohen explains, '[w]ell, I don't like questions and answers, but I do like a story' (85). Issy's story is contained and concealed in her recurring dream of a terrible burning heat, and this phantasy of fire acts as metonym for the widespread pain and persecution faced by many potentially innocent individuals during the witch trials. Just as Issy's own origins as the daughter of an accused witch have to be reclaimed and resolved, so too does the cultural narrative of the voiceless witches according to the novel's structural thrust.

The Casebook

Stories—and their ability to enlighten or deceive—are important for much of Burgess's work, from the historical narratives of *Burning Issy* to the layers of postmodern fictions in *Sara's Face* and the 'found' stories of *Nicholas Dane* and *Kill All Enemies*. There is great opportunity for future examination of truth and meaning in his fiction, using critical tools of deconstruction, postcolonialism, or queer theory for instance. There is also scope for future explorations of Burgess's writings on the edge—his Twittertales, blogging and cross-platform TV and gaming drama series for the BBC, 'The Well' (2009)—as well as adaptations of his work for stage, TV and film, and his novelization of *Billy Elliot* (2001). The current volume of essays will provide a useful starting point for new critical consideration of Burgess's work.

The first section of this Casebook acts as an introduction to the themes of controversy, cultural context, gender and sexuality, with Chris Richards, Michele Gill and Joel Gwynne working in dialogue with each other to discuss some of the best-known novels for young adults. They represent an important strand of critical enquiry that has thrived during the period in which Burgess has been writing: namely the investigation into identity, its constructed nature, and its manifestation in both fictional portrayals and broader socio-cultural discourses. Richards opens the discussion by alerting the reader to the complexities of Burgess's authorial persona, exploring his public engagement with 'domains of consumption' and probing his claims for an authentic rendering of adolescent boys in *Doing It*. Richards also provides a useful overview of the contested term 'young adult', demonstrating how Burgess has positioned himself within the field of YA between the schools market and popular media in order to appeal to a broad audience of adults and teenagers. Gill picks up on the question of authentic boyhood, placing Burgess's YA fictions alongside other narratives of young masculinity. She argues that *Doing It* and *Kill All Enemies* go some way to challenge dominant ways of thinking about boys which have centred on sexuality, violence, educational failure and emotional limitations. Like Richards, she acknowledges the role that real readers have in constructing their own versions of masculinity through actively engaging with Burgess's work on their own terms. Gwynne, the final voice in this trio of chapters, holds a mirror up to Gill's observations about boyhood in his discussion of postfeminist identities in *Junk*, *Doing It* and *Sara's Face*. Through analysis of the adolescent female body and sexual expression he makes claim to a feminist reading of Burgess, suggesting that these YA novels dramatize debates about girlhood and challenge conventional ideas that girls require private space and emotional fulfilment in order to mature both socially and sexually. According to Gwynne, Burgess's fictions show gender roles 'in transition' and promote the concept of the 'can-do' girl rather than the 'at risk' girl.

The first section of this collection is, therefore, socio-cultural in focus, but these contributors also demonstrate the strengths of literary criticism in uncovering nuances in Burgess's works and the value of theoretical lenses in locating them in broader scholarly debates. The following chapters by Kay Sambell, Robyn McCallam and John Stephens, and Mel Gibson concentrate more explicitly on fictional and stylistic qualities, examining form, genre and theme. Sambell is also interested in identity, but as a postmodern literary device that is fragmented and playful. She analyses *Sara's Face*, a modern melodrama which tells the story of a teenage girl with body dysmorphia who is so obsessed with celebrity that she is willing to allow the rock star Jonathan Heat to steal her face. Sambell notes the influence of journalism and new media on both the construction of Sara herself (who is 'nothing but a bundle of texts') and on the nature of the novel's fictional status. She argues that this most experimental of Burgess's works is a 'producerly' text that asks readers to enter into the game of meaning-making, yet without alienating them through overly avant-garde strategies. McCallum and Stephens bring to bear their expertise in narratology to produce a reading of Burgess's Volsung Saga novels.

They show how '[f]ictional technique is always implicated in how a novel offers possibilities of thematic meaning' and demonstrate how shifting narrative perspectives encourage a dynamic development of ethical understanding by the reader. Their careful reading of two of Burgess's most challenging works, *Bloodtide* and *Bloodsong*, moves from a consideration of how individuals respond to the needs and rights of others, to broader discussions of the nature of evil, the moral imperatives of science and technology, and the relative ontological status of human and posthuman characters: their chapter demonstrates both the complexity of Burgess's narrative structures and the richness of his fiction in philosophical terms. Burgess's picturebook co-produced with illustrator Ruth Brown, can be considered to be in stark contrast to the multi-narrator, mythic retellings of the Volsunga Saga, but Gibson's chapter shows how even in this seemingly innocuous form, Burgess can challenge expectations. Gibson demonstrates how *The Birdman* constructs a reader who must deploy knowledge of other texts 'to enhance their understandings of the narrative', and who will confront horror and ambiguity through a relatively simple reading experience. She identifies key intertexts amongst theatrical traditions, children's literary myth, fairy tale and Burgess's other story of magical metamorphosis, *Lady*, highlighting throughout the ambivalent nature of winged creatures.

The final section of the Casebook includes chapters by Peter Hollindale, Pat Pinsent and Karen Williams, and builds on themes of human and animal identity touched upon in earlier chapters, turning mainly to Burgess's fiction for younger readers to continue an exploration of his philosophical approach to the status of *homo sapiens*. Hollindale's chapter usefully identifies a sequence of animal novels—*The Cry of the Wolf*; *Tiger, Tiger*; *Kite*; *Lady: My Life as a Bitch*; and *Bloodsong*—which he argues are 'just as radical and challenging as Burgess's social realist fictions'. Hollindale pays attention to stylistic and formal qualities of the language used to describe human and animal perspective, showing how Burgess 'steps into the bubble' of animal perspective, particularly in his earlier novels. This chapter argues that animals generally have an 'enhanced value and status' in comparison to humanity and demonstrates how, in his later works, Burgess moves towards conjoining animal and human in new forms of being. Pinsent focuses on the human side of the equation, exploring relationships between child protagonists and outsider characters, including elderly people and those with mental disabilities. Drawing on traditional literary critical methodology in identifying themes and highlighting symbolism in Burgess's work, she argues that the harsh realities faced by the heroes of *An Angel for May,*

Loving April and *The Ghost behind the Wall* have perhaps 'predisposed them towards an initially unlikely sensitivity to others who are also on the edges of society'. The shift in emphasis away from Burgess's young adult fiction helps to offer alternative views on the construction and reconstruction of identity as being not only a task for the youthful but an important part of human experience across ages, abilities and social backgrounds. Pinsent also leads her reader through some of the meanings that can be found in animal figures and symbolic settings in Burgess's work, which paves the way for Williams' chapter. Williams reads *The Earth Giant* (1995) and *The Baby and Fly Pie* (1993) through the lens of ecocriticism, a stimulating and relatively recent theoretical approach. She shows how Burgess anticipates some of the theoretical interest in interrogating binary oppositions of animal/human, urban/rural, and culture/nature: revealing, for instance, the city to be both a 'noxious stereotype' and 'an evolving, contested habitat' in its own right. The countryside too, can be wrenched from traditions of the romantic child of nature and be shown as both 'an escape from urban toxicity and a paradoxical "alien" space filled with danger'. Williams is interested in how animals and humans appear in symbiosis within Burgess's fictional ecosystems, demonstrating through his writings how intertwined we humans are with the world around us.

These final chapters share with the previous six an interest in the way that Burgess's fictional universe is carefully crafted with an awareness of socio-environmental realities that young readers must face every day. In a final chapter, I interview the author to reflect on his passion for gathering 'found stories' and to try to make links between his writing about contemporary British youth and the experiences of young people in other places and times, in novels such as *Burning Issy*. It is Burgess's desire to challenge conventional understandings about young people that emerges most clearly in his recent work, where he continues to promote the idea that 'teenage qualities are really rather splendid'.[51] It is the purpose of this collection to encourage a critical recognition of Burgess's own splendid qualities.

Notes

1. David Rudd, 'Melvin Burgess', in Jack Zipes (ed.), *The Oxford Encyclopedia of Children's Literature* (Oxford: Oxford University Press, 2006) Oxford Reference http://www.oxfordreference.com.
2. Carol Tilley, 'Melvin Burgess', in Bernice E. Cullinan, Bonnie Kunzel and Deborah Wooten (eds.), *The Continuum Encyclopedia of Young Adult Literature* (New York and London: Continuum, 2005): 118.

3. Libby Brooks, 'The Truth about Kids: An Interview with Melvin Burgess', *The Guardian*, 13 August 2001, Features: 6.
4. Bill Moulan, 'Heroin Addiction, Brutality and Prostitution: It's the New Children's Book Prize Winner; TEACHERS OUTRAGED BY LIBRARIANS' CHOICE', *The Daily Mail*, 17 July 1997: 17. The 1996 Carnegie Medal was announced in summer 1997. This practice of awarding the medal in the year following publication was in place until 2007.
5. In Melvin Burgess, 'Sympathy for the Devil', *Children's Literature in Education* 35(4) (December 2004): 293.
6. Nicolette Jones, '"It's Not Books that Corrupt"', *The Times*, 17 July 1997.
7. The term 'hatchet job' is referred to in Burgess's 'Sympathy for the Devil' (297), and seems to have come from a comment on the *Guardian Unlimited* website, no longer accessible (http://guardian.newspaperdirect.com).
8. Anne Fine, 'Filth, Whichever Way You Look at it', *The Guardian*, 29 March 2003, Saturday Review: 33. Fine produced this book review based on reading proofs released two months before the planned publication of *Doing It*. The novel's launch date was subsequently brought forward.
9. Nicholas Tucker, 'Angels with Dirty Minds', *The Independent*, 17 May 2003, Features: 29. See also Justine Picardie, 'Boys' Own Stories', *The Daily Telegraph*, 5 April 2003: 2; Kit Spring, 'The Beastly Boys: Melvin Burgess's Book Has Been Called Vile, but That's Just How Teenagers Are', *The Observer*, 13 April 2003, Review: 15; Chris Brown, 'Review of *Doing It*', *School Librarian* 51(3) (Autumn 2003): 164.
10. Clare Walsh, 'Troubling the Boundary between Fiction for Adults and Fiction for Children: A Study of Melvin Burgess', in Pat Pinsent (ed.), *Books and Boundaries: Writers and their Audiences*, Papers from the NCRCL/IBBY conference held at Roehampton Institute London on 15 November 2003 (Lichfield: Pied Piper, 2004): 142–53; Kimberly Reynolds, 'Baby, You're the Best: Sex and Sexuality in Contemporary Juvenile Fiction', in *Radical Children's Literature: Future Visions and Aesthetic Transformations in Juvenile Fiction* (Basingstoke: Palgrave Macmillan, 2007): 122. *Jouissance* is a term from Lacan's writings, and in psychoanalysis refers to painful sexual pleasure.
11. See Claudia Nelson, 'The Unheimlich Maneuver: Uncanny Domesticity in the Urban Waif Tale', in Kerry Mallan and Sharyn Pearce (eds.), *Youth Cultures: Texts, Images, and Identities* (Westport, CT and London: Praeger, 2003): 109–21; Reynolds, 'Baby, You're the Best'; and Carolyn Smith, 'Exploring the History and Controversy of Young Adult Literature', *New Review of Children's Literature and Librarianship* 8(1) (2002): 1–11. Future explorations in this direction might also consider links and associations with contemporaries such as Philip Pullman, David Almond, Geraldine McCaughrean or Neil Gaiman.

12. Burgess, 'Sympathy for the Devil': 299–300.
13. *Ibid.*: 300.
14. See http://www.melvinburgess.net/andersenreissues.html.
15. Peter Hollindale, 'Why the Wolves Are Running', *The Lion and the Unicorn* 23(1) (1999): 97–115.
16. Carol Otis Hurst, 'Review', *Teaching Pre K-8* 23(7) (April 1993): 74.
17. Aisling Foster, 'Children's Books for Christmas: Adventure Playground of Suspense', *The Independent*, 25 November 1990, Sunday Review: 39.
18. Susan Oliver, 'Review of *The Cry of the Wolf*, *School Library Journal* 38(9) (September 1992): 250.
19. 'Review of *The Cry of the Wolf*, *Kirkus Reviews*, 15 October 1992.
20. http://www.melvinburgess.net/andersenreissues.html.
21. See Rachel Falconer, *The Crossover Novel: Contemporary Children's Fiction and its Adult Readership* (Abingdon and New York: Routledge, 2009) for more discussion of this phenomenon.
22. Melvin Burgess, Letter to Robert Westall, n.d., Seven Stories: The Centre for Children's Books, Robert Westall MSS, RW/14/04/05.
23. Hurst, 'Review'.
24. Janet Todd, *Sensibility: An Introduction* (London: Methuen, 1986): 4.
25. 'Found Fiction: An Interview with Melvin Burgess', Chapter 10 in this Casebook.
26. John Stephens, '"And it's So Real": Versions of Reality in Melvin Burgess's *Junk*', in Heather Montgomery and Nicola J. Watson (eds.), *Children's Literature: Classic Texts and Contemporary Trends* (Basingstoke: Palgrave Macmillan and the Open University, 2009): 321–2.
27. David Rudd, 'A Young Person's Guide to the Fictions of *Junk*', *Children's Literature in Education* 30(2) (1999): 119–26; Maria Lassén-Seger, *Adventures into Otherness: Child Metamorphs in Late Twentieth-Century Literature* (Åbo: Åbo Akademi University Press, 2006).
28. See also Walsh, 'Troubling the Boundary between Fiction for Adults and Fiction for Children'.
29. Stephen Thomson, 'The Real Adolescent: Performance and Negativity in Melvyn Burgess's *Junk*', *The Lion and the Unicorn* 23(1) (January 1999): 26.
30. Melvin Burgess, *Nicholas Dane* [2009] (London: Puffin, 2010): 408.
31. Grahame Smith, 'Charles Dickens', *The Literary Encyclopedia* (first published 8 January 2001 at http://www.litencyc.com).
32. Chapter 10, 'Found Fiction'.
33. Melvin Burgess, '"The Rioters Did What We've Been Doing for Years; When the Chance Came to Get Something for Free They Grabbed It"', *The Times*, 7 September, 2011, T2 Review: 4–5. Dickens' *Household Words* ran from 1850 to 1859 and published 'material of social import' as well as 'informational articles, and material for entertainment'. Anne Lohrli, *Household Words: A Weekly Journal 1850–1859 Conducted by Charles Dickens* (Toronto: University of Toronto Press, 1973): 4.

34. Nicholas Tucker, 'Review of *Nicholas Dane*', *The Independent*, 17 July 2009.
35. On his website: http://www.melvinburgess.net/Nickdane.htm.
36. Elsewhere, I have described the novel as playing with 'the idea of teenage desire gone wild and become animal': Alison Waller, *Constructing Adolescence in Fantastic Realism* (London: Routledge, 2009): 51.
37. The phrase appears in a number of sources, but Burgess published the phrase first in 'Fictional Males Lose the Plot', *Times Educational Supplement*, 12 May 2008: 23.
38. Melvin Burgess, *Doing It* (London: Andersen Press, 2003): 95.
39. Interestingly, the US television adaptation of *Doing It* called *Life as We Know It*, which ran on ABC between 2005 and 2006, substituted much of this very British discourse of innocence with a more glamorous—yet less biologically explicit—portrayal of beautiful youth.
40. Melvin Burgess, 'Lost your Virginity, Son? Let's Have a Party', *The Times*, 5 July 2010, Features: 44–45. See also 'Sympathy for the Devil'.
41. Burgess, 'Lost your Virginity, Son?'
42. Lydia Kokkola, 'Metamorphosis in Two Novels by Melvin Burgess: Denying and Disguising "Deviant" Desire', *Children's Literature in Education* 42(1) (March 2011): 56–69.
43. Natasha Walter, 'Reading between the Lines', *The Independent*, 10 August 2001, Comment: 5.
44. See also Walsh, 'Troubling the Boundary between Fiction for Adults and Fiction for Children' and Chris Richards, 'Writing for Young Adults: Melvin Burgess and Mark Haddon', in *Forever Young: Essays on Young Adult Fictions* (New York: Peter Lang, 2008): 51–64.
45. See Jonathan Douglas, 'Robert Cormier Meets Melvin Burgess', *ACHUKAbooks* (http://www.achuka.co.uk/special/cormburg.htm).
46. Melvin Burgess, *Loving April* [1995] (London: Puffin, 1996): 120.
47. Chapter 10, 'Found Fiction'.
48. Jerome de Groot, *The Historical Novel* (Abingdon: Routledge, 2009): 4.
49. Melvin Burgess, *Burning Issy* [1992] (London: Andersen Press, 2012): 2.
50. Chapter 10, 'Found Fiction'.
51. Melvin Burgess, 'Then, Thank God, We Grew Up', *The Guardian*, 27 May 2006.

Part I
Controversy and the Cultural Context

1

'One of the Boys'? Writing Sex for Teenagers in *Doing It*

Chris Richards

Introduction

The emergence of young adult literature has a rather uncertain history in the activities of publishers, libraries and education through the later decades of the twentieth century. Jack Zipes has argued, of both young adult and children's literature, that such literature is largely an adult matter, negotiated between adult interests in institutions entirely of their making. His essay, provocatively entitled 'Why Children's Literature Does Not Exist',[1] follows an argument made by Jacqueline Rose in 1984—on 'The Impossibility of Children's Fiction'—and shares some ground with, for example, Roberta Seelinger Trites and Alison Waller, both of whom have pursued a more particular focus on the 'institutional' formation of a young adult literature.[2] The paradox Zipes highlights is that, on the whole, such literatures are not produced by children or by teenagers, nor are they even necessarily read by them—at least not without extensive adult mediation. So the implication that the texts so designated belong to the young is, for Zipes, thoroughly misleading:

> There is always an implied audience or audiences, and the implied audiences of a children's book are constituted first and foremost by an editor/agent/publisher, then by a teacher/librarian/parent, and finally by children of a particular age group. Only rarely does an author write expressly for a child or for children, and even then, the writing is likely done on behalf of children, that is, for their welfare, or what the author conceives of as a children's audience or childhood.[3]

In the production of texts for children and young people, a central issue must be that of how the 'child' or 'youth' audience is constructed.

Questions about the characteristics, interests, needs and desires of the young circulate between adult participants in the processes of book publishing, marketing and distribution and in the reception and mediation of texts by adults such as parents, librarians and teachers. Ideas about what children are like, and what is appropriate for them, have their history too.[4] There is no stable and entirely consensual understanding of what childhood or youth are and where their boundaries can be drawn; 'childhood' and 'youth' are contested terms.[5] In some institutional settings, such as schools, a particular set of psychological themes may reliably inform the way young people are placed and what is expected of them, often in relation to ideas of development, progress and maturation. But, elsewhere—in the domain of the commercial media, for example—those same children and young people will find themselves addressed in rather different ways, not least as consumers and as 'free' agents in pursuit of pleasure.[6]

This chapter will examine Melvin Burgess's novel *Doing It* (2003)[7] in the context of the author's career as a writer for children and teenagers. Among writers whose work addresses children and young people, Burgess is perhaps relatively unusual in explicitly engaging with these conflicts between domains of consumption both in articles and in interviews.[8] *Doing It* proved to be particularly controversial and was the occasion for extended commentary and debate. From the standpoint of an adult writer defining his professional career entirely within the field of children's and young adult fiction, Burgess has offered a commentary on the production of his own novels and the choices he has made. What authors have to say about their own work is always of interest, and his explanations are given considerable attention here, but reading his novels also needs to be further informed by wider debates around the construction of 'audiences' or 'readers' in contemporary publishing. In particular, it is important to focus on the idea that books for children and young people are a form of provision for their needs by adults skilled in judging what is appropriate and desirable. This has been the priority for publishing and, with occasional exceptions, young people are not themselves expected to represent their own engagement with 'being young', either in old or new media (short stories and novels or online writing). Attempts to facilitate young people as writers have been made but these are marginal to the activities of commercial publishing both in the 'schools market' and in the wider book trade.[9]

For publishing, 'young adult', by contrast with 'crossover', is a category inseparable from education and its division of young people into age phases, with children grouped year by year and relocated institutionally at key moments such as the transfer from primary to secondary school. Indeed, 'young adult' is a regulatory category indicating that the texts assigned to it are not for younger children and that some of their characteristics are appropriate to 'adolescence'—such characteristics typically include some acknowledgement of sexual interests and perhaps heightened tensions and emotional conflicts between teenage characters. Texts labelled in this way are deemed to be for young people, both in the sense that there is an emotional and experiential correspondence between the text and the reader, and because they provide moral guidance, if perhaps only minimally and implicitly, in showing the consequences of some actions. Indeed, 'moral risk' may be registered in some novels primarily in the narrative display of outcomes such as pregnancy, addiction and educational failure rather than through a more overt discourse of judgement.[10] The emergence of young adult fiction in the latter half of the twentieth century was closely aligned with the history of English teaching in schools and with related developments in school library policy and provision.[11] At least in Britain, the *category* 'young adult' really has relatively little currency outside education and the organization of that area of publishing addressing the 'educational market'. In the wider context of commercial media, 'teen' and 'teenage' are far more prominent in those discourses that intend to address young people themselves. Teen carries less of the implied admonishment that lingers in the use of 'young adult'—that implication that those addressed as 'young adult' are being reminded to learn the sense of responsibility that is attributed to being a properly mature adult. Texts—films, comics, magazines, computer games, music—located in the non-educational commercial domain and sold directly to young people themselves are *not* positioned primarily as offering instruction in how to be 'grown-up'—though particular examples that can be read as doing so are not difficult to find.

However, especially since the later 1990s, the idea of young adult fiction has become a little more complicated. 'Crossover' fiction has emerged as a more firmly identifiable category and one that, because it extends the potential market, has been pursued by publishers with some enthusiasm.[12] The positioning of new titles as for readers both teenage and adult, and outside the institutional structuring of age phases in education, is one significant strategy. Mark Haddon's *The Curious Incident of the Dog in the Night-Time*, published in the same year as *Doing It*, was launched in two different editions.[13] In the United States, Francesca Lia Block's five Weetzie Bat novels (1989–95) were reissued together in one volume as *Dangerous Angels* in 1998 and without any of the previous educational and American Library Association endorsements.[14] These two examples represent related but distinguishable tendencies. I have discussed Block elsewhere in some detail, and Haddon in an essay where I explicitly contrast his stance with that adopted by Burgess.[15] With *The Curious Incident of the Dog in the Night-Time*, a novel about a teenage boy was presented as sufficiently complex and challenging to attract the attention of adult readers. In some ways, this was consistent with Haddon's own account of his reasons for writing something very different from his previous work for children.[16] *Dangerous Angels* was offered more as a contribution to the flexible extension of youth as a lifestyle lived across age phases and well into adulthood—in their 1998 relaunch, the novels became a series of 'magical realist' reflections on a 'younger adult' rather than a more circumscribed 'teenage' way of life. Both Haddon and Block were positioned in the 'crossover' strategy pursued by publishers but their writing was recruited to an adult readership in rather different terms. Melvin Burgess, whose writing has also been associated with 'crossover' fiction, is different again from both Haddon and Block, not least because he has more consistently pursued a professional identification with writing for young people.

Writing *for* the teenage reader

Burgess has drawn attention to the wider patterns of consumption typical of young people in the past two decades, citing both the variety of media to which they have access and the virtual irrelevance of the boundaries associated, in the United Kingdom, with the work of the British Board of Film Classification.[17] The full texts of his articles are archived on his own website—itself indicative of his public self-positioning as an author-celebrity and as a speaker on behalf of young people's interests. Here, writing in 2000, he enthusiastically embraces the wider media culture both for its pleasures and its financial rewards:

> Teenage fiction is an area that has developed out of recognition in recent years. I can't recall any books written specifically for me when I was that age. Now the range of books increases every year [...]
>
> Books occupy a very curious position as far as teenagers are concerned. Although there is no censorship for books for any age group, they have lagged behind the other media in the kind of material they present to young people. The film industry, the music industry, computer games, magazines, comics—they all know very well about the youth

> market. There is an age group of about fourteen to twenty five that is extremely profitable for everyone.[18]

In the same year—and perhaps with the recent publication of *Bloodtide* (1999) in mind, given its arguably cinematic violence—he makes a similar case:

> Teenagers as a group consume entertainment—often narrative entertainment—by the barrel load, and the kind of thing they choose for themselves in film, magazines, gaming, music and TV, come largely from that cultural area. Who can blame them? It's so rich—sexy, loud, violent, ironic and cruel, but also beautiful, dreamy and intense. Schools have an obvious problem with this kind of thing […] one reason why books for teenagers have been so slow to take on the experience of other media.[19]

The identification of a disjunction between the way in which young people are positioned and addressed in school and by the media has consistently informed the development of his career, at least since the mid 1990s with the publication of *Junk* (1996).[20]

To some extent Burgess has been able to contribute to the continuing process of redefining how teachers should engage with the popular media and especially with the representation of sex and drug use, in the late twentieth and early twenty-first centuries. In London, the English and Media Centre published a study guide to support the teaching of *Junk* and Michael Rosen made the novel central to an article on social realism in children's literature, '*Junk* and Other Realities'.[21] More broadly, media studies teachers, often caught up in the vicissitudes of teaching horror or other apparently transgressive texts, could acknowledge that Burgess was attempting to reanimate an old media form in circumstances where many argued that it was irrelevant to young people's lives.[22] There was a great deal of common ground. Indeed, generationally, Burgess belonged with some of the leading figures in the development of media education—David Buckingham, like Burgess, was born in 1954. A shared generational experience of childhood and youth in the 1950s and 1960s by no means entails any particular stance in relation to youth culture and popular media, but perhaps a sense of frustration and confinement within the narrow constraints of the school curriculum in that period does persist. Burgess ruefully remarks that '[w]riting books that schools feel happy with is the sensible option—at least I know the market is there' but adds '[w]riting books that borrow style and imagery from other media isn't going to make my life any easier […]. But, being mad, I expect I'll do it anyway'.[23] Much more strongly than either

Haddon or Block, Burgess thus locates himself as writing for young people of school age but also frequently seeks to disrupt the implicit imperatives of educationally located young adult fiction.

However, the disruptive tactics adopted by Burgess and articulated in his claims about his own work are pursued on ground very different from the mainly 'poststructuralist' approaches to language and representation long familiar in media studies and related fields. Chris Barker explains that 'for poststructuralism there can be no truths, subjects or identities outside of language, a language which does not have stable referents and is therefore unable to represent fixed truths or identities'. Going further he notes that what we say, about ourselves or anything else, is 'dependent on the prior existence of discursive positions. Truth is not so much found as made and identities are discursive constructions'.[24] Discussing young people's own writing in school, Gemma Moss argues similarly that the 'truth' of experience cannot be represented authentically by adopting a realist genre: 'the reality we seek to disclose [...] is just as much a matter of convention as the genres we seek to discard; it is no more natural, no more the product of the direct apprehension of experience than the texts we dislike'.[25] In media studies, claims to be able to convey the 'truth of reality' are always regarded as, indeed, 'claims'—rhetorical strategies to secure an audience's acceptance of the particular version of reality being 'promoted'. Judgements between competing versions have to be made but can never be pursued by arguing that one *authentic* representation can be produced, conclusively fixing the truth in question.

Perhaps Burgess would agree with much of this. But his emphasis on 'authenticity', on addressing teenagers 'directly', in their terms, using their 'language', reiterated across a number of articles and interviews, implies a kind of privileged capture of young people's experience.[26] He concludes his article 'Teenage Fiction Comes of Age': 'I want people to be able to pick up one of my books and think—I know this stuff and I know these people; this is mine'. This is his professional project and he explicitly disowns 'reminiscences about some old bloke's first sexual experience back in the sixties'.[27] Of course, as an old bloke whose first sexual experiences were in the 1960s, he might well write about himself with an at least equal claim to authenticity—though that is not a claim that would escape the poststructuralist critique. The central issue here is that of how he constructs his novels to address and represent young people in these realist and experiential terms. The work of doing so is not confined to the text alone but includes the design of the book cover, the comments made in articles and interviews and his authorial presence online. For example:

> If you are aged sixteen or seventeen and you want to read fiction that talks about your life—your recreation, your sex life, your feelings and emotions—you're either stuck with stuff about twenty-somethings, or [...] soft stuff that seems to be written for younger readers, or [...] some polite, carefully edited stuff that doesn't dare talk about reality.[28]

Burgess claims to successfully address young people, especially boys, and to do so in terms that they accept and enjoy—nothing too 'soft' or too 'polite'. The idea of representing the real authentically is one key theme in the construction of his career and he is presented, and presents himself, as an adult writer who will 'dare' to talk about young people's realities.

'Their language': sexwords

Perhaps one of the most controversial aspects of *Doing It*, its apparently frank and explicit sexual language, is also an implicit claim to authenticity in representing teenage boys and, in addressing them as readers, offering them a sense of recognition. Mikhail Bakhtin comments on the relationship between the language of the 'speaker' and the addressee in his discussion of genre:

> Both the composition and, particularly, the style of the utterance depend on those to whom the utterance is addressed, how the speaker (or writer) senses and imagines his addressees, and the force of their effect on the utterance. Each speech genre in each area of speech communication has its own typical conception of the addressee, and this defines it as a genre.[29]

I want to consider the extent to which Burgess's repertoire of 'sexwords'[30] might, in Bakhtin's terms, underpin his claim to know his teenage audience and if it is also somewhat idiosyncratic, an aspect of an authorial 'idiolect'.[31]

Given Burgess's attention to the wider media 'world' inhabited by his readers, it could be argued that, with some justification, he mostly follows the evaluative map of language use broadly established in the mainstream British media. He thus addresses his readers in accord with measures of offence current in the public domain. Rather than attempting to reflect the actual speech of any particular group of young people, *Doing It* follows a generic representation of young people's sexual language familiar from film and television, if, in 2003, still relatively unusual in print fiction published for teenagers. In addressing boys, the recognition Burgess appears to seek is that of a repertoire already familiar to them in those other media and, perhaps, in part adopted by them in their everyday language use.

To some extent, the linguistic repertoire of *Doing It* participates in, and further contributes to, an internationally marketed 'Britishness'. In the USA, *Junk* was published as *Smack* and with a glossary giving the US equivalents of some eighty 'British' words and phrases.[32] In *Doing It*, sexual terms such as 'shag' and 'snog' might require some translation—though 'British' film and television have made these more familiar outside the United Kingdom. In addition, the following words for parts of the body prevail: 'bollocks', 'arse', 'knob' (sometimes penis), 'pubes', 'pubis', 'tits', 'hole', 'minge', and 'fanny' (sometimes pussy). Some of these—'fanny' and 'minge', for example—are, again, likely to be construed as distinctively 'British'; so too are 'prat', 'twat', 'wanker', 'bum', 'fag', 'bloke' and 'slag'. But, whether or not this is the authentic language of even a particular sub-category of teenage boys in Britain is difficult to verify.[33] It appears to be a version of British youth talk shaped by the standards and customs of British media rather than an attempt to replicate any particular pattern of use among young people themselves. Furthermore, it can also be understood as Burgess's own distinctive repertoire, not entirely and peculiarly his of course, but in terms of the privileging of some words over others ('knob' and 'minge' most obviously), a strong authorial inflection of the 'British' vocabulary he has chosen to use.

Perhaps further support for my argument that Burgess is writing largely within the current mainstream standards of the British media can be found in noting those words used infrequently or only with a derogatory rather than sexual meaning. 'Cunt', in the plural, occurs once as abuse shouted by Zoe at her parents (128). 'Cunt', despite attempts to reclaim it, is still regarded as irretrievably nasty and in the media it remains a term used to convey contempt.[34] 'Dick' figures in the text perhaps once or twice, 'cock' never. Similarly 'fuck' is never used with its sexual meaning but as abuse, 'fuck off' and 'fuck you', or to suggest defeat—'fucked'. 'Screwed', with its sexual meaning, appears once. 'Shag', widely used in British television and film, has become a seemingly more acceptable, if crass, euphemism, where 'fuck' is mostly regarded as more contentious, usually requiring warnings in advance on television, for example. Though Burgess clearly intends to achieve some degree of authenticity in his rendering of teenage sexual talk, and has some interest in challenging the existing conventions for young adult fiction, his preferred vocabulary mostly avoids the most controversial words or declines to give them their sexual meanings. It may be that confining them, where they are used, to the status of swear words avoids any more direct attempt to question, and thus to engage, the (hetero)normative sexual vocabulary likely to be in common use among his readers.

Anne Fine's notoriously condemnatory review[35] of *Doing It* found considerable offence in Burgess's use of language. Her review suffers from the use of decontextualized quotation to support moral disgust, citing such lines as 'tits and minge are actually very important things to me in a girlfriend' without regard for their almost invariably humorous intent or their purpose in constructing several bemused and emotionally uncertain characters. More importantly, the central problem with Fine's review is that she assumes that the novel will achieve the kind of direct connection and allegiance suggested in the title of this chapter—as if Burgess can connect with and write from the perspective of 'one of the boys'. The polarization she attempts, with her outrage spoken on behalf of young women and girls, and Burgess firmly 'othered' on the side of the 'sexual bullies', suppresses the questions that needed to be posed and given serious consideration. For example, how might teenage girls actually respond to Burgess's novel? And how might their sexual interests be represented in young adult fiction? In reporting on undergraduate students' engagement with *Doing It* I found some evidence that Fine's attempt to represent the sensibilities of young women simplifies, at the least, a more complex and diverse array of positions than she appears to have imagined.[36] Fine's 'solidarity' with her gender also neglects the possibility that there may be many male readers of *Doing It* who find it offensive or find little that relates to their own feelings and experiences.

I have suggested that the use of language does not necessarily correspond to that used by the novel's readers or indeed any other actual group of young people. The suggestion that Burgess is able, through writing of this kind, to become 'one of the boys' is one that I make ironically—an implicit claim to be met with considerable scepticism. Perhaps the distance between themselves and their 'constituencies' that neither Burgess nor Fine acknowledge is evident in their apparently similar designation of sex as 'dirty'. Fine's review, 'Filth, whichever way you look at it', and her references to 'this grubby book', the publishers' 'grubby little lives' and the novels' 'vile, disgusting musings' reanimate the past menace of the 'dirty book'. Both in *Doing It* and in articles and interviews, Burgess also refers to sex as 'dirty', 'really filthy', involving acts of 'rampant rudeness'.[37] Drawing on this discourse on sex may well imply, whatever their personal realities, self-location for both the novelist and the reviewer as troubled adults, still struggling to come to terms with the embodied reality of sexual life. For Burgess, 'filth' may suggest a kind of earthy physicality rather than the moral pollution implied by 'dirt'. Indeed, Burgess frequently, in the novel and elsewhere, declares sex to be 'gorgeous'. But *Doing It* is above all a comic and not an erotic novel. To achieve some degree of erotic power it would need to go much further, perhaps both in the use of sexual language and in the narration of sexual action; and neither Burgess nor Fine acknowledge that this is one of its more significant limitations.

In one further respect Fine and Burgess share some common ground. Both suggest a kind of gender essentialism. Fine writes of how 'young girls' will react and what damage will be done to their self-esteem. She invokes an undifferentiated category (all young girls everywhere?) and attributes to them both vulnerability and naivety—rather ironically both of which Burgess mostly manages to avoid in his representation of girls and their actions in *Doing It*. But Burgess does tend towards a comparable essentialism in his representation of male sexuality and the culture of masculine friendship. He presents a monolithic, undifferentiated view of such male culture, projecting into the construction of the characters and the relations between them one kind of white, lower middle-class, heterosexual and homosocial conviviality. Though, as noted above, he is dismissive of writing that might be a vehicle for sexual reminiscences in the 1960s (his own youth), the novel does claim, implicitly, that 'we were like this, so this is how it is':

> For research, I went around all my friends and acquaintances and asked everyone I knew for their early knobby stories—everybody has one—and I came out with a great stack of tales, some crude, some pathetic, some funny, some charming, but all with something to say. Out of these, I assembled the events in *Doing It* around three lads I knew when I was younger.[38]

The retrospective recovery of a circumscribed friendship network's sexual experiences, though not represented in the novel as belonging to his own generation and his own particular social milieu, contributes to a depiction of teenage masculinity to which many (male) readers, including those close to Burgess in age, may feel no particular affinity. A lively example of a disengagement from *Doing It* by male readers emerged during a BBC TV Newsnight Review discussion between Will Self and Mark Kermode in 2003.[39] Both refused to recognize their own teenage experience as represented by the novel, suggesting that Burgess does not quite get the age register right and that the boys behave like early rather than late teenage characters. Self claimed that teenagers would feel preached at by the novel, while Kermode suggested that reading a 40-year-old man's words masquerading as those of adolescent boys was 'rather creepy'. Unsurprisingly, as adult critics perhaps unusually reading a young adult novel, both recoiled from the suspicion that they were thus positioned as in need of moral guidance.

For these critics, Burgess's attempts to engage young people through detailed and explicit accounts of teenage experience clearly failed on this occasion. There are questions of critical standpoint (adult, middle-class, highly educated readers) that should qualify complete acquiescence in their judgements.[40] However, whatever their own limitations, they do highlight the problems that arise, and that Burgess invites, in reading *Doing It* as an 'authentic' portrayal of teenage boys. Differences in class, ethnicity and sexuality, most obviously, significantly complicate *any* attempt to represent teenage boys' experience as of an enduring and singular kind. But the strength of the novel lies in its comic structure.

Comic perspectives on the teenage boy

If Burgess fails to offer a sufficiently differentiated perspective on male sexuality, and attributes to his seventeen-year-old characters the preoccupations some would associate with much younger boys, he does construct a narrative that, within the form of the comic novel, allows for more credible explorations of the emotional vicissitudes of sexual activity. The narrative trajectories of the three central male characters are sufficiently troubled and potentially destructive to allow the comic rendering of their circumstances worthy of serious attention. Curiously, Fine entirely ignores the embedding of the most offensive talk in these trajectories and the guarded friendship between the three boys, Jonathon, Dino and Ben. It is their dilemmas that provide the substance of a novel that, otherwise, might fail to address either the teenage audience Burgess claims or the wider readership publishers seek to attract. Ben's affair with a manipulative teacher in her twenties and the growing loneliness, despair and isolation following from his promise of secrecy is perhaps the most bleak and disturbing narrative strand. Jonathon's vulnerability to the stigma of having a 'fat' girlfriend, and the further complication that he imagines he has cancer of the penis, allow for some quite subtle explorations of distress, anxiety and embarrassment.

Dino's arrogance, sexual opportunism and self-obsession provide a further basis for exploring multiple disjunctions and misunderstandings. Indeed, Burgess's approach, shifting between narrative viewpoints, is especially effective in extending the threads of bewilderment and misunderstanding between all concerned. Such 'play' with areas of knowledge, mostly putting the reader in a position to see more than the characters know themselves, but *also* to see how each 'feels', places *Doing It* with its almost entirely non-comic predecessor *Junk*, where the narrative shifts from character to character throughout the novel. However, in *Doing It* Burgess uses *both* omniscient narration—describing and explaining events beyond the knowledge of any one character and also commenting on the thoughts and feelings of the core protagonists—*and* first-person narration by several of those main characters. By both means Burgess shifts 'focalizations'. Jonathan Culler usefully defines focalization by differentiating between two meanings of 'point of view', a phrase we use a lot in talking about the novels we have read: 'Discussions of narrative frequently speak of the "point of view from which the story is told", but this use of *point of view* confuses two separate questions: who speaks? and whose vision is presented?'[41]

Dino, whose feelings both of frustration and self-satisfaction are made visible, sometimes within the same chapter, through 'his' first-person narrative (for example, Chapter 17: 134–5) and through the 'omniscient' 'third-person' narration (135–9), thus both exhibits his arrogance and is explained as an actor in events he cannot fully understand or control. But the third-person narration in combination with other characters' first-person narratives also tells us things he cannot know. For example, at the end of Chapter 24 (third-person narration), Zoe, with whom he has had sex, is told that he is also continuing a relationship with Jackie; she responds: '"Chuck him?" said Zoe. "I'm going to fucking destroy him"' (206). We know, and Dino doesn't, that revenge awaits him. Such turns, familiar enough in continuing serials (soaps) on television, contribute to the narrative dynamic and invite engagement, even concern and empathy, from readers positioned as 'above' the events. In this respect, *Doing It* offers readers a position at some distance, perhaps implicitly more 'mature', looking back to events and situations that are familiar and painful but also 'understandable'.[42] Adult readers might thus feel included in the field of the novel's implied readership and that therefore this is not *just* a novel for teenagers.

Readers are also invited to witness the unruly, confused and inadequate attempts to think through their circumstances by each of the three main male figures. In each case, their resources are shown to include elements borrowed from popular cultural narratives, some associated with earlier childhood. For example, Dino's power fantasies are reminiscent of the children's picture book *Angry Arthur* in which Arthur's anger becomes all consuming, destroying just about everything around him.[43] Dino, walking away after being told to 'fuck off' by Jackie (the girl he pursues throughout the novel), is abruptly repositioned through third-person narration as a child actor in his own solipsistic drama:

> As he walked sadly back home alone, Dino distracted himself by imagining that a mighty power-beam grew out of each of his temples, destroying everything they touched. All that lay behind his step was crushed by his passing. Trees, houses, lampposts, even small hills were all reduced to trash or broken neatly off where the beam struck them. If he stood on tiptoe, he could peer over the devastation. The world below his nose was a tangled mass of rubble and destruction. (33)

Later, when Dino has to deal with his own parents' crises as well as his own faltering attempts to have a 'relationship', a key chapter is entitled 'Dino the Destroyer' (Chapter 22). Ben's attempts to withdraw from the 'predatory' embrace of his teacher, Alison, are rendered in terms derived, in part, from computer games:

> From next door came a terrible strangulated, groaning roar. It seemed to express agony, rage and lust all at the same time. He'd never heard anything like it. There was something chitinous about it, as if a giant insect had suddenly discovered its mouth had air, and was giving voice to the accumulated desires and appetites of its kind for the past three hundred million years. With a cry he dropped the tea bags and ran next door. Alison was stretching out her legs. (272)

The strategy that secures his eventual escape depends on finding and bringing into play a monster even more powerful and, for Alison, terrifying—her own mother. This resolution, enabled by transposing the complexities of his relationship to the narrative logic of fantasy play, returns Ben to his own teenage world, paradoxically both successfully 'moving on' and failing to engage as an adult-in-a-relationship.

Similarly, Jonathon imagines that he has 'magical helpers' (148–9). The comedy here is that they are so rule-bound that he has to dismiss almost every wish he can think of as unlikely to be acceptable to them and, as they fade from his thoughts, he concedes 'Childish or what?' (152). From the first page of the novel, he deals with sex through a relentless stream of variously harsh and cynically offensive jokes.

Meanwhile, in his private reflections, he is constructed almost as a bewildered child. His gradual recognition of female sexual desire—demonstrated by Deborah—is rendered in language that is also, strikingly, like that used by Burgess 'speaking-as-himself':

> Sex is ...well it's so rude, isn't it? You wouldn't think girls would like sex. You'd think it's too rude for them [...]. And yet apparently even the nice ones like you sticking the rudest thing you have on your whole body up the exact, rudest part of their body that they have! It doesn't make a lot of sense to me. (145)

To some extent, Burgess constructs the three central male characters as children, little boys lost among knowing girls and sexually mature women and, at the same time as pursuing physical encounters with them, perplexed by the emotional dynamics in which they are caught up as incompetent actors. It is this aspect of the novel that perhaps led both Will Self and Mark Kermode to deny any sense of recognition in their reading, as if Burgess has 'recaptured' a childhood or youth that *remains* his own fabrication.[44] But perhaps such broad realist expectations are misplaced in reading a comic novel where the disjunction between thought and action is, as in *Junk*, central. It might reasonably be suggested that 'incoherence' is fundamental to Burgess's representation of 'youth' or 'adolescence' in *Doing It*—and possibly of sexual relations more broadly. As 'he' (Jonathon, but also 'Melvin Burgess') says: 'It doesn't make a lot of sense to me'. Such a perspective may, or may not, engage teenage readers but it appears integral to Burgess's own comic pessimism and, despite his disclaimers, might even be read, therefore, as displaced autobiography rather than the 'knobby' book for boys he intended to write.

Some concluding thoughts

As is usual in reading and talking about novels, and in writing about them as I have in this chapter, the characters come to occupy the foreground, almost as if they step forward to claim their substance as fully constituted beings. Pick up a copy of *Doing It* and the cover itself initiates this process before the book is even opened. On the back of the Andersen Press hardback edition (2003) the three boys are named (the girls are not): 'Dino, Jon and Ben have three very different problems but they've all discovered sex'. The Penguin paperback (2004) also lists the three boys by name, introducing each with a sentence pinpointing their respective dilemmas. Such naming invites us to accept what Roland Barthes calls the 'ideology of the person': we assemble characters from 'semes' despite their 'instability [...] dispersion, characteristic of motes of dust, flickers of meaning'.[45] Barthes argues that 'the person is no more than a collection of semes', converging through the use of a proper name:

> The proper name enables the person to exist outside the semes, whose sum nonetheless constitutes it entirely. As soon as a Name exists (even a pronoun) to flow toward and fasten onto, the semes become predicates, inductors of truth, and the Name becomes a subject.[46]

In talking about novels, it is very difficult *not* to persist with the illusion that the characters are real people. So, again on the back cover of the Penguin edition, *The Times* comments: 'Excellent. The sex lives of seventeen-year-old boys are skilfully dissected.' That readers do (sometimes) accept, with conviction, that Dino, Ben and Jonathon are credible seventeen-year-old boys is apparent.[47] But if they are discussed only as if they are real teenage boys, we may forget to consider and to question their *textual function* both in articulating a variety of discourses around sex and power and in displaying emotional disjunction. If we neglect the artifice of their construction, we risk being drawn into reading *Doing It* as a *revelation of* teenage life rather than a comic re-staging of disparate narratives of sexual misadventure from a fraction of Burgess's own generation.

The first enigma we are presented with by the cover of—and publicity for—almost any novel is its title: in this case, *Doing It*. 'Doing what exactly?' we are invited to wonder and thus, so the hermeneutic logic goes, we are drawn into the narrative.[48] With the hardback edition 'doing it' is imprinted in red letters on a silver wrapped condom. But the author's name is presented in large white letters occupying nearly a quarter of the black cover. So the enigma, in one sense already resolved by the condom, is not quite what it seems. In this case it is more like posing the question—'What has Melvin Burgess done *now*?' The book, though no longer published by Andersen Press, is positioned in a narrative of growing notoriety centred on the author-celebrity himself—after *Junk*, after *Lady: My Life as a Bitch*, what next? We are enticed to read on and find out just 'how far' he will go—in a curious parallel with the linear and goal-oriented sexuality condensed in the novel's title. Zipes, again, remarks that the 'design and appearance of the book became increasingly important because, as a commodity, the book signified something about the character of the person using it',[49] but here the book cover signifies something about the career of the author, highlighting, and promising, increased transgression. The

Penguin edition has an image of a girl's legs with her knickers being pulled back on, her naked bottom just outside the frame of the cover. The name Melvin Burgess is positioned just above the centre line, superimposed on the girl's slightly bent knees. Again, the proper name of consequence is not, it seems, a character in the novel but the author himself. But, as I have argued, this may be especially appropriate to the text enclosed in these covers, with its very particular resurrection of male sexuality.

Notes

1. In Jack Zipes, *Sticks and Stones: The Troublesome Success of Children's Literature from Slovenly Peter to Harry Potter* (New York: Routledge, 2001): 39–60.
2. See Jacqueline Rose, *The Case of Peter Pan: Or the Impossibility of Children's Fiction* (London: Macmillan, 1984); Roberta Seelinger Trites, *Disturbing the Universe: Power and Repression in Adolescent Literature* (Iowa City: University of Iowa Press, 2000); Alison Waller, *Constructing Adolescence in Fantastic Realism* (London: Routledge, 2009).
3. Zipes, *Sticks and Stones*: 44.
4. See David Buckingham, *After the Death of Childhood: Growing Up in the Age of Electronic Media* (Cambridge: Polity Press, 2000); David Buckingham, Hannah Davies, Ken Jones and Peter Kelley, *Children's Television in Britain: History, Discourse and Policy* (London: British Film Institute, 1999); Nancy Lesko, *Act your Age! A Cultural Construction of Adolescence* (London: Routledge, 2001).
5. Chris Richards, *Forever Young: Essays on Young Adult Fictions* (New York: Peter Lang, 2008). See also Chapter 2 of Chris Richards, *Teen Spirits: Music and Identity in Media Education* (London: UCL Press, 1998).
6. Jane Kenway and Elizabeth Bullen, *Consuming Children: Education-Entertainment-Advertising* (Buckingham: Open University Press, 2001); David Buckingham, *The Material Child: Growing Up in Consumer Culture* (Cambridge: Polity Press, 2011).
7. Melvin Burgess, *Doing It* (London: Andersen Press, 2003) and (London: Penguin, 2004). All further textual references in the chapter are to the 2003 edition.
8. See http://www.melvinburgess.net/
9. I have discussed young people's writing—and its presence online—in Chapter 1 of *Forever Young*. Of course, there have been some prominent, though exceptional, instances of young writers getting published while still teenagers—see S. E. Hinton, *The Outsiders* (London: Gollancz, 1970) and Nick McDonell, *Twelve* (New York: Grove/Atlantic, 2002), for example.
10. See John Stephens, 'And it's So Real': Versions of Reality in Melvin Burgess's *Junk*', in Heather Montgomery and Nicola J. Watson (eds.), *Children's Literature: Classic Texts and Contemporary Trends* (Basingstoke: Palgrave

Macmillan and the Open University, 2009): 320–8; Trites, *Disturbing the Universe*.

11. Richards, *Forever Young*.
12. See David Belbin, 'What Is Young Adult Fiction?', *English in Education* 45(2) (2011): 141.
13. Mark Haddon, *The Curious Incident of the Dog in the Night-Time* (London: Cape, 2003) and (London: David Fickling Books, 2003) (children's edition).
14. Francesca Lia Block, *Dangerous Angels* (New York: Harper Collins, 1998).
15. See Chris Richards, 'Addressing "Young Adults"? The Case of Francesca Lia Block', in Nicole Matthews and Nickianne Moody (eds.), *Judging a Book by its Cover: Fans, Publishers, Designers, and the Marketing of Fiction* (Aldershot and Burlington VT: Ashgate, 2007): 147–60; Chapters 2, 3 and 5 in Richards, *Forever Young*; Chapter 7 in Chris Richards, *Young People, Popular Culture and Education* (London: Continuum, 2011).
16. Kate Kellaway, 'Autistic differences', *The Guardian*, 27 April 2003 (http://www.guardian.co.uk/books/2003/apr/27/fiction.guardian childrensfictionprize2003).
17. www.bbfc.co.uk/
18. Melvin Burgess, 'Teenage Fiction Comes of Age', *The Bookseller*, 11 August 2000 (archived at http://www.melvinburgess.net).
19. Melvin Burgess, 'Ban Sex and Drugs? Not in my Book', *Times Educational Supplement*, 7 July 2000 (archived as 'Rethinking Literacy' at http://www.melvinburgess.net).
20. Melvin Burgess, *Junk* (London: Andersen Press, 1996); see also *Bloodtide* (London: Andersen Press, 1999); *Lady: My Life as a Bitch* (London: Andersen Press, 2001).
21. Jenny Grahame, *Making Junk: From Page to Screen* (London: English and Media Centre, 1999); Michael Rosen, '*Junk* and Other Realities: The Tough World of Children's Literature', *The English and Media Magazine* 37 (Autumn 1997): 4–6.
22. The novel is an 'old media' form. See Richards, *Forever Young*; Sara Bragg, *Media Violence and Education: A Study of Youth Audiences and the Horror Genre* (unpublished PhD thesis, University of London, 2000); Sara Bragg and David Buckingham, *Young People, Sex and the Media: The Facts of Life?* (Basingstoke: Palgrave Macmillan, 2003); Sara Bragg and David Buckingham, 'Too Much, too Young? Young People, Sexual Media and Learning', in Feona Attwood (ed.), *Mainstreaming Sex: The Sexualization of Western Culture* (London: I. B. Tauris, 2009): 129–46.
23. Burgess, 'Ban Sex and Drugs? Not in my Book'.
24. Chris Barker, *Cultural Studies: Theory and Practice*, 3rd edn (London: Sage, 2007): 20–1.
25. Gemma Moss, *Un/Popular Fictions* (London: Virago, 1989): 116.
26. See, for example, Melvin Burgess, 'Sympathy for the Devil', *Children's Literature in Education* 35(4) (December 2004): 289–300.

27. Burgess, 'Teenage Fiction Comes of Age'.
28. Melvin Burgess, '*Junk/Smack*' (www.melvinburgess.net).
29. Mikhail Bakhtin, *Speech Genres and Other Late Essays* (Austin, TX: University of Texas Press, 1994): 95.
30. Jane Mills, *Sexwords* (Harmondsworth: Penguin, 1993).
31. Milka Ivic defines the idiolect as 'the whole of the speech characteristics of an individual, including all personal nuances'. Milka Ivic, *Trends in Linguistics* (The Hague: Mouton, 1965): 82.
32. Melvin Burgess, *Smack* (New York: Avon Books, 1999): 289–93.
33. For sociological evidence from past decades see Paul Willis, *Learning to Labour: How Working-Class Kids Get Working-Class Jobs* (London: Saxon House, 1977): 43–7; Sue Lees, 'How Boys Slag Off Girls', *New Society*, 13 October 1983: 51–3; Sue Lees, *Losing Out: Sexuality and Adolescent Girls* (London: Hutchinson, 1986); Roger Hewitt, *White Talk Black Talk: Inter-racial Friendship and Communication amongst Adolescents* (Cambridge: Cambridge University Press, 1986): 126–99; Valerie Hey, *The Company She Keeps: An Ethnography of Girls' Friendship* (Buckingham: Open University, 1997): 71–83; Beverley Skeggs, *Formations of Class and Gender: Becoming Respectable* (London: Sage, 1997): 118–38.
34. In the USA, see Eve Ensler, *The Vagina Monologues* (London: Virago, 2001); Inga Muscio, *Cunt: A Declaration of Independence* (Emeryville, CA: Seal Press, 2002). In Britain, see Angela Carter, *The Bloody Chamber and other Stories* (London: Vintage Classics, 1995); Germaine Greer, *The Madwoman's Underclothes: Essays and Occasional Writings, 1968–85* (London: Picador, 1987); Mills, *Sexwords*: 54–5.
35. Anne Fine, 'Filth Whichever Way You Look at It', *The Guardian*, 29 March 2003.
36. Richards, *Forever Young*: 55–60; See also Belbin, 'What Is Young Adult Fiction?': 137.
37. Burgess, 'Sympathy for the Devil': 296; *Doing It*: 60, 145.
38. Burgess, 'Sympathy for the Devil': 296.
39. BBC TV Newsnight, 'Review: *Doing It*', 28 April 2003.
40. Richards, *Forever Young*: 59–60.
41. Jonathan Culler, *Literary Theory: A Very Short Introduction* (Oxford: Oxford University Press, 2000): 88.
42. *Ibid.*: 91–2.
43. Hiawyn Oram and Satoshi Kitamura, *Angry Arthur* (London: Red Fox, 1993 and London: Andersen Press, 2008).
44. See Zipes, *Sticks and Stones*: 44.
45. Roland Barthes, *S/Z*, trans. Richard Miller (London: Cape, 1975): 19.
46. *Ibid.*:191.
47. Richards, *Forever Young*: 55–60.
48. Barthes, *S/Z*: 19.
49. Zipes, *Sticks and Stones*: 47.

2

'Keeping it Real': The Debate for Boyhood and its Representations in *Doing It* and *Kill All Enemies*

Michele Gill

Introduction

> There's no shortage of people willing to sneer at young men for their clumsiness, their shyness, their lack of social skills and to attack them for their attitude to girls. Men, perhaps not in society at large but in fictions, often don't get a good deal these days. There's the action man, the cool dude, the oaf, the wimp; not much else [...] I wanted to do some psychological realism and show that young men aren't just blundering buffoons, teetering on the edge of sexual violence all the time, but sensitive as well as coarse, thoughtful as well as lustful, vulnerable as well as crude; and above all, irreverent and funny.[1]

Discussing his reasons for writing the novel *Doing It* (2003),[2] Melvin Burgess highlights a number of complex issues surrounding the question of what it means to be a boy at the beginning of the new millennium. He makes an important distinction between the actual lives of men and boys and discursive representations of boyhood which have dominated popular culture for the past two decades. Specifically, he suggests that in contemporary fiction male characters are represented through a very limited range of stereotypes while acknowledging that men as a social group may still get 'a good deal' in Western societies.

While I disagree with Burgess's assessment of male fictional character representations,[3] his suggestion that young men in contemporary society are often interpreted and portrayed negatively, tunes into a wider debate on boyhood *per se* which was taking place in the media, popular writing and academic literature in Western societies at the time *Doing It* was published. The images of contemporary boyhood which stemmed from these various sources were especially influential during the 1990s and the early years of the new millennium, and defined the way boyhood has been understood in popular culture. Burgess, in discussing what he considers to be the paucity in fictional representations of boys, in fact highlights one of the key flaws in much of the popular writing and some academic debate: an inability to make distinctions between young men, who are largely represented as an indistinct, homogenous group and on the whole positioned very negatively. In this cultural narrative, fears were expressed about boys' lives: perceived failures in relation to education, involvement in gang culture and the attendant violence associated with this lifestyle, as well as an inability to engage in meaningful emotional relationships, were key themes which appeared in popular discourse.[4] However, the interpretation of this negative imagery, specifically the reasons suggested as being responsible for the problematic nature of boys' lives, was to evolve into a divisive political debate. Positioned as both troubled and troubling, at the beginning of the new millennium boys' lives were certainly in the spotlight.

In this chapter I discuss some of the narratives which have grown up around boyhood in popular writings and academic literature during the 1990s and into the new millennium and consider how they have been interpreted in two novels by Melvin Burgess—*Doing It* which was published at the time when the debate for boyhood was especially vocal and *Kill All Enemies*, published more recently in 2011[5]—specifically analysing representations of male friendships, romance and issues around male violence. In concluding, I suggest that Burgess has largely achieved his goal of portraying multidimensional male characters, albeit within a framework of white, middle-class, heterosexual masculinity, and that the characterizations offer a more complex source of imagery around contemporary boyhoods than have come out of the majority of popular culture in recent times. Yet these representations are also potentially problematic in that they portray young men—as Burgess intended—as being 'sensitive', 'vulnerable', 'funny', but also 'coarse', 'lustful' and 'crude' and the latter create unease because they represent a version of being male which has generally been discredited in Western cultures. However, if the imperative is to portray boyhood as complex and multidimensional, is it plausible for elements which are considered unpalatable or inappropriate simply to be ignored or 'written out' if they actually form part of the make-up of some boys and young men? Assuming that readers accept Burgess's account of boyhood as 'authentic' (and this is not necessarily the case as discussed by Chris Richards in Chapter 1), then they are left with a dilemma as to whether this is ultimately a version of boyhood which can be condoned.

The 'universal boy'

One of the important outcomes of second-wave feminism in relation to academic research was to put men on the agenda as a category open to investigation. Initially an area of inquiry in the domain of feminist scholars, the study of men's lives developed into the field of Men's Studies, growing from the late 1970s when research focused on men as socially privileged in relation to women, to analysing various aspects of men's lives and experiences and later, the dynamics between men themselves in relation to social power structures which culminated in the seminal work of R.W. Connell, *Masculinities*, published in 1995.[6] However, this proved to be a highly divisive area of research, exemplified by the men's movements which grew up from the 1970s, specifically the politically polarized groups of profeminist and mythopoetic men.[7] While undoubtedly there are positive outcomes from male organizations which promote social justice and equality, there are also examples of groups that try to reinforce or stabilize men's privileged positions in both private and public spaces. Consequently, such groups can be described as engaging in backlash politics rather than seeking out social justice in spite of their desire to improve the lives of men and boys. Nevertheless they remain significant because of the influence they have had on the landscape of Men's Studies through their writings and social presence and specifically, their debates about boyhood which, on the whole, position boys as a victimized yet homogenous group.

Kenneth Kidd argues that much of the debate around boyhood—what he terms 'boyology'—is, in the case of the USA, a reflection of conservative politics, found in groups such as the Mythopoetic Men's Movement. He continues:

> The boys' movement is imagined variously as a pioneering defence of boyhood, as a rejoinder to an exaggerated girl crisis, and as a parallel crisis that also demands attention. The rhetoric of the boy crisis is at once sexist and indebted to feminism; it also echoes the language of civil rights while ignoring racial and class biases of our culture. That the new boyology should function as a referendum on feminism and indeed all of the social reforms of the last thirty-plus years isn't surprising, as boyology is at heart a conservative American ideology of masculine self-making.[8]

Kidd's suggestion that 'boyology' is ultimately a defensive reaction to the changing political landscape appears to be borne out by the stance taken by a number of commentators on the subject of boyhood. For example, writing in the USA in 2000, Christina Hoff Sommers highlights concerns about the ways in which boys are perceived in contemporary society, suggesting that, '[i]t's a bad time to be a boy in America. As the new millennium begins, the triumphant victory of our women's soccer team has come to symbolize the spirit of American girls. The defining event for boys is the shooting at Columbine High.'[9] Sommers, then, implies that boys have become entwined in, and are possibly being defined by, a discourse which equates them with violence and failure. However, her argument is deeply divisive in that she pits boys against girls and goes on to suggest that many of the woes which are heaped upon young men are due to a feminization of society which privileges and benefits girls, especially in relation to education.[10]

At the same time, another strand of the 'crisis' discourse suggests that it is the consequences of traditional versions of masculinity—understood to privilege independence, rationality, competitiveness—which are harmful to boys, creating something of a paradox at the heart of this narrative which is never fully resolved: are boys under threat because traditional versions of being male are becoming feminized, not allowing them to express their maleness, or is traditional masculinity damaging boys because it stifles emotional maturation and engagement, making young men hard, aggressive and sometimes violent. Both narratives run through the literature without resolution but equally position boys as being victimized and devoid of individual agency, giving credence to Kidd's argument that for many commentators this is essentially a political debate rather than an enquiry into the lived experiences of individual boys.

The way that the concept of masculinity is interpreted in relation to boyhood in discourses proposed by the Mythopoetic Men's Movement and others such as Sommers, imply that it is essential, yet the very fact that Connell points to the potential for different versions of hegemonic masculinity suggests a sense of fluctuation, that there are multiple ways of being male which are therefore related to social conditions as opposed to being solely biological. This position is one which Kerry Mallan highlights in her discussion of masculinity representations in literature for young people:

> The apparent security that comes with the notion of 'a central essence to being male' has been eroded and masculinity can no longer be fictionalized as a stable, coherent and universal attribute of men. Rather, masculinity is being re-defined (however provisionally) not as a 'singular', 'given', or 'natural' attribute of men, but as a social and political construction that is temporally and historically shaped.[11]

While a discussion about the nature of gender *per se* and its definition as a performative entity[12] is beyond the scope of this chapter, nevertheless it is important to establish that masculinity is understood here as being socially constructed rather than simply an essential part of the individual. This potentially affords more flexibility to boys and young men in their personal identity formations although it is important that the regulatory nature and power of socially privileged versions of masculinity also be acknowledged. Through his fictions Burgess emphasizes a sense of plurality, portraying various ways of being young and male while simultaneously suggesting that there are characteristics which young men embody, thus making his position ambivalent, something I discuss further in relation to the novels *Doing It* and *Kill All Enemies*.

Boyhood to boyhoods

Whatever the perceived reasons for the 'crisis' in boyhood—too much 'traditional' masculinity; too much feminization—a feature of this narrative is that very little distinction is made between boys, leading to the question of who the boys being described by Sommers (and other writers taking this approach) actually *are*.[13] Very little reference is made to race, class, or sexuality, all major factors in boys' constructions of their individual personal identities. Like the writings which have come out of the Mythopoetic Movement, specifically the formative text, *Iron John* (1990) by Robert Bly,[14] much of this material takes as its subject the white, middle-class, heterosexual male. However, there have been examples of qualitative research which examine boys' lives by focusing on diversity.[15] These studies all emphasize the importance of making distinctions in relation to the key life factors above, as evidenced in the findings of Niobe Way and Judy Chu in their study of ethnically diverse boys in the USA. They suggest that in the vast majority of research the experiences of white, middle-class boys have come to represent all boys, writing out and making invisible all forms of diversity and conclude that, 'the findings from these studies are commonly used to generalize all boys rather than serving as a framework for understanding the specific experiences of white middle-class boys'.[16]

Qualitative research opens up the possibility of allowing boys to talk about their own lives and how they experience being young and male in a culture which frequently vilifies and victimizes them in equal measure. One example of such insight comes from the work of Stephen Frosh *et al.*, which is based on in-depth interviews carried out with both boys and girls in a London school about their experiences of young masculinities. This includes the ways in which boys construct their gendered identities in relation to the privileged versions of hegemonic masculinity which they encounter in their daily lives. Although hegemonic masculinity is frequently interpreted as being a version of 'traditional' masculinity in that it is understood to represent characteristics such as independence, rationality, competitiveness and physical strength, R.W. Connell points out that, '[h]egemonic masculinity is not a fixed character type, always and everywhere the same. It is, rather, the masculinity that occupies the hegemonic position in a given pattern of gender relations, a position always contestable.'[17] This becomes evident in the interviews conducted by Frosh and his associates as issues around ethnicity in particular featured centrally in the ways that many of the boys described their experiences of being young and male.

While it may seem obvious to suggest that boys are individuals who experience life in different ways depending on their unique circumstances, material such as the work of Sommers exemplifies that this is not always the case in popular writing about boyhood. Without considering difference and the distinctive experiences of boys, the idea of boyhood ultimately becomes nothing more than a blank canvas onto which society's hopes and fears about young men are projected. Annette Wannamaker makes this point in relation to American boyhood: while acknowledging that there are a number of concerns about boys in contemporary society in the USA, verified in statistical data, which show boys to be struggling in some areas of their lives, she seeks to stress the difference between perceptions of and opinions about boys as a category and real boys' lives: 'If what we, in the contemporary United States, *think* about boys matters more than what boys actually *are*, then our boys are in big trouble because they are, at least within popular discourse, in the midst of a crisis.'[18] She goes on to acknowledge the importance of individual agency and the complex nature of personal identity formation, but suggests that this may be suppressed in public discourse as boys come to represent simultaneously the hopes and fears of a society.

Doing boyhood in *Doing It*

Although fiction is another example of cultural imagery which exists at a discursive level, its composition means that it has the potential to present nuanced portrayals of being male rather than anonymous, homogenized boyhoods. Fiction can therefore have an impact on how boys are interpreted in culture, something which Melvin Burgess was aware of in publishing *Doing It*.

Burgess's novel is irrevocably associated with the subject of teenage sex, due in no small part to the furore which surrounded its publication; in particular Anne Fine's scathing review.[19] As Roberta Seelinger Trites argues in *Disturbing the Universe*, the ways in which representations of young people engaging in sex are presented in children's and YA literature has long been a contentious issue and the negative consequences of being sexually active have generally been emphasized ahead of any potential enjoyment.[20] It is debatable whether Burgess's novel can be understood entirely as an example of this type of 'morality' tale since it avoids the spectre of teenage pregnancy or serious heartache which are usually features of such works, but it does follow some of the narrative threads which abound in such novels: for example, each of the boys learns a lesson about sexual relationships in the course of the story and becomes more thoughtful as a consequence. Ultimately, although *Doing It* initially appears to challenge the conventions of literature for young people with graphic sexual descriptions, it is, in the end, more conservative in terms of the narrative outcomes.

In the novel, Burgess introduces three key romantic relationships, each featuring one of the boys; Dino, Ben and Jon. The boy who most closely represents an example of 'traditional' masculinity is Dino: outwardly confident, good looking and popular, he appears to be the epitome of success. However, what is interesting about Burgess's portrayal of Dino is that after a series of very humorous incidents during which he thoroughly discredits himself, Burgess still affirms Dino as a success in spite of his many mistakes and the dubious character flaws which he embodies and persists with even after the humiliations. Burgess does not describe Dino's exploits through the framework of a cautionary tale; instead he implies that he *will* learn from the events which unfold but at the same time, his behaviour will not change dramatically because basically there is nothing wrong with him. The conceit which Dino illustrates, his belief that girls find him irresistible—'You ask anyone, there's loads of other girls would love to go out with me, they'd shag me tomorrow if I went up and asked' (30)—is in total contrast to the situations in which he finds himself as self-delusion mounts. Paradoxically, this makes him a more likeable character for the reader, even though his behaviour and attitudes remain largely reprehensible. For example, when his parents separate he is both furious and disconsolate and is further outraged because he feels that Jackie, his girlfriend, does not support him enough. It is left to Ben to patiently point out why: '"You two timed her. She was upset"' (322). Dino, however, remains upset, seeing the world only from his own rather self-obsessed perspective.

One of Dino's more unpleasant moments occurs when he challenges Jon about his interest in Deborah, drawing attention to her weight, although he knows that Jon likes her. After Dino and Ben see Jon kissing her at a party, a discussion ensues in which Ben tries to emphasize Deborah as a person with feelings, warning Jon not to hurt her, but Dino persists in objectifying her by highlighting her weight: '"Fat's fat. That's all there is to it"' (71). Jon is portrayed as less confident than Dino and is torn between his feelings for Deborah and how he is judged by his peers; initially he tries to convince himself that he doesn't like her because he knows that his male peers will mock him, as evidenced by Dino's behaviour. However, although Jon is portrayed as less self-assured than Dino, he too is not above some outrageous behaviour. He is very interested in having sex and although he has reservations about acknowledging Deborah as his girlfriend in public, privately he is very happy for her to 'take him in hand'. For instance, although he is reluctant to be seen leaving Dino's party with her, when they are alone he has no qualms about enjoying himself: '"I've been waiting to get you on your own all night," she told me, and lifted her eyebrows up and gave me one of those big lovely smiles, so I knew what was in store. And of course Mr Knobby, the traitorous little fletch, stood up at the mere thought' (93).

Throughout the narrative the descriptions of how the boys indulge in their sexual relationships are graphic but equally humorous, due to their general hopelessness. It is actually the way in which the boys objectify women and girls in all-male conversations which is rather more disquieting. At the outset, when the reader meets the three boys for the first time, they are discussing the 'merits' of a girl from school as opposed to a homeless woman:

> 'OK,' said Jonathon. 'The choice is this. You either have to shag Jenny Gibson—or else that homeless woman who begs spare change outside Cramner's bakers.'
>
> Dino and Ben recoiled in disgust. Jenny was known as the ugliest girl in the school but the beggar woman was filthy. Her teeth!
>
> 'You are so gross,' said Ben disgustedly. (1)

The way in which the boys talk about female characters can justifiably be described as disrespectful because it is. However, whether this becomes the definitive reading of the text rests on how the reader interprets Burgess's constructions of the boys in the narrative: their buffoonery and general showing off conceals a world of insecurities which implies that these outward displays do not represent the whole picture, as discussed earlier in relation to Dino. Burgess certainly proposes that this vulgar behaviour is part of the make-up of each of the boys, and is therefore intrinsic to the narrative, but ultimately it does not constitute their entire composition. It is this contradiction which prevails throughout the novel, creating more complex portrayals but also potential 'disquiet' as the three boys remain unapologetic even as they gain valuable life experiences: Burgess appears to imply that even as they mature they may still be 'filthy' but for him this is authentic, one of many aspects of the male character, and therefore entirely acceptable.

Interpreting Burgess's portrayals of the boys and their sexual behaviour in relation to the debates around boyhood, presents a rather complex picture: the passages where they discuss girls, boasting about their own sexual prowess, initially reinforce some of the stereotypes about boys and romantic relationships, positioning the boys as predatory and emotionally disengaged. These have been key narrative threads in relation to 'crisis' yet, as already discussed, Burgess suggests that these characteristics are part of the make-up of boys and young men. Much of the popular writing on boyhood positions young men as being victimized and the stance taken by Suzanne Enck-Wanzer and Scott Murray in discussing the ways in which teenage boys are mediated through *Cosmo Girl!*, a magazine intended for a teen girl readership, can be interpreted in this way. They suggest that the young man constructed in the magazine is 'one who is sexually assertive, emotionally evasive, and naturally prone to aggression'[21] and this 'message' is conveyed to girl readers, creating expectations around male behaviour and reaffirming a specific, traditional way of being male. However, it is the potential impact for teenage boys that is the focus of Enck-Wanzer and Murray as they conclude that this type of representation means 'boys are in turn interpolated into these positions in ways that strip them of agency and determination as individuals and diversity as a group'.[22] This argument has validity as these kinds of cultural representations potentially pressurize boys to behave in particular ways, creating expectations around how to be male. However, I would suggest that this is making an assumption about how boys may respond to this imagery and therefore divests them of agency and diversity, the very problem which Enck-Wanzer and Murray are trying to highlight in relation to the cultural narrative invested in the magazine. There is certainly a suggestion that the boys in Burgess's narrative are trying to emulate a dominant cultural image which privileges the confident, sexually proactive male; in particular Dino, who thinks of himself as a 'babe magnet'. Therefore an argument could be made for the boys being victimized by their need to conform to expectations of male sexual behaviour. However, the overriding impression which emanates from the narrative is that the ways in which the boys go about romantic relationships is a consequence of their inexperience, due to age rather than a default in hegemonic masculinity constructions.

Burgess undermines the idea of the predatory male not only through the comical exploits of the boys but also through his portrayals of the female characters in the novel (a subject which is discussed further by Joel Gwynne through the lens of changing female sexuality in Chapter 3). Burgess describes Ben, Jon and Dino as being 'handled' by the girls they become involved with. Burgess uses multiple narrators which allow him to suggest that girls can be equally active in seeking out sexual relationships: giving the reader access to both the interior and exterior worlds of his characters, he shows not only the difference between private hopes and public expectations but also what he perceives are the similarities between male and female attitudes and behaviour in relation to sex. In a discussion of contemporary sexual behaviour, Michael Kimmel proposes that male and female sexual behaviour is now less distinct; while intimate relationships have become more feminized, sexual behaviour has become more masculinized, concluding that '[w]hile men's sexual behaviour has hardly changed, women's sexuality has changed dramatically, moving increasingly closer to the behaviour of men'.[23] Certainly Burgess portrays both male and female characters as interested in sex. Jackie's friend Sue is incredulous that Dino could be of any use other than for sexual pleasure: 'Shagging him is the single possible reason for going out with Dino. If you don't shag him, why bother?' (56). Dino is objectified in the same way as the female characters in the opening scene, although the girls' behaviour here may also be an example of bravado, masking other, more personal feelings. Nevertheless, through Sue's eyes Dino is seen as merely a sexualized body, albeit an attractive one, which can be negotiated without too much emotional investment.

While Burgess destabilizes the idea that only boys are proactive in seeking out sexual relationships at the cost of deeper, more emotional, committed relationships, the tone throughout remains playful, humorous, non-judgemental. At the same time, the resolution of each of the narrative strands suggests that successful romantic relationships involve both emotional and sexual intimacy. The relationship which is presented as most likely to endure is the one which evolves between Jon and Deborah, who are friends as well as sexual partners. Observing them together, Ben is described as recognizing the intimacy which exists between them, their physical closeness symbolic of the whole relationship: 'He [...] saw that they'd leaned close together already, noses almost touching across the little wooden table. Sweet. He'd never seen Jon look so happy' (329).

Perhaps the boy with the most unconventional character is Ben. From the outset he is portrayed as being less concerned about how he is perceived than the other boys. As discussed earlier, he insists on Jon treating Deborah well while the other boys in their peer group objectify her, and he doesn't mind being out of tune with his peers which potentially positions him as 'other'. Because his friends are unaware of his relationship with Ali Young, his single status and apparent lack of interest in girls leads Dino to consider if he might be gay. While Dino, in one of his more enlightened moments, goes on to state that he doesn't care either way, the fact that Ben is considered 'suspect' because he doesn't necessarily conform to the hegemonic masculinity of his peer group indicates the pressure which can potentially be exerted in directing boys towards the normative masculinity performances expected within their social landscape. However, Burgess does not pursue the implications of 'otherness' in relation to boyhood, instead creating a range of diverse versions of being male, albeit within the boundaries of heterosexual relationships, which in Ben's case is his secret affair with his teacher.

When Ben finally decides to take action to decisively end his relationship with the increasingly unstable Ali, he contacts her mother who attacks him, ruefully pointing out, 'Yes, every schoolboy's dream, I expect. [...] I suppose you had a great time boasting to all your mates about it' (317). Initially this does seem like a dream situation but ironically Ben doesn't tell anyone until the pressure becomes too great and he confides in Jon, desperate to find a way out of the situation. However, the way in which Burgess portrays the relationship is complex: on one level Ali Young is in charge as she is older and sexually more experienced. The first time that they have sex Ben is still a virgin and it occurs to him that he is being taken advantage of: 'Ben found himself thinking that this was how young girls must feel when they are seduced by an older man. He was so bewildered and sexed up he could hardly think. There was no question of him having any choice about what was happening' (27). However, he also enjoys himself, a great deal, and concludes that, 'Ok, the whole thing had been awkward and embarrassing as well—but it was easily the nicest half an hour he'd ever had in his life. Fleshy, filthy and holy. It had everything' (28).

In discussing the way in which relationships between older women and boys are mediated in Western culture, Matthew B. Prickett argues that as a society we find it difficult to interpret these relationships as abuse because 'we see them as a rite-of-passage or as an "initiation" for teenage boys'.[24] He goes on to suggest that this is because there is a tradition of young men being encouraged to be proactive in seeking out sex in order to prove themselves as men. This can simultaneously be interpreted as positive in terms of validating traditional masculinity but also problematic because it negates the need for emotional engagement, again highlighting opposing narratives surrounding boyhoods and how they should be encouraged to evolve. Certainly Burgess is reluctant to position Ben as a victim and the fact that he is the one who eventually takes steps to end the relationship ultimately leaves him in a more powerful position, although not entirely unscathed by the experience.

While Ben is portrayed as more perceptive than Jon or Dino, as evidenced in his attitude towards Deborah, he too has the potential to be coarse, joining in with the general 'banter' about girls and sex. This suggests that Burgess's purpose is not to construct stereotypes of acceptable versus unacceptable versions of being male; instead he creates boys who fluctuate between gross, funny and sensitive, in both romantic relationships and friendships.[25]

Doing It is dominated by relationships and Burgess portrays the complexities and challenges which face teenage boys as they manoeuvre and try to balance competing demands. Through his characterizations of Dino, Ben and Jon, Burgess shows that intimacy and disclosure are potentially challenging because of the regulatory nature of 'traditional' forms of masculinity which encourage boys to be competitive and suspicious of each other. However, through the interactions which take place between them, Burgess implies that these relationships are valuable to each of them in terms of their emotional security and confidence. This does not mean, however, that they are immune to the influence of the larger peer group and although Ben and Jon are affected less than Dino by peer interactions, all three regularly become involved in behaviour that is vulgar; intended to impress. However, the humour which is employed throughout signals that Burgess does not intend this to be problematic, but rather the consequence of age and immaturity, and certainly not wrong.

Different, but the same

In *Kill All Enemies*, Burgess returns to his now familiar style of multiple narrators; in this case they include Billie, Rob, Chris and intermittently Hannah, Billie's care worker who works at The Brant, a Pupil Referral Unit, where all three teens end up. As with the boys in *Doing It*, the different voices offer perspectives on each other and consequently highlight the inconsistencies in each others' stories which reveal the unreliability and vulnerability of each of the young narrators. Here the humour and frivolity of *Doing It* is replaced by a more serious tone as the teens face difficult challenges in their lives around violence, isolation, and being positioned as outsiders. The themes at the heart of the narrative are therefore closely associated with the 'crisis discourse', yet unlike *Doing It*, there is no sense of Burgess focusing on boyhood *per se*: being male is not central to the crises faced here and this perhaps reflects the less politicized landscape in which the novel was published or simply that Burgess did not set out with the same purpose when writing *Kill All Enemies*.

From the outset the narrative is engulfed by a sense of rage as all three teen narrators are embroiled in abusive relationships, both physical and emotional, and are viewed as problematic by the majority of adult characters who surround them. However, Burgess does not pit teens against adults with the young people positioned as victims. Instead, he creates a more complex set of relationships in which the three teens contribute to their own problems. At the same time he does portray the young people sympathetically, empathizing with their sense of frustration and the lack of control they have over their own lives.

Billie is a fourteen-year-old girl who is living with foster carers following the breakdown of her own family. She blames these circumstances on her mother's problems with alcohol but as the narrative unfolds it becomes clear that her own behaviour is also a factor: she regularly has furious violent outbursts which leave her and others physically and emotionally scarred. Her reputation goes before her, something she is aware of, and although she tries to control her behaviour, in stressful situations she comes out fighting and is described as taking some satisfaction from this. For example, after being attacked in a park by a group of girls, Billie makes it her business to find out who they are and goes looking for revenge which she exacts in such a way that the reader is left in no doubt that this has become a way of life: '"Kill the bitches!" I screamed, and Jane and Sue let out a yelp by my side. We went in, I had to jump up at Betty to get my head anywhere near her fat snotty nose, but I felt it crunch lightly, that soft crunch you get, when you know you've broken something inside' (96). Burgess does provide a back story for Billie which explains some of her behaviour and through Hannah's narrative the reader is made aware of Billie's vulnerability. On meeting her for the first time, Hannah recognizes that Billie is trying to protect herself, 'scowling away like

Dennis the Menace, this black cloud hanging over her. Well, I'd seen that scowl before. That wasn't anger. That was her way of trying not to cry' (108). Nevertheless there remain some very unlikable aspects to her character which Burgess does not seek to hide by presenting her as solely a victim of her circumstances. Like the boys in *Doing It*, Billie is described through both positive and negative narratives which results in a more complex, yet troubling, characterization.

Attending her latest school, one in a long line from which she ends up being excluded, Billie meets Rob who she rescues from bullies, although she cannot understand why he is allowing himself to be beaten up as physically he is a large boy. However, unknown to Billie, Rob is also being bullied and beaten up by his stepfather, Philip, and feels crushed and ashamed because he is unable to help his mum, a victim of domestic violence:

> 'How rubbish am I?' If I was worth anything, I'd be down there as soon as he raised his voice to her. I'm a big lad—big as Philip, I reckon. But I never do. You know why? Because I'm too scared. I'm a coward. I sit up here instead, playing computer games and pretending nothing's happening. (54)

Although he is still a child and is being beaten up by a man, Rob feels that he should be able to take on Philip, to 'be a man'. The subject of male violence has been at the centre of concerns about young men, yet at the same time, boys have traditionally been encouraged to stand up for themselves which highlights the contradictory landscape presented to them: at once they are encouraged to defend themselves but are then vilified for the logical outcome of this behaviour. In the case study carried out by Frosh *et al.*, they found that many young men do indeed protect themselves and maintain their positions in the peer group through a suggestion of being able to prove themselves in situations involving real or threatened violence.[26] Ultimately Burgess portrays Rob taking on Philip after he hits Davey, Rob's younger brother, and beating him in a physical fight which suggests that in some circumstances reverting to traditional understandings of being male are necessary to survive. Rob is aware of the irony in using physical violence and stops short of causing serious injury because he doesn't want to be the kind of man that Philip represents. Standing over Philip with a knife in his hand, he has a choice:

> 'You haven't got the guts, have you?' he said.
>
> 'You'd love that, wouldn't you?' I said. I didn't know what I was going to say; it just came out. 'If I did that, you'd have won, because then I'd be

> just like you. But you haven't, and I'm not. So why don't you just fuck off out and get on with your miserable, sad, bullying little life, before I kick your sorry arse through that door.' (303)

Rob is portrayed as more sensitive than the other two teens, similar to Ben in *Doing It*—he is kind and caring towards his mother and younger brother and a loyal friend to both Billie and Chris, even in the most difficult of circumstances—yet in standing up to Philip he must use the 'weapons' of traditional masculinity which again highlights the pervasive nature of hegemonic versions of being male and the challenges which boys face in negotiating them as they grow and mature. As in *Doing It*, uncertainty arises as to how Burgess positions traditional masculinity. While he certainly does not condone Philip's violent domestic abuse, he does suggest that Rob's response is acceptable in this context which potentially creates unease about how to respond to the narrative. Are there circumstances in which violence is acceptable? Billie tries to control her rage while Rob needs to unleash his anger: in both cases this is necessary for the individual to build a life and a sense of belonging yet there remains a sense of a retreat to traditional stereotypes of being female and male respectively.

While Rob and Billie battle to survive in very difficult circumstances, Chris, a boy from a middle-class home, initially appears to create problems for himself. He is constantly in trouble at school through his refusal to do any homework and is generally unruly in the classroom, leading to friction with teachers. His dissent frustrates his parents and this leads to yet more conflict as they try to 'control' his behaviour. Eventually everyone loses patience and he is excluded from school and sent to The Brant. Perceived failure in education has been central to anxieties around boyhood and was the focus of much of the debate which suggested that education had become too feminized, privileging girls at the expense of boys, as highlighted above. However, Burgess's portrayal of Chris in relation to education is rather ambivalent: Hannah eventually uncovers a problem with dyslexia which accounts for many of his problems, especially his unwillingness to do homework, but he remains antagonistic towards formal schooling and returns to his former school to exact revenge on one teacher with whom he had a particularly fractious relationship. This ends with him chasing both the teacher and deputy head with a fire extinguisher:

> I got 'em so good, they started slithering around on the foamy goo and ended up on their bums, nowhere to go, nowhere to hide, covered in white foam like a pair of penguins in batter. I emptied the extinguisher and then I swung it round and chucked it through the window. *Crash!* I love the

> sound of breaking glass. Then I turned round and I walked out of that useless dump forever. (308)

As this comic sequence of events is the culmination of the narrative, it could be argued that Burgess valorizes misbehaviour in his teen characters in the same way as he represents some of the more challenging characteristics of young males in *Doing It*. Ultimately he may make the same claim for *Kill All Enemies* as he did for the earlier novel; that he is aiming to portray more nuanced and multidimensional characters which young readers can relate to. That this doesn't necessarily result in positive role models is likely to be more problematic to adult gatekeepers than a teenage audience. In this instance, finding each other allows the characters to grow: Billie begins the slow process of trying to trust people again, Rob finds the strength to stand up to Philip and the school bullies and Chris begins to find his place in the world. The 'Kill All Enemies' of the title is actually a heavy rock group which Rob becomes a member of, with Billie adding some vocals. Chris suggests himself as their manager and finds to his surprise that he belongs and finally feels comfortable. To the adults around them, these relationships may appear dysfunctional but they are significant to all three youths and as research has suggested, friendships which may appear anti-social to those outside can still have a positive effect on the young people involved.[27]

Rather than an interpretation of contemporary boyhoods, *Kill All Enemies* portrays the challenges faced by young people who are considered problematic by society and perhaps tunes into a more current debate which highlights anxieties about youth more generally concerning lawlessness and anti-social behaviour. However, in common with *Doing It*, the novel portrays ambivalent characters who do not necessarily resolve the unease which exists around youth in contemporary Western societies.

What crisis?

In relation to the crisis discourse specifically, *Doing It* and *Kill All Enemies* respond in a number of complex, and at times contradictory, ways: as discussed throughout this chapter, Burgess explores the challenges which his fictional boys face in developing personal relationships, in the face of fears about personal vulnerabilities or ridicule whether in respect of friendship or romance. This is a theme which has been significant in both popular and academic writing about boys' lives due to concerns about a lack of emotional engagement created by adherence to traditional Western models of being male. However, Burgess suggests that it is possible to develop and maintain such relationships regardless of the tensions which may surround them, a stance which challenges the opinion that boys are necessarily unable to create and maintain meaningful intimate relationships. Simultaneously he portrays the boys as vulgar, offensive and generally sexist while in the company of other boys and is resolute that this too is part of the make-up of teenage boys. In discussing violence, specifically in relation to Rob in *Kill All Enemies*, Burgess delivers another ambivalent response: he portrays Philip the stepfather as an abhorrent bully but Rob employs the same strategy in ending the bullying, beating up Philip. Although he stops short of using the knife there is still a suggestion that to defeat a physically violent bully, further violence is necessary and Rob feels empowered by his response.

Burgess presents some challenging behaviour in both novels, suggesting that it is part of the make-up of boys—and girls—related in part to their youth and immaturity but not necessarily problematic. However, whether this is what commentators who bemoan the feminization of boys' masculinity would consider to be an appropriate source of positive cultural imagery in relation to representing 'real boys' is questionable and this highlights the dilemma of Burgess's writing. As I suggested at the beginning of this chapter, if we want to portray boyhoods as multidimensional and to give boys more complex and nuanced cultural representations of being male, can we then edit out characteristics which we don't find acceptable? Burgess has certainly achieved his goal of portraying young men as 'sensitive as well as coarse, thoughtful as well as lustful, vulnerable as well as crude; and above all, irreverent and funny' and therefore offers versatile and potentially perceptive portrayals of being young and male in the face of a cultural narrative which cites crisis while reducing boys to a homogenous mass. Whether readers can ultimately accept Burgess's interpretations of what it means to be young and male in the twenty-first century, however, is very much open to debate.

Notes

1. Melvin Burgess, 'Sympathy for the Devil', *Children's Literature in Education* 35(4) (2004): 296.
2. Melvin Burgess, *Doing It* (London: Andersen Press, 2003). All further references in the chapter are to this edition.
3. My PhD thesis explores representations of boyhoods in contemporary YA fiction and I found a diverse and nuanced range of male characters. See

Michele Gill, *Making Men: Representations of Boyhoods in Contemporary Young Adult Fictions* (unpublished thesis, Newcastle University, UK, 2012).

4. In a 2005 article for *The Guardian*, 'In the Hood' (13 May 2005), Gareth McLean discusses mediated perceptions of young people and why they are portrayed as dangerous in contemporary society.
5. Melvin Burgess, *Kill All Enemies* (London: Penguin Books, 2011). All further references in the chapter are to this edition.
6. R.W. Connell, *Masculinities* (Berkeley, CA: University of California Press, 1995).
7. In *Politics of Masculinities: Men in Movements* (Thousand Oaks and London: Sage, 1997), Michael Messner outlines the key men's movements which originated in the 1970s and the implications of the positions they take up in relation to social justice through gender equality.
8. Kenneth Kidd, *Making American Boys: Boyology and the Feral Tale* (Minneapolis: University of Minnesota Press, 2004): 170.
9. Christina Hoff Sommers, *The War against Boys: How Misguided Feminism Is Harming our Young Men* (New York: Simon and Schuster, 2000): 18. The now infamous Columbine High School massacre took place on 20 April 1999. Two students, Eric Harris and Dylan Klebold, killed twelve students and a teacher before committing suicide. For a detailed study of the events and the implications of the killings see D. Cullen, *Columbine* (New York: Twelve, 2009).
10. See Victoria Foster, Michael Kimmel and Christine Skelton, 'What about the Boys? An Overview of the Debates', in Wayne Martino and Bob Meyenn (eds.), *What about the Boys? Issues of Masculinity in Schools* (Buckingham: Open University Press, 2001): 1–23 for a discussion of the different positions which have been taken up in relation to boys and education.
11. Kerry Mallan, 'Men / Boys Behaving Differently: Contemporary Representations of Masculinity in Books for Young People', *English in Australia* 131 (2001): 57–8.
12. Judith Butler, *Gender Trouble: Feminism and the Subversion of Identity* (New York and London: Routledge, 1990).
13. Other examples of books which address boyhood from the same perspective as Sommers include: Steve Biddulph, *Raising Boys* [1997] (Sydney: Finch Publishing, 2003); Dan Kindlon and Michael Thompson, *Raising Cain: Protecting the Emotional Lives of Boys* (New York: Ballantine Books, 1999); and Michael Gurian, *The Minds of Boys: Saving our Sons from Falling behind in School and Life* (San Francisco, CA: Jossey-Bass, 2005).
14. Robert Bly, *Iron John: Men and Masculinity* [1990] (London: Rider, 2001).
15. Examples include: Mike O'Donnell and Sue Sharpe, *Uncertain Masculinities: Youth, Ethnicity and Class in Contemporary Britain* (London and New York: Routledge, 2000); Stephen Frosh, Ann Phoenix and Rob Pattman, *Young Masculinities: Understanding Boys in Contemporary Society* (Basingstoke: Palgrave, 2002); Niobe Way and Judy Y. Chu (eds.), *Adolescent Boys: Exploring Diverse Cultures of Boyhood* (New York: New York University

Press, 2004); and Niobe Way and Jill Hamm (eds.), *The Experience of Close Friendships in Adolescence* (San Francisco, CA: Jossey-Bass, 2005).

16. Way and Chu, *Adolescent Boys*: 1–2.
17. Connell, *Masculinities*: 76.
18. Annette Wannamaker, *Boys in Children's Literature and Popular Culture: Masculinity, Abjection, and the Fictional Child* (New York: Routledge, 2008): 1.
19. Fine's attack on *Doing It* appeared in *The Guardian* newspaper and claimed that the novel was filth and an insult to both boys and girls. 'Filth, Which Ever Way You Look at It', *The Guardian* online, 29 March 2003.
20. Roberta Seelinger Trites, *Disturbing the Universe: Power and Repression in Adolescent Literature* (Iowa City: University of Iowa Press, 2000).
21. Suzanne Enck-Wanzer and Scott A. Murray, '"How to Hook a Hottie": Teenage Boys, Hegemonic Masculinity, and *CosmoGirl!* Magazine', in Annette Wannamaker (ed.), *Mediated Boyhoods: Boys, Teens, and Young Men in Popular Media and Culture* (New York: Peter Lang, 2011): 58.
22. *Ibid.*: 70.
23. Michael S. Kimmel, *The Gender of Desire: Essays on Male Sexuality* (New York: State University of New York Press, 2005): 11.
24. Matthew B. Prickett, '"Who Is the Victim Again?" Female Abuse of Adolescent Boys in Contemporary Culture', in Annette Wannamaker (ed.), *Mediated Boyhoods: Boys, Teens, and Young Men in Popular Media and Culture* (New York: Peter Lang, 2011): 39.
25. For a more detailed discussion of boys' friendships in *Doing It*, see my earlier paper: 'Best Mates: An Exploration of Male Adolescent Friendships in Contemporary Young Adult Fictions', *New Review of Children's Literature and Librarianship* 14(1) (April 2008): 1–17.
26. Frosh *et al.*, *Young Masculinities*: 83.
27. William W. Hartup, 'Adolescents and their Friends', in Brett Laursen (ed.), *Close Friendships in Adolescence* (San Francisco, CA: Jossey-Bass, 1993): 3–22.

3

The Girl and the Streets: Postfeminist Identities in *Junk*, *Doing It* and *Sara's Face*

Joel Gwynne

Introduction

In *Learning Curves: Body Image and Female Sexuality in Young Adult Literature*, Beth Younger contemplates the status of young adult fiction in contemporary literary culture and society. As a genre 'uniquely subject to social supervision and frequent challenges', Younger contends that YA fiction is 'an important source of cultural information for young readers in that it portrays adolescents negotiating the social and sexual standards of the dominant culture'.[1] Produced by adults yet consumed by young readers, the genre occupies a sensitive and often contentious space, and for this reason the cultural information presented by adult authors to their potentially impressionable audience has long been the target of intense critical attention. Yet Younger's study is perhaps representative of a pattern in recent years in which girlhood studies has emerged more expansively as a pronounced site of critical interrogation. Since the mid-1990s, popular culture and academic scholarship has witnessed 'an incredible proliferation of images, texts and discourses around girls and girlhood',[2] exploring not only the relationship between culture and gendered identities, but also the role of social institutions in the formation of femininities. As Angela McRobbie notes, the 1990s saw female youth—rather than 'youth' in more general terms—positioned as a site of political investment and utilized as a metaphor for social change, with girls and young women 'recognized as one of the stakes upon which the future depends'.[3] This recognition of the importance of girls and young women in society has been further evidenced by what Anita Harris has described as a widespread investment in them as 'new kinds of workers, consumers, and citizens', with their 'relationship to the labor market, their patterns of consumption, and their sexual lives'[4] the subject of close attention by the state, the private sector, researchers and the media. While young working women have achieved high media visibility as the new professionals of the new millennium, female adolescents have attained equal visibility in terms of 'health alerts about their sexual behavior' and 'educational discourse and policy preoccupied with girls outperforming boys'.[5]

YA fiction reflects the contemporary concerns of female adolescence and deserves feminist critical attention, especially for its representations of young female bodies. Sinikka Aapola, Marnina Gonick and Anita Harris have documented that adolescence and the process of becoming an adult is a 'deeply gendered and gendering experience',[6] and specifically female experiences have largely been explored in the work of prominent women writers of YA fiction such as Judy Blume, Malorie Blackman, Sarah Dessen and Elizabeth Scott. Melvin Burgess publishes against this trend as a male writer who has established a reputation for producing fiction that is uncompromisingly realist in its depiction of the lived experiences of female adolescents. Yet, despite the critical attention paid to themes of substance abuse, prostitution and underage sex in his novels,[7] there has been no sustained discussion of how Burgess's female characters reflect the wider cultural aftershock of second-wave feminism, especially in relation to the construction of postfeminist identities and the reconfiguration of traditional gender roles. In this chapter, I am concerned with demonstrating how Burgess's novels reflect aspects of postfeminist discourse by situating the sexually active adolescent body as a site of constantly negotiated empowerment, and in doing so present a dramatic modification of conventional representations of adolescent female sexuality and femininity. Through an analysis of *Junk* (1996), *Doing It* (2003), and *Sara's Face* (2006), this chapter will examine how Burgess reconstructs femininity by positioning female sexual expression as 'agentic'[8] and the body as a site of self-regulation and excess. It will also focus on how Burgess's novels invoke contemporary moral panics surrounding notions of contemporary girlhood in crisis, and how this conceptualization is inseparable from postfeminist discourse. Prior to doing so, it is therefore important to locate and contextualize not only the emergence of the term 'postfeminism', but also its relationship to female adolescence in popular culture and academic discourse.

Postfeminism and girlhood

Media attention to the status of young women in Western societies has often been inseparable from considerations of the relative success and perceived failures of second-wave feminism as a socio-political movement. Whether in the employment and economic market as consumer-citizens, or in secondary schools and sixth-form colleges as exemplars of academic success, the heightened visibility of young women in society is a pattern that has permitted media commentators to proclaim the twenty-first century as a 'post-feminist' epoch in which feminist activism is no longer necessary. While 'post-feminism' and 'postfeminism' could be understood as distinctly different terms—with the former representing a historical period and the latter a cultural sensibility—it should be noted that in both instances the prefix 'post' is ambiguous, and can be understood as suggesting either a period 'after' feminism or, more optimistically, as denoting 'a genealogy that entails revision or strong family resemblance'.[9] The term can represent both a repudiation and affirmation of feminist politics, depending on how it is deployed in a certain cultural context. Even though many critics have drawn attention to the apparently empowering aspects of postfeminist discourse—comprising philosophies that espouse equality, inclusion and free choice—they have also highlighted how this celebration of the power of the individual is part of a more insidious process whereby the social constraints placed upon contemporary girls and women are deemed inconsequential. From this critical perspective, feminism is 'absorbed and supplanted by "postfeminism" in such a way that the complexity of contemporary feminist theories and activisms is lost'.[10] McRobbie extends this line of enquiry by stating that, 'postfeminism positively draws on and invokes feminism as that which can be taken into account, to suggest that equality is achieved, in order to install a whole repertoire of new meanings, which emphasize that it is no longer needed, that it is a spent force'.[11]

These critical appraisals appear to conclude that postfeminist ideology is ultimately disempowering; however, McRobbie's reference to the manner in which postfeminism 'positively draws on and invokes feminism' suggests that postfeminist sensibilities do not entirely, or even deliberately, reject feminism. Indeed, postfeminism has been read as offering liberating possibilities to women as a sensibility indicative of a post-traditional era characterized by dramatic changes in social relationships and conceptions of agency. Sarah Gamble astutely notes that postfeminism is a 'flexible ideology which can be adapted to suit individual needs and desires',[12] and is a discourse which refuses 'any definition of women as victims who are unable to control their own lives.'[13] This positive conceptualization of postfeminism has been most visibly discernible in representations of youthful femininity in popular culture. Even though female adolescents have always embodied powerful feminist potential—their ability to negotiate gender roles an 'unconstrained freedom representing the most fearsome threat to male control'[14]—the figure of the girl has been resurrected in contemporary popular culture and utilized to demonstrate the empowering possibilities of reconfigured femininity. This resurrection has followed a historical trajectory in which postfeminist sensibilities have also emerged, and Sarah Projanksy notes that 'the current proliferation of discourse about girlhood literally coincides chronologically with the proliferation of discourse about postfeminism'.[15] Discourses affirming girlhood as an empowering period of social development have been most conspicuously mobilized through the rhetoric of 'Girl Power' that began to dominate consumer culture in the mid-1990s, raising 'a series of striking questions about the relationship between feminism, femininity and commercialization'.[16]

Academic enquiry into these questions has been predominantly concerned with the political origins of 'Girl Power' and its comparative depoliticization in popular culture. While many second-wave feminists perceived 'girlyness' and its association with normative femininity as an artificial and disempowering man-made construct, this conceptualization was challenged through the third-wave feminist 'Riot Grrrl' movement whose, 'choice of mixing and matching frilly dresses with combat boots' epitomized the third-wave's 'contradictory and ambiguous relationship to mass consumer society and traditional forms of femininity'.[17] The movement politicized the notion that women are capable of performing feminine and feminist identities simultaneously, yet it is the Spice Girls who are commonly associated with the problematic mobilization of this message in consumer culture. As Jessica Taft observes, by the 1990s, the discourse of Girl Power had 'been deployed by various elements of popular culture and the mainstream media in a way that constructed a version of girlhood that excludes girls' political selves'.[18] Initially a subcultural political statement, Girl Power became co-opted in postfeminist media culture to imply that 'girls have attained all the power they could ever want, and there is nothing left to be done'[19] in terms of women's progress in society. Regardless of whether Girl Power is positioned as empowering or disempowering, it is clear that constructions of femininity have radically transformed in Anglo-American society and popular culture. This forces the reader and critic of YA fiction to consider how these changes are conceived and negotiated in texts produced by popular authors, most notably in terms of body image and attitudes to female sexual expression. If postfeminist culture is indeed indicative of dramatic changes in female gender roles and conceptions of agency, then how are these embodied in Melvin Burgess's novels? Do Burgess's female characters succumb to the multifarious sexual pressures placed on young women in society, or do they experience their bodies and sexuality as conscious and empowered agents? In order to answer these questions, it is important to begin by demonstrating how Burgess's girls reflect contemporary concerns surrounding the notion of girlhood in crisis.

Girls in crisis, girls as agents: negotiating the adolescent female body

Younger claims that adolescent females are 'among the most powerless in our culture', as 'while their bodies are continually viewed and desired, ultimately young women have little control of their lives'.[20] Burgess's novel *Sara's Face* is concerned with the seventeen-year-old protagonist's desire to transform her body in order to attain a level of fame that parallels her idol, Jonathan Heat. Yet, while the narrative of a young woman's attempts to achieve visibility in society locates the novel as an inscription of postfeminism, what is most striking is the way it invokes a number of contemporary debates surrounding the status of female adolescents in Western societies and the material reality of girlhood as an experience. The first page of the novel is important:

> [Sara] comes down to us as a mystery, a figure without explanation. Her refusal or inability to speak has led to endless speculation about her, but the story of her hopes and dreams, and her role in the terrible way they were fulfilled, remain elusive. How much did she plan? Was she in control the whole time, or was she just the innocent victim of Heat and his surgeon, Wayland Kaye? It's the purpose of this book to try to cast some light on the girl herself.[21]

Sara embodies the cultural experience of girlhood as an ambiguous territory of both empowerment and disempowerment. By presenting Sara's silence as either a 'refusal or inability to speak', the narrator summons larger questions surrounding the levels of agency that girls experience in their lives. In positioning Sara as potentially occupying polarized locales—as either 'in control' or an 'innocent victim'—Burgess's novel represents a wider pattern in popular culture whereby female adolescence is simultaneously and contradictorily depicted as an experience of crisis and an experience of liberation, the latter conceived as freedom from the gendered constraints of adult womanhood. Appola, Gonick and Harris have termed these opposing cultural trends as the 'Girl Power' discourse and 'Reviving Ophelia' discourse,[22] the second an allusion to Mary Pipher's bestselling *Reviving Ophelia: Saving the Selves of Adolescent Girls*, in which girlhood is depicted as a period of psychological crisis from which young women never truly recover. Connected to these antithetical cultural trends, Harris observes that contemporary girls are constructed as either 'can-do' girls or 'at risk' girls, with the former hailed as 'optimistic, self-inventing, and success-oriented' and the latter a focus of 'more general moral concern about juvenile delinquency, nihilism, and antisocial attitudes'.[23] Like the 'can-do' girl and 'at risk' girl, Burgess's Sara Carter is a character whose agency is positioned in constant flux. Despite 'her assertive stance', she is described as possessing 'something vulnerable about her' (51), and 'comes down to us as such a tangle of contradiction' (140). The ambivalence of Sara's agency is most apparent in the novel's exploration of female body dissatisfaction, where Burgess's presentation of Sara's level of control over her own body is complex. Sara's dissatisfaction with her body is framed in the language of psychiatric pathology—'Her dissatisfaction with her appearance was so profound, [Kaye] believed, that she suffered from a permanent sense of self-alienation from her own body' (199)—yet even this pathologization is subtly agentic. When she injures her face on an iron—an event that leads to the cosmetic surgery she desperately desires—the audience is informed that her 'accidents have come under much suspicion' as Sara may have 'engineered them herself' (21). Sara simultaneously embodies the 'at risk' girl who self-harms due to low self-esteem and the 'can-do' girl who engineers for herself opportunities for cosmetic self-improvement.

The adolescent female body has become a site in which debates surrounding the 'can-do' girl and the 'at risk' girl are heavily invested. The vast majority of these debates concern the pressures placed on young women to valorize an impossibly narrow model of slim, Caucasian feminine attractiveness, and women's desire/ability to function as agents in the process of positive identity creation. Issues surrounding young women's crisis of self-esteem over their body shape are widely documented, yet Jane Victoria Ward and Beth Cooper Benjamin comment that 'the site of change has moved from the collective to the individual', and 'strategies now focus increasingly on changing the girl herself (or sometimes her parents), rather than changing the culture to accommodate her developmental needs'.[24] In accordance with the neoliberalization of contemporary Western cultures—in which the individual rather than society is positioned as ultimately responsible for his/her social welfare and self-management—young women are increasingly held accountable for their physical condition. Before examining how this operates in *Sara's Face*, it is important to connect the subject of young women's bodily crisis to the wider global development of neoliberal 'new femininity'.

In *Reclaiming the F Word*, Catherine Redfern and Kristen Aune comment that, '[m]any cultures now assume that something is fundamentally wrong with the natural female body and that women are duty-bound to reshape ourselves'.[25] In a continuation of long-standing cultural narratives that reify the importance of female desirability, the global media has in recent years employed the 'makeover' narrative to further entrench the notion that female desirability is a goal to be relentlessly pursued. In postfeminist media culture, the makeover narrative has become 'a mainstay of advice columns and entertainment literature targeted at women',[26] and the process of 'becoming' feminine is framed as a form of liberation, inviting women to reject the notion of a 'stable, untested and fixed' self and embrace female identity as 'subject to a multiple and on-going process of revision, reform and choices'.[27] Scholars have located this conceptualization of new femininity at the centre of the sexualization of Western cultures and the mainstreaming of the porn industry, with Feona Attwood stating that '[d]iscourses of sexual agency have been seen as central to the development of new femininities, part of a broader shift in which older markers of femininity such as homemaking skills and maternal instincts have been joined by those of image creation, body work and sexual desire'.[28] New femininity could thus be understood as a subversive form of modern female identity in its ostensible rejection of the passivity and dependence associated with traditional femininity. It is, however, important to emphasize that this positioning ultimately represents modification rather than repudiation. Shelley Budgeon observes that even though females under neoliberalism 'must be assertive, autonomous, and self-determining', they 'must also retain aspects of traditional femininity, including heterosexual desirability and emotional sensitivity to others'.[29]

Returning to Burgess, *Sara's Face* engages with this opposition between traditional femininity and new femininity in terms of both female sexuality and body image. Even early in the novel it is clear that Burgess is concerned with exploring the difficulties young women confront in attempting to negotiate the contradictory space they must inhabit in culture. This is first discernible in Burgess's treatment of Sara's sexuality. As a desirable teenager, Sara 'began to attract a great deal of attention from boys, which she suffered with a kind of bemused tolerance' (13). Yet, when the newspapers 'tried to make out that she slept with a great many of those boys', she 'liked it that people thought that about her' even though she 'wanted only to do it with someone special' (14). Sara represents, then, the challenges that young women confront in a society that encourages women to cultivate an image of active sexuality while conforming to traditional notions of romantic love. In terms of body image, Sara also occupies an ambivalent space between traditional and new femininity, as both a passive consumer of society's commercialized images of beauty and an entrepreneuring, ambitious young woman who takes charge of her self-presentation. Estella Tincknell notes that women's 'achievement of a limited social and political autonomy in the twenty-first century' has been 'paralleled by a renewed discursive emphasis on femininity as a pathological condition, this time recast as a relentless drive for physical perfectibility'.[30] Burgess's novel demonstrates the psychological trauma that may occur when young women inevitably fall short of achieving their target of physical perfection, with Sara declaring to her boyfriend, '[y]ou ought to be grateful I've got my clothes on—it's such a mess underneath. Talk about cellulite. It's revolting. This tit's practically under my arm when I lie down. What good's that on a photo shoot?' (6). Sara feels 'fat and ugly', even though the 'briefest glance at any photograph would tell anyone else that none of this was true' (21), demonstrating her internalization of the narrow standards of beauty disseminated by the fashion industries through the mass media.

While it could, therefore, be easy to read Sara as an example of the 'at risk' girl who is a victim of media and social pressure, Burgess complicates this reading by investing his character with a level of subjectivity in the process of makeover and bodily renewal. Sara becomes a 'can-do' girl who is 'getting [herself] really sorted out' by 'eating really healthily' and 'getting loads of exercise' (61). She is, at this point in the novel, preparing her body for cosmetic surgery, and Burgess manages to execute a sophisticated balancing act between accentuating her subjective experience of empowerment while centralizing the social forces that precipitate her desire to reshape her body: 'My skin is glowing. I've had my hair done. Look at me: I look like something out of a magazine. If Mark could see me now—wow. Well, boy, you lost what you ain't never gonna get' (61). Sara experiences the makeover process as agentic—even though this pleasure derives from her new bodily location in the mainstream of commercial femininity—and perceives the makeover as not only a form of self-improvement, but even artistry: 'People say I'm good-looking like that, but there's loads of girls prettier than me, or sexier than me or, whatever. That's not the point. Anyone can be pretty these days' (10). Sara declares 'if you want to be a work of art, you have to suffer a bit' (7), and is highly aware of her motivations: 'People say, What's the point if you have natural good looks, but that's not the point. The point is, this is art. It isn't natural, that's the point. Art makes things unnatural' (62). Burgess emphasizes the possibility of Sara's agency by providing two explanations for her willingness to perform facial surgery, the 'view of the courts', that she 'was either forced or fooled, perhaps both', and a more empowering interpretation, that 'she was complicit in her own fate—that she made a deliberate sacrifice for the sake of her own ambition' (157). In his exploration of Sara's management of her body and the wider culture's construction of female desirability, Burgess thus locates his protagonist as embodying competing narratives about girlhood, as either an experience of crisis or an experience of postfeminist empowerment and choice.

Junk: femininity, public space and sexual agency

Burgess's novels frequently convene the 'can do' and 'at risk' into the same space by placing female adolescents in vulnerable positions while demonstrating their strength in adversity. Female strength is shown through dramatic modifications of dominant femininities, expressed in non-traditional attitudes to sexuality and the ownership of self and body. If postfeminism is indicative of the emergence of women who are 'both feminine and feminist at the same time, merging notions of personal empowerment with the visual display of sexuality',[31] then Burgess's *Junk* can be viewed as a case study of female adolescent gender roles in transition. Even though the novel situates girlhood as a location of crisis—Gemma Brogan nonchalantly asks the reader, '[w]as being bored a reason for running away to the city at fourteen years old?'[32]—Burgess employs this context of crisis to demonstrate the political reasons behind Gemma's decision to leave the parental home. The novel strongly suggests that the family nucleus—the preserve of parental authority and primary inscriber of traditional gender roles—is a microcosm of a society culpable in its refusal to acknowledge the changing status of contemporary girlhood in the aftermath of feminism.

Indeed, while the most conspicuous crisis in *Junk* is manifested in the drug abuse and prostitution that consumes Gemma after she leaves the parental home, these are themselves symptomatic of a wider crisis concerning gender roles and material space. Ever since the publication of Betty Friedan's *The Feminine Mystique* (1963), the private and domestic sphere has long been associated with fostering a detrimental and constraining normative femininity, with young women 'confined to the family home until they have established an appropriate heterosexual relationship'.[33] In a more contemporary milieu, Gemma Brogan's decision to flee the domestic space and mark her entrance into the world can be connected to more expansive moral panics surrounding teenagers' occupation of public spaces. As Gill Valentine, Tracey Skelton and Deborah Chambers assert, the 'space of the street is often the only autonomous space that young people are able to carve out for themselves, and hanging around, and larking about, on the streets, in parks and in shopping malls, is one form of youth resistance (conscious and unconscious) to adult power'.[34] This form of resistance may not appear to be specifically gendered, yet Harris observes that young women's 'apparently increasingly delinquent behavior is seen as one of the main reasons why the streets are no longer safe'.[35] In popular journalism, the emergence of girl gangs and increased levels of violence among female adolescents has been directly linked to the aftermath of feminism as 'byproducts of girl power out of control'.[36] Burgess does not appear to corroborate this particular moral panic, and instead demonstrates that female resistance to the private sphere is a feminist issue by constructing the public sphere as a location that affords greater levels of agency to young women.

Young women's occupation of the public space of the streets is motivated by different reasons compared to their male peers. Burgess engages with the specifically gendered causes of female resistance by locating the home and societal institutions as inadequate for female adolescent growth and entry into womanhood. The female characters of *Junk* demonstrate that reconfigurations of femininity cannot be tolerated in the reactionary location of the parental home. This is conveyed clearly at the beginning of the novel, when Gemma's father suspects that she may have had intercourse with her boyfriend, Tar. Referring to young women's sexual conduct more generally, Gemma's father states, '[h]er reputation is a girl's greatest asset', a view that Gemma sees as 'Stone Age!' (7). Gemma's response—'"What about her GCEs?" I said. "What about her ability to put her lipstick on properly?"' (7)—positions her in a postfeminist frame of reference, merging 'feminine and feminist at the same time'[37] by illustrating the importance of both academic achievement and feminine adornment. In the domestic sphere, Gemma's parents do not know how to manage her resistance to traditional femininity. While normative femininity is marked by a woman's ability to be caring, sensitive and nurturing, Gemma is 'not all that interested in niceness' and 'just want[s] to have a good time' (72). She is a character for whom 'sarcasm flows in [her] veins like blood', ensuring that her behaviour is not even received positively on the rare occasions that she does demonstrate a more conventional femininity: 'I couldn't even be good without arousing suspicion' (65). It is only after leaving the parental home that Gemma finds social acceptance, largely due to meeting peers who also reject conventional femininity. Gemma's initial meeting with another homeless girl, Lily, has a dramatic effect on her: 'Did you ever see someone and think straight away, I want to be that person? [...] This girl—nothing mattered to her' (120). For Gemma, Lily is 'the magic girl' (123) who discards 'all the rules' (120), and it is her neoliberal ideology of postfeminist empowerment that Gemma finds intoxicating: 'You can be anything, you can do anything, you can be anything, you can do anything' (259). Even though Lily's perspective is highly naïve—and, of course, distorted by heroin consumption—for Gemma it represents a long overdue affirmation of agency. Even after she begins working as a prostitute—which critics could perhaps interpret as proof that she is indeed *unable* to control her life—Gemma remains self-aware and reflective: 'Me, I've made my own choices and I'm happy with it. Yeah. Yes, I am. I'm in control of my life and I love it, and I love myself and I love Tar and I love my friends' (193). After experiencing the freedom of the streets, Gemma comments, 'I didn't look-like *anyone's* daughter any more, let alone Mr and Mrs Brogan's' (99). Now transformed by her experience in the public sphere, Gemma is unable to return home.

In *Junk*, the unregulated streets encourage agency in young women by providing a context in which their strength and vitality can be made visible, and the gendered terrain of the novel is clearly postfeminist in its accentuation of female strength juxtaposed with male fragility. Unlike Gemma, Tar has experienced a physically abusive home environment, rather than one that is merely ideologically constrictive, and leaves home as he 'needed a bit of space' (107). From the perspective of Vonny, Tar is unable to fully recover from his traumatic experiences as 'you didn't get any space when Gemma was around. She filled it all up' (107). Gemma's vibrancy is situated as an obstacle to Tar's convalescence, further marking her as non-nurturing and unconventional in gender orientation. Even in their consumption of heroin, Gemma is depicted as stronger than Tar in a manner that collapses bodily strength and psychological strength to the same parameters: 'Now she takes loads and loads again. She frightens me, she takes so much. She says that's because she's stronger than anyone else. Well, she is' (174). Burgess illustrates Gemma's vigour in a number of ways that can be connected to a generalized repudiation of femininity, most obviously in her emotional relationship with Tar. Even though she eventually falls in love with Tar, this occurs organically, and she is not constructed as a character who privileges romantic love as a central component of her identity, nor as one who specifically pursues attaining a romantic relationship.

Indeed, if we recall Harris's observation that young women do not usually escape the domestic sphere until securing an 'appropriate heterosexual relationship',[38] it is interesting that, in contradistinction, Gemma only feels comfortable entering such a relationship *after* enjoying freedom in the public sphere. In the early stages of the novel, it is clear that Tar is emotionally invested in Gemma, yet her response to his declarations of love is revealing: 'I felt so sorry for him, but I hadn't anything else to give him, you know?' (80). Even after losing her virginity to Tar, Gemma 'felt that someone could come along and blow hard and [she would] fly away from him' (80). For Gemma, the emotional intimacy and commitment that Tar expects represents a life of conformity and tradition, and it does not take long for other characters in the novel to realize that, 'Gems was feeling a bit tied down' (134). While Tar is a character who has 'had a hard time' (134) and hopes to take refuge in a loving relationship, Gemma 'wanted to take the place by storm' (134). After meeting Lily—who provides a model of hedonistic femininity—Gemma begins visiting nightclubs where all the girls 'looked like right *slags*' and 'didn't care about *anything*' (104, original emphasis). Gemma follows suit, rips a hole in her tights and takes to the dance floor while considering the potentially liberating possibilities of promiscuity: 'I looked around, and I thought, You can have a one-night stand every now and then without being a complete slut, right? And I fancied this guy. He had the right look. I mean, I wouldn't say I wanted to spend my life with him but I was ready for whatever was coming my way' (104). By constructing Gemma as a character who is not, by the mere fact of her sex, inclined to seek out emotional intimacy and long-term companionship, Burgess thus reflects a wider trend inherent in the 'can do' and 'at risk' discourses concerned with changing notions of female sexual conduct. In postfeminist culture, there has been great attention paid to the visible sexual agency of young women, sparking a number of debates regarding whether this should be a cause for concern or a cause for celebration. With this in mind, it is important to draw parallels between *Junk* and *Doing It*, the latter a more pronounced articulation of these debates, and to do so it is necessary to first lay the critical terrain of contemporary sexual politics.

Junk and *Doing It*: sexual politics

Gemma's non-traditional attitude to romance and female sexuality can be seen as merely one of the ways in which Burgess's novels show young women actively engaged in negotiating femininity and feminine roles in heterosexual relationships. This may appear to be a positive shift, for feminist critics have long positioned the heterosexual relationship as a site of male oppression in which women acquiesce to the sexual demands and unrealistic expectations of their partners. Yet, while many second-wave feminist critics identified sexual oppression as a highly political issue experienced in the private sphere, contemporary feminists have become increasingly concerned with the public pressures that young women confront in highly sexualized Western cultures. In the context of the 'pornografication'[39] of Western cultures and the mainstreaming of the sex industry, Gemma's attitude to promiscuity could be read as indicative of what Natasha Walter has described as a 'new culture of shags and threesomes, orgies and stranger fucks' which 'seems to be replacing the culture in which sex was associated with the flowering of intimacy'.[40] Walter argues that the 'highly sexualized' cultural landscape of contemporary Britain is 'tolerated and even celebrated' as it rests on 'the illusion of equality', a postfeminist climate in which it is perceived as 'unproblematic that women should be relentlessly encouraged to prioritise their sexual attractiveness'.[41] Locating the sexualization of Western cultures in popular culture, Gail Dines implicates the mainstreaming of the sex industry, observing that magazines like *Cosmopolitan* 'teach women how to perform porn sex in a way that is all about male pleasure'.[42] In 'porn culture', it is the 'sheer ubiquity of the hypersexualized images that gives them power since they normalize and publicize a coherent story about women, femininity, and sexuality'.[43]

Like Dines, the cultural commentator Ariel Levy has expressed concern regarding what she terms the rise of 'raunch culture' and the emergence of 'female chauvinist pigs' who deliberately 'make sex objects of themselves and of other women'.[44] Connecting this to postfeminist culture, Laura Harvey and Rosalind Gill have noted that the postfeminist subject is 'incited to be compulsorily sexy and always "up for it"',[45] while McRobbie states that young women endorse 'the ironic normalization of pornography' by wearing T-shirts bearing phrases such as 'Porn Queen' or 'Pay To Touch'.[46] Like Walter, McRobbie interprets the normalization of porn culture as an indication of the status of feminism in popular culture, arguing that the 'phallic girls' who embrace porn culture present the 'impression of having won equality with men by becoming like [their] male counterparts'.[47] She continues to ascribe the 'phallic girl' to discourses of the 'at risk' girl, young women who are 'asked to concur with a definition of sex as light-hearted pleasure, recreational activity, hedonism, sport, reward and status' and whose 'seeming masculinity enhances her desirability since she shows herself to have a similar sexual appetite to her male counterparts'.[48] McRobbie's position can be read as a critique of the manner in which postfeminist media culture has co-opted the values of third-wave 'power feminism', a form of politics that fosters solidarity between women 'through shared pleasures and strengths, rather than shared vulnerability and pain',[49] a sensibility that is, according to Naomi Wolf, 'unapologetically sexual' and 'understands that good pleasures make good politics'.[50] Regardless of how the audience may interpret both recent challenges to traditional femininity and the increased sexual activity of young women in both the UK and US, what remains clear when reading Burgess is that his novels are fully engaged with these cross-cultural transformations. In both *Junk* and *Doing It*, Burgess's girls emblematize the changing face of contemporary sexual politics and the effect on adolescent sexuality.

This is most apparent through both attitudes to sexual intimacy and the manner in which the female characters actively negotiate sexual boundaries. In *Junk*, while Tar is not afraid to express his *emotional* attachment to Gemma, she is not afraid to express her *physical* desire for him. Tar is 'about a foot taller', however it is she who takes control: 'I pulled him on me so he was leaning against me. I could see from his face what I was doing to him' (70). Burgess devotes several extended passages to describing the effect that Lily has on Gemma's understanding of the power of female sexuality: 'She had this black net string vest on. [...] I mean, you could see everything. It was quite long for a vest but even so when she bent over to put on a new cassette you could see her bare bum. Everyone was watching her —but it wasn't just because she was more or less naked. She had the power' (119). Burgess makes it clear that—from Gemma's perspective—Lily is not simply a powerless object of the male gaze: 'She was everything that was going on in that room' (199). While these examples from *Junk* demonstrate a shift in young women's relationship with their own bodies, it is *Doing It* that depicts with greater force a narrowing space between male and female sexual conduct. The novel presents several alternatives to conventional femininity through the characters of Jackie, Sue and Siobhan (Zoe). Comparing Jackie and Siobhan, Dino remarks that 'Siobhan shags and Jackie doesn't' (134), yet the two girls do not represent a Madonna/whore dichotomy of innocence/experience, as Jackie 'juggled Dino and Simon, trying to decide what to do' (55). Jackie's dilemma is manifested in a realization that while Simon is more suitable as a partner, Dino is more sexually attractive to her. Sue provides a distinctly postfeminist resolution to this dilemma by encouraging Jackie to 'shag Dino's brains out for a few weeks, give him the elbow and go back to Simon for a mature, lasting relationship' (55). For Sue—who 'ate Dinos for breakfast' (16)—sex is 'the single possible reason' for going out with him (56), and Jackie is tempted after a long-term relationship with Simon that has made her feel like she has missed out on gaining sexual experience. Burgess conveys Jackie's changing priorities through vivid symbolism, commenting that Jackie's 'heart had burrowed its way down and made a cozy little nest for itself just below her womb, where it snuggled in and pulsed and glowed and purred happily' (17).

While it could be argued that Jackie's sense of 'missing out' on gaining sexual experience is a product of the cultural pressures placed on young women (as identified by Walter, Dines and Levy), it is beyond dispute that Burgess constructs her experiences of sexual desire and sexual encounters as pleasurable. Jackie is aware that, as a female, society expects her to establish an emotionally intimate and secure relationship before having sex, that the 'official line was that she didn't feel sure of his feelings for her and that she was waiting for their relationship to grow' (47). Despite this rationalization, her 'hormones had another, simpler plan' (47), and she admits to being 'desperate' to sleep with Dino (56). By constructing an adolescent female character who feels like 'weeping with [sexual] frustration' (56), and whose kisses 'went further than she intended' (11), Burgess demonstrates that female sexual desire can be as consuming as male desire, subverting a long-standing patriarchal assumption that sexual activity is an experience that females submit to rather than seek out. Dino himself reflects on the mythologies surrounding girls' alleged sexual passivity: 'He remembered what someone had once said to him about girls: if you don't ask you don't get' (98). While Burgess's novel debunks this myth through Jackie's expression of sexual desire and Sue's 'phallic girl' persona, it is another character, Deborah, who demonstrates the highest degree of agency in her negotiation of sexual boundaries. Even though Deborah is overweight and does not conform to the ideal image of feminine desirability, she attracts Jonathon by forcefully initiating almost all of the sexual acts they perform together. It is Deborah who 'came right up to' Jonathon and 'put her hand on it' (94). After Jonathon ineptly performs oral sex on Deborah she responds, 'I'll show you how another time' (95). Deborah is sexually active and skilled, while Jonathon is sexually passive and inexperienced. Indeed, all of the male characters in *Doing It* are positioned as novices who desperately seek the guidance and approval of females, with Dino waiting for sexual consent from Jackie, Jonathan guided by Deborah, and Ben receiving a literal sex education from his teacher, Miss Young. Burgess is perhaps proposing that, while society may expect adult women to conform to sexually passive roles, female adolescence constitutes a period in which gender roles can be tried, tested and negotiated, and young women can learn to participate in relationships that can—at least notionally—represent models of future agency in adulthood.

Conclusion

Valerie Walkerdine has claimed that female adolescents have been historically defined by their 'ability to create close and lasting personal relationships'.[51] The valorization of female adolescence as a period of romantic asexuality can, in patriarchal society, be attributed to the manner in which young women have been socialized to believe that sexual activity must occur after emotional intimacy has been established. Even though prominent feminists like Kate Millet have commented that '[s]ex itself is presented as a crime to children',[52] female adolescence remains unclaimed in feminist discourse as a territory of sexual expression, with Caitlin Fisher making the astute observation that 'few public narratives have been generated by feminism about sexually desiring girls'.[53] For Fisher, feminist narratives have been unable to claim a theoretical space for the 'empowered and erotically complicated'[54] girlhood she vividly recalls. Yet in Burgess's *Doing It*, Jonathan's response to the complicated reality of girlhood is worth quoting at length, if not for its eloquence then for its reclamation of girlhood sexuality in a manner that Fisher may approve:

> Sex is … well it's so rude, isn't it? You wouldn't think girls would like sex. You'd think it's too rude for them. Doing sex with a girl, it's a bit like putting a frog down their backs or scaring them with dead mice or throwing worms at them. They're such sensible, grown-up sorts of people. And yet apparently even the nice ones like you sticking the rudest thing you have on your whole body up the exact, rudest part of their body that they have! It doesn't make a lot of sense to me. (145)

Jonathan's appraisal demonstrates the crucial role that fiction plays in compensating for the omissions of scholarly criticism and popular culture. In this chapter, I have aimed to explore how Burgess's novels construct a fictional landscape that permits the reclamation of alternative experiences of girlhood outside of traditional discourses of chastity and vulnerability. I have demonstrated how Burgess's female characters construct their embodied sexual subjectivities, and create sexual relationships amidst contradictory discourses of femininity, sexuality and agency. I have also illustrated how contemporary female adolescents actively participate in sexual cultures that transgress conventionally romantic sexual scripts, and in doing so demonstrate a number of postfeminist sensibilities. If women's sexuality in society is, as Lynne Segal notes, subject to 'a host of sanctions and constraints—legal, social and ideological',[55] then regardless of how we position Burgess's girls—as either empowered 'can do' girls or 'at risk' girls in crisis—his novels are important in their problematization of public narratives of female sexuality that largely focus on sexual behaviour confined to the realms of social acceptability.

Notes

1. Beth Younger, *Learning Curves: Body Image and Female Sexuality in Young Adult Literature* (Lanham, MD: Scarecrow Press, 2009): xi.
2. Sinikka Aapola, Marnina Gonick and Anita Harris, *Young Femininity: Girlhood, Power and Social Change* (Basingstoke: Palgrave Macmillan, 2005): 18.
3. Angela McRobbie, *Feminism and Youth Culture* (London: Macmillan, 2000): 200–1.
4. Anita Harris, *Future Girl: Young Women in the Twenty-First Century* (London and New York: Routledge, 2004): 16.
5. *Ibid.*: 13.
6. Aapola *et al.*, *Young Femininity*: 132.
7. See, for example, John Stephens, 'And it's So Real': Versions of Reality in Melvin Burgess's *Junk*', in Heather Montgomery and Nicola J. Watson (eds.), *Children's Literature: Classic Texts and Contemporary Trends* (Basingstoke: Palgrave Macmillan, 2009): 320–9.
8. This chapter will deploy the term 'agentic' as representing the notion that individuals are not entirely governed by external cultural forces, but are able to resist these forces and make choices in the world as self-determining agents.
9. Stephanie Genz and Benjamin Brabon, *Postfeminism: Cultural Texts and Theories* (Edinburgh: Edinburgh University Press, 2009): 3.
10. Sarah Projansky and Leah R. Vande Berg, 'Sabrina, the Teenage? Girls, Witches, Mortals and the Limitations of Prime Time Feminism', in Elyce Rae Helford (ed.), *Fantasy Girls: Gender in the New Universe of Science Fiction and Fantasy* (Lanham, MD: Rowman and Littlefield, 2000): 15.
11. Angela McRobbie, 'Postfeminism and Popular Culture: Bridget Jones and the New Gender Regime', in Diane Negra and Yvonne Tasker

(eds.), *Interrogating Postfeminism: Gender and the Politics of Popular Culture* (Durham, NC: Duke University Press, 2007): 28.

12. Sarah Gamble, 'Postfeminism', in Sarah Gamble (ed.), *The Routledge Companion to Feminism and Postfeminism* (London: Routledge, 1998): 44.
13. *Ibid.*: 44.
14. Frances Gateward and Murray Pomerance, 'Introduction', in Frances Gateward and Murray Pomerance (eds.), *Sugar, Spice and Everything Nice: Cinemas of Girlhood* (Detroit: Wayne State University Press, 2002): 13.
15. Sarah Projansky, 'Mass Magazine Cover Girls: Some Reflections on Postfeminist Girls and Postfeminist Daughters', in Diane Negra and Yvonne Tasker (eds.), *Interrogating Postfeminism: Gender and the Politics of Popular Culture* (Durham, NC: Duke University Press, 2007): 42.
16. Aapola *et al.*, *Young Femininity*: 27.
17. Dawn Heinecken, 'Toys Are Us: Contemporary Feminisms and the Consumption of Sexuality', in Ann C. Hall and Mardia J. Bishop (eds.), *Pop-Porn: Pornography in American Culture* (Westport, CT: Praeger, 2007): 125.
18. Jessica K. Taft, 'Girl Power Politics: Pop-Culture Barriers and Organizational Resistance', in Anita Harris (ed.), *All about the Girl: Culture, Power and Identity* (London and New York: Routledge, 2004): 69.
19. Taft, 'Girl Power Politics': 72.
20. Younger, *Learning Curves*: 25.
21. Melvin Burgess, *Sara's Face* [2006] (London: Penguin, 2008): 1. All further references in the chapter are to the 2008 edition.
22. Aapola *et al.*, *Young Femininity*: 40.
23. Harris, *Future Girl*: 25.
24. Jane Victoria Ward and Beth Cooper Benjamin, 'Women, Girls and the Unfinished Work of Connection: A Critical Review of American Girls' Studies', in Anita Harris (ed.), *All about the Girl: Culture, Power and Identity* (London and New York: Routledge): 19.
25. Catherine Redfern and Kristen Aune, *Reclaiming the F Word: The New Feminist Movement* (London: Zed Books, 2010): 24.
26. Brenda Weber, *Makeover TV: Selfhood, Citizenship and Celebrity* (Durham, NC and London: Duke University Press, 2009): 1.
27. Hilary Radner, *Neo-Feminist Cinema: Girly Films, Chick Flicks and Consumer Culture* (London and New York: Routledge): 6.
28. Feona Attwood, 'Through the Looking Glass?: Sexual Agency and Subjectification Online', in Rosalind Gill and Christina Scharff (eds.), *New Femininities: Postfeminism, Neoliberalism and Subjectivity* (Basingstoke: Palgrave Macmillan, 2011): 203.
29. Shelley Budgeon, *Third Wave Feminism and the Politics of Gender in Late Modernity* (Basingstoke: Palgrave Macmillan, 2011): 54.
30. Estella Tincknell, 'Scourging the Abject Body: Ten Years Younger and Fragmented Femininity under Neoliberalism', in Rosalind Gill and Christina Scharff (eds.), *New Femininities: Postfeminism, Neoliberalism and Subjectivity* (Basingstoke: Palgrave Macmillan, 2011): 83.

31. Genz and Brabon, *Postfeminism*: 92.
32. Melvin Burgess, *Junk* (London: Penguin, 1996): 2. All further references in the chapter are to this edition.
33. Harris, *Future Girl*: 101.
34. Gill Valentine, Tracey Skelton and Deborah Chambers, 'Cool Places: An Introduction to Youth and Youth Culture', in Tracey Skelton and Gill Valentine (eds.), *Cool Places: Geographies of Youth Cultures* (London: Routledge, 1998): 7.
35. Harris, *Future Girl*: 119.
36. *Ibid.*: 29.
37. Genz and Brabon, *Postfeminism*: 92.
38. Harris, *Future Girl*: 101.
39. See Brian McNair's *Striptease Culture: Sex, Media and the Democratization of Desire* (London: Routledge, 2002).
40. Natasha Walter, *Living Dolls: The Return of Sexism* (London: Virago, 2010): 101.
41. *Ibid.*: 119.
42. Gail Dines, *Pornland: How Porn Is Hijacking our Sexuality* (Boston, MA: Beacon Press, 2010): 107.
43. *Ibid.*: 109.
44. Ariel Levy, *Female Chauvinist Pigs: Women and the Rise of Raunch Culture* (London: Pocket Books, 2006): 4.
45. Laura Harvey and Rosalind Gill, 'Spicing it Up: Sexual Entrepreneurs and *The Sex Inspectors*', in Rosalind Gill and Christina Scharff (eds.), *New Femininities: Postfeminism, Neoliberalism and Subjectivity* (Basingstoke: Palgrave Macmillan, 2011): 56.
46. Angela McRobbie, *The Aftermath of Feminism: Gender, Culture and Social Change* (London: Sage, 2009): 17.
47. *Ibid.*: 83.
48. *Ibid.*
49. Genz and Brabon, *Postfeminism*: 69.
50. Naomi Wolf, *Fire with Fire: The New Female Power and How it Will Change the 21st Century* [1993] (London: Vintage, 1994): 149.
51. See Valerie Walkerdine, *Schoolgirl Fictions* (London: Verso, 1990).
52. Kate Millett, 'Beyond Politics?: Children and Sexuality', in Carol Vance (ed.), *Pleasure and Danger: Exploring Female Sexuality* (London: Pandora Press, 1989): 218.
53. Caitlin Fisher, 'The Sexual Girl Within: Breaking the Feminist Silence on Desiring Girlhoods', in Merri Lisa Johnson (ed.), *Jane Sexes it Up: True Confessions of Feminist Desire* (New York: Four Walls Eight Windows, 2002): 55.
54. Fisher, 'The Sexual Girl Within': 54.
55. Lynne Segal, *Is the Future Female? Troubled Thoughts on Contemporary Feminism* (London: Virago, 1987): 72.

Part II
Form, Style and Genre

4

Beyond Face Value: Playing the Game with *Sara's Face*

Kay Sambell

Introduction

Melvin Burgess is perhaps best known for incorporating challenging subject matter into his work for young readers and in this regard *Sara's Face* (2006) is no exception.[1] At face value, the book deals with some bold and arguably contentious material which seems likely to chafe at the boundaries of what some adult gatekeepers view as appropriate fare for young readers. After all, the novel introduces body hatred, cosmetic surgery, addiction, self-harm, teenage sex, mental instability and narcissism, not to mention the horror of the image of a jailed man, his face sliced away until it looks 'like a bag of butcher's meat' (30). It is not hard to imagine why, given his propensity to use such provocative material, Burgess has earned himself such a reputation as the 'enfant terrible'[2] of the children's book world. Nor, in the light of this reputation, is it difficult to imagine why so much critical endeavour has been targeted on illuminating the social and ethical dimensions of his work.

By contrast, in this chapter I aim to look beyond the subject matter of *Sara's Face* to illuminate the novelist's fondness for daring innovation and playful experiment. The overall aim is to illustrate the narrative playfulness which characterizes Burgess's work more generally, showing his propensity to experiment with challenging stories at level of form, as well as content. I will particularly concentrate on showing how *Sara's Face* sets up an elaborate, extremely complex debate about the representation of Sara herself. In so far as the novel refuses to resolve this debate, teasingly maintaining her identity throughout as a complex system of multiple interpretative possibilities, it breaks the bounds of the traditional children's novel and shows instead a range of metafictional qualities. Underlying these qualities is a 'heightened sense of the status of fiction as an elaborate form of play'.[3] Indeed, as my own employment of metaphors of the face and body demonstrates throughout the essay, the very title of Burgess's novel knowingly offers playfully slippery semantic possibilities.

According to Robyn McCallum, the majority of fiction written for children is associated with narrative strategies which embody conventional expectations about meaning and closure.[4] These 'readerly' texts serve to position readers in restricted and relatively passive subject positions, so that the text itself appears to offer an apparently neutral or transparent medium which 'allows the utmost identification with the author's intention'.[5] In stark contrast to this relatively conservative, controlling model of writing for young readers, *Sara's Face* employs a plethora of narrative and discursive techniques as strategies which tend to distance readers from the text instead. These tactics position readers in more active interpretative and interrogative roles, engaging them explicitly and playfully in the active production of meaning.[6]

In this chapter I will show how Burgess foregrounds technique and structure in *Sara's Face*, so that the novel consciously displays its conventionality, explicitly revealing its conditions of artifice and thereby exploring and questioning the problematic relationship between life and fiction.[7] I will suggest, then, that the novel markedly displays some of the experimental features of postmodern, metafictive or 'writerly' texts which have been documented by critics like Geoff Moss, Dudley Jones, Kristin Cashore and Stephenie Yearwood.[8] I will argue that it joins what Maria Nikolajeva suggests is 'an ever growing segment of contemporary children's literature [which] is transgressing its own boundaries',[9] countering the traditionally received 'text' of children's literature itself.[10]

This is not to say, however, that *Sara's Face* mirrors the more difficult, avant-garde texts that are commonly associated with experimental or metafictive texts for adults. In fact, what Burgess offers may be more in line with what Yearwood notes are the growing number of popular (rather than fringe, auteur or minority appeal) books for young adults which use postmodernist ideas and techniques to raise questions about identity,[11] self-fashioning and the ways in which reality is mediated, represented, constructed and ascribed with meanings.

The importance of intertextuality in *Sara's Face*

In what follows, I will demonstrate how Burgess achieves his experimental effects in *Sara's Face* by drawing inventively on a range of popular fictive practices which have characterized the recently changing face of UK journalism, especially in its appropriation of celebrity culture. The novel tells the story of the disturbing ways in which a seventeen-year-old girl, Sara, becomes fatally embroiled in the bizarre world of a legendary rock star, ultimately undergoing a face transplant in her quest for celebrity status. The body of *Sara's Face* offers a pastiche of journalistic devices, including transmedia storytelling, celebrity-as-text and sensational cinematic excess. These act as intertextual references to the popular fictions of the mass media and are used in the novel to construct and represent the eponymous Sara. Burgess also plays ingeniously with the ways in which the frame narrative of *Sara's Face* stands in relationship to the fictive practices of the celebrity-focused journalism that he draws upon.

It is important to emphasize my view of intertextuality, which does not claim that the intertextual aspects of *Sara's Face* relate to specific sources. That is, the references do not function as direct allusions to particular news stories that have been circulated, or specific celebrity figures, nor do they allude directly to specific films, magazines and so on. Instead, the novel's intertextual references are more general and indicative of the new rules of the game that are arguably in play in contemporary journalism, defined in its broadest sense. As the book unfolds, these strategies are variously employed to make clear that Sara is positioned within a new kind of space altogether, one which does not simply mirror the world or offer us Sara as a character in a realistic sense. Sara herself is never physically present throughout the body of the text; instead, her image is only made visible through the fictions that are typically broadcast via the fictional worlds of popular media.

This narrative strategy draws attention to the ways in which Sara, as a character in the novel, is actually nothing but a bundle of texts. In this way Burgess uses intertextual representation to show how meaning is produced at the point of interaction with texts. This strategy opens up all kinds of playful possibilities which I will outline throughout the chapter. In effect, it allows for the prospect that Sara, at least in part, creates herself, as she plays with meaning in innovative and potentially mischievous ways, producing media representations which tell and spin her own story. In other words, as a knowing consumer and producer of popular fictions herself, Sara becomes an active and powerful player in the fictive games on offer in the new journalism. However, the intertextual play simultaneously allows for the possibility that Sara is, equally, exploited by popular media, falling victim to its manipulative, deceitful and offensive practices. In this sense, *Sara's Face* sets itself up an elaborate game, based, it seems, on deciding whether Sara is in control of, or controlled by, the characters in Heat's house, her situation and the fictions by which she is made to exist. At face value, this seems to be a question of working out how far Sara knowingly manipulates, or passively becomes, the journalistic hype which surrounds her. The novel, however, is arranged in such a way that her status in relation to the multiple texts through which she is constructed remains ambiguous. Instead of resolution, the book offers a mind-boggling array of interpretative possibilities for understanding Sara. These are considerably heightened because of the new rules of the game embodied in the changing face of tabloid journalism.

The changing face of British journalism

S. Elizabeth Bird argues that 'tabloidization' is a vaguely defined term that has been used since the 1980s to refer to stylistic and content changes in journalism.[12] It is typically associated with a perceived decline in traditional journalistic standards and has come to define a particular kind of colourful narrative which appeals to public demand for sensationalism. According to media commentators like David Marshall[13] and Philip Schlesinger[14] the emergence of the contemporary celebrity system exerted a powerful effect on tabloid journalism in the decade preceding *Sara's Face*. The public became progressively preoccupied with famous people, to the extent that techniques formerly reserved for writing about entertainment stars were expanded and appropriated to secure coverage of the famed and notorious in politics and other more serious spheres. The tabloidization of the increasingly competitive newspaper market meant that the new trick was to gain visibility, publicity and profile. In this context, good copy began to replace the notion of information that was fit to print. Further, the idea of fame, as opposed to talent or policy, became the presiding principle for individuals to be deemed newsworthy. Celebrities were, at root, simply known for being well known, rather than for anything important that they said or did.

In the scramble to press an individual's image on the public imagination, new and dubious tactics emerged. The public taste for scandal, gossip and stories about individual falls from grace enabled parallel professions to journalism to spring up, including the spin doctor, the publicist and the Internet muckraker. Press agentry—the skill of making a person more successful—often involved the 'puffery or exaggeration of events for greater impact'.[15] The sheer fabrication of newsworthy items, as epitomized in the ludicrous but hugely effective 'Freddie Starr Ate My Hamster!' headline, was not uncommon, bringing a carnivalesque, excessive quality to some reporting. Furthermore, according to Su Holmes and Sean Redmond,[16] any previous distinctions about achieving an appropriate balance between private and public spheres began to be seriously eroded where the construction of the famous was concerned. So while the opportunity for ordinary individuals to achieve celebrity status expanded dramatically, exemplified in the popular television show *Big Brother,* it often involved renegotiating the rules of the game with regard to what might produce shame and embarrassment. Commonly, for instance, individuals set themselves up for the total exposure of their private lives in order to become celebrities.

At every level, then, according to these commentators, the ploy was to become an excellent exponent of the media game, selling oneself to acquire the media coverage required to keep one in the public eye, and spinning stories about oneself to win popularity or neutralize negative press. To expose oneself to the media was, however, a dangerous game to play, as no-one was immune from becoming a victim of the public appetite for denigratory stories, exposés, scandals and ruination.

Introducing the rules of the game in *Sara's Face*

Sara's Face firmly locates itself within the broad narrative landscape of the new journalism in its opening lines, as follows: 'the story of Jonathon Heat and Sara Carter [...] is common currency, revealed to us through a thousand newspaper headlines, magazine articles, news bulletins, TV shows and an endless commentary on the radio' (1). The frame narrative signals that *Sara's Face* is not going to work in a simple or straightforward manner. The book immediately announces its departure from more traditional plot-driven formats by explicitly drawing attention to the nature of its own artifice. The overly obtrusive unnamed narrator explains that he is 'a novelist doing a journalist's job' (2). He goes to extraordinary lengths to describe the means by which he has produced the book, which, he claims, has been commissioned to 'throw light' on the girl behind the headlines. He offers readers tantalizing glimpses of the sensational things that have happened to Sara, but rather than rushing headlong into Sara's side of the story, he explains, at length, the problems he has encountered in trying to follow his brief. These centre on the difficulties of interpreting the many versions of events that he has uncovered.

On one level this opening seems to establish the apparently straightforward game on offer in *Sara's Face:* to work out Sara's true meaning. The narrator heavily underlines the key question: 'Was she in control the whole time, or was she just the innocent victim of Heat and his surgeon, Wayland Kaye?' (1). He assures readers that he has done his best to throw light on Sara. However, there are subtle clues that, as a character, the narrator may not be all that he seems. He seems incongruously naive, for a novelist, in his declared amazement at how difficult it has proved to investigate 'positive truth', because everything is filtered through 'what people want you to know' (2). This raises questions about the reliability and authority of the narrator, and his relationship to the main character, Sara, which are returned to forcefully at the end of the book. The deeper game at play in *Sara's Face* revolves around more subtle questions. In a world of spin, image and profile, what, at any point, is the status of the text we are reading? Who is speaking? Above all, which of the characters—including Sara and the narrator—is playing who?

Transmedia storytelling and self-publishing

While the narrator implies that he will help readers to read beyond the mass media constructions of Sara, in practice he reveals her through them, and she proves utterly impossible to pin down as a result. In part, this effect is achieved by allowing Sara the possibility of constructing herself in the novel via her own use of a range of narrative tactics associated with the new journalism. Sara appears to be a consummate producer of fictive media texts. Indeed, the first direct image of her in the novel takes the form of a video diary, which, it seems, she created several weeks before the scandalous affair with Heat erupted. On the one hand this intertextual reference frames her as a victim of celebrity culture. She appears to be pretending to be a guest on a chat show and her dialogue suggests she is obsessed with a desire for fame and glamour, even to the extent of craving surgery which helps her avoid looking like the 'blubber bunny' she claims she now is. Perceived through media-effects discourses such as those discussed by Joel Gwynne in the previous chapter, which view the young as particularly prone to be damaged and moulded by popular media,[17] Sara may seem hopelessly vulnerable, sick and at risk. She can also be seen, of course, as a victim of intrusive public interest in her private life, with her privacy invaded.

On the other hand there are clues in the video diary that Sara is not a cultural dupe or naive innocent when it comes to popular culture. She expresses unsettlingly well-developed ideas about fame and the way it provides power in the context of the new journalism. She knows how to spin her story, artfully constructing a series of filmed images of herself for future public consumption. She seems acutely aware she is being watched, to the degree that she may knowingly fabricate the video log to narrate herself in particular ways. Indeed, she may be performing victimhood deliberately as a strategic ploy. For example, Sara's first video diary entry is accompanied by a commentary which draws attention to the ways in which she dramatically and self-consciously stages her own presentation:

> *(She stares into the camera with a frightened/expression. Then she catches sight of her expression and raises a hand to the lens.)*
> Cut
> *(She wipes away her tears and turns off the camera.)* (11–12)

There is no definitive way for readers to decide how knowing or unwitting Sara is in relation to the text she creates. There are, however, strong signs that she fully understands the ways in which, as Henry Jenkins observes, new platforms like blogging open up avenues for self-publishing and transmedia storytelling which represent a shift in how popular culture becomes produced and consumed.[18] Sara's films may demonstrate her capacity to spin and construct desired identities in radically new ways, across multiple media. The act of producing these fictions might allow her to take control of the information about her which is brought to the public attention, possibly in an attempt to knowingly manipulate others' perceptions. After all, Sara is in control of the camera, and knows how to play the game. In this sense Sara can be seen as her own director: she even announces 'Cut!' (12) when she wants the camera to stop rolling.

There are other intertextual references in the body of the book which suggest that Sara exercises high levels of control in the world of the new journalism. Early in the novel, for instance, the narrator reports a story that Sara's best friend, Janet, told him about a whistle-blowing incident in which Sara mobilized the local press while at school: 'The story, as Sara had realised at once, was a beauty' (18). It is blown out of all proportion by the papers, although Sara, too, appears to have lied, or embellished the details, presumably for maximum effect. Once again, in the context of the incident Sara constructs herself as a helpless victim in the public eye, but there are strong clues that her public image cannot be taken at face value. Furthermore, the incident not only suggests her flair for fabrication, but also her understanding of the ways in which, as Richard Berger and Julian McDougal suggest, in the context of transmedia storytelling ordinary contributors can submit stories which become framed, 'reworked and recycled in mainstream popular media, in an endless process of "remediation" (Bolter and Grusin 2000)'.[19] It seems, then, that Sara knows how to wring power from the large corporations and publish herself in manipulative ways.

But the incident also demonstrates how the story, once in the public domain, spirals out of Sara's control and divides public opinion. Sara's relationship to the fictions of transmedia storytelling is presented as problematic and in question on a number of levels.

Celebrity-as-text

Throughout the novel Sara gains another dimension through her association with the idea of celebrity figures themselves as becoming particularly rich popular texts, whose significance can be read in multiple ways. This intertextual reference opens the possibility that Sara knowingly constructs herself as what John Fiske calls a 'producerly text'.[20] Fiske asserts that top-selling performers like Madonna become exemplary popular texts precisely because they embody so many contradictions.[21] He argues that, in this context, excess and textual unspecificity mean that, far from being self-sufficient, adequate texts in themselves, they vitally become provokers of multiple meanings. These meanings, however, can only be realized in their multiple and often contradictory circulations, whereby the celebrity figure means different things to different people, according to the discursive frames brought by different audiences. Producerly texts (that is, texts that are selected by the people to be made into popular culture) equate with writerly texts, in that they foreground their own textual constructedness, thereby challenging the reader to participate in the construction of meaning via a process of constant rewriting. However, because writerly texts are often associated with 'difficult, avant-garde literature', this tends to exclude them from mass appeal.[22] By contrast, Fiske suggests the category of the producerly text is needed to describe the *popular* writerly text, a text whose writerly reading is 'not necessarily difficult' in the sense that it 'does not faze the reader with its sense of its shocking difference from [...] the everyday',[23] nor requires the recognition of (arguably elitist) literary allusions to be able to decode it and enter into the type of play offered within its fictive game.

Sara and Heat both share striking similarities with Fiske's definition of producerly texts. Both build and refashion themselves in an ongoing, ever-changing cycle of transformation. Both use excess, bad taste and offensiveness as tricks to gain publicity. Both use the playful freedoms of the carnivalesque, including outrageous disguises, masks and physical transformations to create their image. Both also become popular public texts in the narrative logic of the novel, because of what Fiske calls 'their incompleteness'[24] as constructed texts. Their popularity rests on the realization of their public image as incomplete, indeterminate fictions, which offer their audiences the pleasure of producing and participating in making meanings. The novel makes clear that it is Sara's producerly qualities that are her greatest asset. She has a versatile look which means that she can be read in many ways: 'there was something mask-like about her which gave her an odd look that some saw as surreal, others angelic, and some merely bland' (53). When it comes to Sara's construction as a celebrity in her own right, it is this quality, though, that allows Sara's image to be manipulated and exploited, as well as misinterpreted. There is ample evidence offered that Sara is used, and potentially abused, by the entourage of image consultants associated with Heat's extravagant lifestyle. The stylist, Gray, for instance, successfully produces different images of Sara which achieve 'cult status' because 'her look was so versatile—a different pose or the right lighting could change her whole appearance. The sets showed Sara seductive, cold, aggressive, passive and sexy in turn' (54).

As ever, it is manifestly unclear whether Sara is in control, constructing her own celebrity image, or whether she is constructed by others. In the world of the novel, however, there is ample evidence that Sara spins stories deliberately to control other people. Her best friend, Janet, for instance, explains Sara's extraordinary capacity for performance, 'games of pretence, role plays, that sort of thing' (20). Like Heat, Sara clearly has an uncanny capacity to become other people and, as Janet puts it, to make 'a whole story up' (146). This insight offers the interpretative possibility that Sara so fully understands celebrity performance culture that she can use its rules to produce different versions of herself in order to manipulate other characters in the novel. It may be, for instance, that she is acting, rather than reacting, when she appears to see the ghost of a girl who, allegedly, used to work at Heat's house, but mysteriously went missing. No one but Sara ever sees the horrifying apparition, whose face has been removed. Sara may genuinely believe the ghost exists. Or she may be trying, for a host of complex reasons, to provoke boyfriend Mark into behaving in certain ways. She may, for example, being depicting herself as a victim so that he rescues her. Or she may be trying to use Mark to fuel the stories about Heat's indiscretions, perhaps to cause a scandal and bring about Heat's public demise, or gain publicity for herself. There is no way of knowing. The intertextual references are used to situate Sara as a complex creation with multiple faces, all of which are brought into play by virtue of her own, and other characters' interpretative frameworks.

Nothing succeeds like excess

As the novel progresses, Sara is also increasingly mediated as a text of melodramatic cinematic excess. From this perspective, the stories that are spun about and by Sara are associated intertextually with a compelling but outrageously exaggerated blend of genres. The generic hybridity invoked increasingly inflects towards cinematic fictions, rather than the documentary realism which, at least at face value, opened the novel. Here the intertextual references are used to represent sensational, overblown stories, based upon extreme and absurd narrative formats. The novel becomes packed with chases, near-miss escapes, nightmare visions, body horror, ghosts, secret passages and underground cellars. The gothic is well represented in the labyrinthine passageways that run under Heat's extravagant mansion. The characters, too, become framed as overblown and exaggerated grotesques. They are represented variously as villains, knights in shining armour, mutilators, heroes, damsels in distress, ogres and mad scientists.

On the one hand this tormented view of the world offers evidence of Sara's delusional state and her descent into the madness that Heat's nurse Bernadette, amongst others, is convinced afflicts her. But Sara's visions uncannily begin to resemble the symbolic sets and extreme distortions of a stylized, expressionist horror film. These cinematic qualities also allow Sara the potential to peddle sensational stories which, however absurd and bordering on a pantomime performance, have the power to persuade others that Heat and Kaye are about to perform the unthinkable and steal her face. Sara dubs Kaye 'Dr Ghoul the Face Eater' (205), and spreads the idea that she is about to be operated upon against her will. Bernadette, for instance, does not know whether to believe Sara, as the stories she spins seem so ludicrous. Bernie vacillates, talking herself in and out of belief in the face of these fictions: 'so monstrous, so vile ... [...] of course, so untrue. [...] Oh God! What if they were true?' (231). Finally, though, Bernie is persuaded to see Heat as a monster and Sara as his prey, despite her misgivings.

Maybe Sara knows, then, that nothing succeeds like excess. Her best copy turns out to be the wildest, most implausible fictions of all. In spinning them, Sara shares many of the characteristics William J. Hynes suggests characterize the mythical trickster: shape-shifter, deceiver, trick-player, bricoleur, one who inverts situations and violates taboos.[25] Her sensationalist stories climax in the media hysteria which greets her eviction from Heat's household. Sara and Heat are wheeled out amidst the feeding frenzy of the paparazzi, which, we find, Sara has tipped off before the event. This is the very moment when 'the now famous image of Sara's face, inert in a way no face should ever be' (243) is revealed and circulated around the world. Although Heat, not Sara, is wearing Sara's face after the gruesome operation, Sara has, at last, hit the headlines. Like a trickster god, she has dismantled the social order and, quite literally, brought the house down. However implausible, however extreme, Sara's story captivates the public interest and turns opinion against the rock star. It seems that Sara has effectively become her own publicist and spun her story, making fame into a work of art. Again the cinematic excess, like the former intertextual fictions, offers the possibility that Sara is simply a helpless victim of gross misconduct on others' parts. But the ways in which she has alerted the press strongly imply she knowingly plays a major role in Heat's defamation and the scandal that ensued. Sara may best be seen as a 'calculating cat' (259) who has placed herself firmly among the pigeons. Whether she acts to expose injustice, garner fame from the scandal, or cruelly frame an innocent man, there is no way of telling. By the end of the novel, Sara has been exposed as an extremely unreliable narrator of her own story: full of lies, disguise and deception. It seems, by the climax of the story, that the mystery of Sara's true identity will never be solved. She is simply too good at hiding in plain sight.

Unreliable narrators: the frame narrative revisited

In the epilogue, things appear to change. Just when we believe Sara's story is over, the journalist discovers he has been offered a scoop: the chance to interview Sara in person. This element of the novel is told in the frame narrative, which acts as an additional appendage to the main body of the focused text. At face value, the interview, which is reported by the narrator in the first person, using the past tense, offers us the opportunity to hear Sara's real story, directly from her own mouth. We discover, however, that Sara is now in the guise of a new identity, Lucy. This adds yet another dimension to the multiple ways in which Sara is represented. Moreover, during the reported interview, instead of offering a straightforward revelation or confession, Lucy constructs yet another story which gets added to the heady mix of ways in which we already know Sara. The story Lucy tells is evocatively outrageous, excessive and scandalous, much in line with the stories Sara has spun and the sensationalized media fictions which have surrounded her case. Sara/Lucy reveals, in a journalistic kiss-and-tell format, that she had sex with Heat the night before the operation was due. She also divulges that she went willingly into the operating theatre, rather than being coerced. This acts as a deliciously sensational new turn of events, which potentially throws the previous versions of Sara into some sort of relief. However, as Sara expands on her motivations for knowingly accepting surgery, the truth of the matter—and Sara's true identity—remain steadfastly open to interpretation right to the end.

As usual, the character voices a wide range of possible reasons for her unpredictable, apparently unreasonable behaviour, all of which are plausible, comprehensible explanations. Possibly, for instance, she was driven by love, or indebtedness or pity for Heat, or possibly by a sense of self-hatred in which self-slaughter seemed the only solution to end her inner torment. Or possibly, she claims, she was propelled by the feeling that, with her face removed, she would feel free and be cured. As a self-reflexively producerly text, Sara's closing moments in the novel resolutely retain a strong mixture of contradictory, absurd, yet curiously convincing possibilities. The alternative perspectives she offers may remind readers how much of the character of Sara is constructed by herself, by others and by those who produce, and those who procure, media fictions. They also drive home the possibility that Heat and Kaye are not the predatory monsters they have subsequently been made out to be.

Lucy also indicates that she has moved on and has settled in to her new identity: 'Sara's gone. She really did die [...] But I'm happier like this [...] I know who I am like this' (250). But whether she is lying, or trying to convince the journalist, readers or herself of the reality of her new identity, there is no way of telling. And perhaps, after all, she is still simply spinning another good story about herself to fuel her fame and public image, in an attempt to make sure she remains once again in the public eye. Thus the character's new identity acts as another estranging strategy whereby Burgess insists on the ultimate indeterminacy of knowledge about Sara, thus refusing a single way of engaging with her.

Even when she speaks directly, then, the character proves to be an extremely unreliable narrator of her own story. This has been true throughout the novel, as Lucy admits: 'That Sara!' she exclaimed. 'You couldn't trust a word she said' (253). As a source for the journalist narrator's scoop, Lucy is no more trustworthy. She, like Sara, delights in the slipperiness of language and characteristically speaks about Sara's 'death' in ingeniously ambiguous ways, repeatedly impressing on the journalist that she fully intends to 'let Sara lie' (255). Of course, this may be intended to signify that the character has invented herself as a new person, and is letting go of her damaged past in healthy and productive ways. But it simultaneously signifies Sara's dishonesty and her propensity for deliberately presenting falsehood as truth, for wilfully misleading others and giving fake impressions. Her talent for spinning stories is undeniable but makes her an extremely undependable source. Lucy's unreliability as a narrator, then, acts as a narrative tactic which frustrates conventional expectations about meaning and closure, thereby positioning readers in active, interpretative roles with regard to the multiple meanings of Sara.

On another important level, though, the epilogue finally discloses that Sara actually commissioned the book itself. Here she is seen as a character in search of an author. As a narrative tactic this foregrounds the issue of authorship and returns forcefully to the questions which were posed, but never answered, in the opening frame narrative: Whose story is this? Who speaks? Who is in control of the narrative? In other words, the epilogue reinstates a battle for authorial control over Sara's story between the unnamed narrator and Sara, adding new layers of complexity to the nature of the game on offer in the focused text. In an important sense, the epilogue can be seen as staging a face-off between Sara and the unnamed journalist. This showdown, too, is enacted dramatically, played out in full public view, like so much of Sara's life. It can be viewed as a cat-and-mouse game in which the journalist and Sara tease and torment each other as to whose version of events, and whose identity, will, ultimately be published in the book itself. Yet the question of who wins this authorial battle, and the ownership of the overall book, is also, characteristically, represented ambiguously.

It may be that, in general terms, Sara playfully wins the battle, claiming her story for herself. She appears to be in control of the epilogue. She initiates the interview, safe in the knowledge that the journalist will come running, unable to resist the scoop. She teases the journalist for appearing to imagine, like a novelist, that everything about her mystery will be resolved. She torments him with tantalizingly juicy information, whilst revelling in his inability to verify her reliability as a source. She even asserts that, in practice, she controls what, at face value, seems to be real in *Sara's Face*. Her capacity to see things, invent people, and conjure characters like Katie out of thin air, make her seem like a 'magician' (249 and 255) who can make anything seem real. She suggests that she has extended her creative capacity to forge her own identity in the media fictions about her: she boasts about her ability to achieve what she wanted to achieve by fashioning herself as 'a kind of event, an artwork' (260).

In the epilogue, the narrator observes that Sara no longer needs him and is beginning to dispense with him entirely. He notices that Sara even starts to orchestrate her own interview, side-lining his role in the process and overriding his questions by supplying more interesting, probing ones. On several occasions, her shocking kiss-and-tell revelations reduce him to silence: 'I felt that she had struck me dumb' (260). Throughout the epilogue, Sara mocks his literary status as an accomplished novelist, turning him, comically, into a character in a book who can only employ empty journalistic clichés: 'Coupla tabloid questions? I'm afraid I get as curious as anyone else' (261). The frame narrator acknowledges, too, that on one level Sara holds the whip hand in the book's production process. He grumbles, for instance, that her offer of a scoop was calculated to make him come running to dance to her tune, despite his annoyance about the likelihood of having to rewrite the whole 'wretched thing' (245), just when he was looking forward to working on a new project. He seems childishly peeved that she should try to tell him her side of the story in half an hour. On a number of levels, then, Sara appears to be in control of the book itself. As its commissioner she explicitly issues the orders about its production and tells the narrator that he does not need to rewrite the whole thing after all: 'I don't want you to change a word. Just put me in … as an epilogue. That's all I really am' (263). The journalist appears to agree to her authorial demands, resigning the story to her: 'Why not? It was her story, after all' (263).

This all suggests, then, that perhaps Sara has used the narrator as a tool, such that he has been naively complicit in helping her to publish her story, in the format of the book we are reading. Perhaps Sara chooses this particular narrator to tell her tale because, as she claims, she knows and likes his novels and thinks he will do her justice, maybe because of his reputation for writing sensational stories. Perhaps she selects him to tell her story because she anticipates his journalistic naivety, which leads her to believe he will be easy to manipulate. Whatever Sara's reasons, these levels of reflexivity about authorial control over the book's production all imply that, perhaps, Sara has knowingly successfully established herself, albeit indirectly, as the architect of *Sara's Face*. As such, she has quite possibly created her own character, and the characters that appear to populate the text.

However, another reading is simultaneously made available, in which the unnamed narrator is also, like Sara, an unreliable source, especially when it comes to disclosing his own identity. He may have invented his blundering, journalistic style to present himself in particular, and possibly untrustworthy, ways. Perhaps his apparent naivety and clichéd writing techniques are themselves part of a clever disguise, which the narrator has been wearing like a mask. So whilst it may appear, in the epilogue, to be the case that Sara is in control of the narrator, perhaps it has been the other way around all along, and he has been playing and manipulating her. After all, Sara's voice is, throughout, entirely mediated by him. The epilogue raises additional questions, then, about the narrator's possible motivations for writing Sara's story. For instance, has Sara really been his victim all along, becoming tangled and trapped in his ruthless pursuit of a sensational story to tell? Or has he been in collusion with her, aware of her authority over him from the outset, but failing to disclose that he was in her paid employ? If this is the case, has he been complicit in spinning her story, acting, in effect, as her publicist and fabricating her fame? Or has he, a novelist after all, simply made Sara up, for good copy, so that he can teasingly dupe his readers into somehow believing, or being enthralled by, a story which, at face value, is utterly incredible?

Conclusion

Once questions like this are raised, they are likely to drive readers back to re-read the novel itself, looking for further clues which will give the game away and solve the puzzles about the characters, especially Sara and the narrator, that have been set in motion. The novel is so artfully constructed, however, that these are puzzles that fiendishly refuse to be solved. So while at face value it may seem like *Sara's Face* is, as Philip Ardagh's review admits, 'a roller-coaster of a ride',[26] or, as David Self observes, is 'reminiscent of the soft porn fiction that appears in [...] certain tabloids',[27] in fact it is an immensely ingenious, playfully inventive text, which goes to immense pains to disguise its own meticulous construction. And while the narrative tactics obtrusively position the book and the stories within it as works of fiction, at no point are readers able to be certain of the status of any fiction, however much they travel back and forth, reading and re-reading the book. *Sara's Face,* and the texts which it draws upon, are unstable, indeterminate, ambiguous creations which continually foreground the narrative constructedness of texts and the fictionality and artifice of their stories.

There is a final playful sting in the tail of the novel, however, which also lies in the novel's intertextual references to the new journalism and celebrity culture. Any reader who goes in search of evidence of 'real' press coverage of Sara Carter will find absolutely no trace of her fictional identity, although, interestingly, they might find a series of eight scenes dramatizing Sara's vlogs, which were published as part of an innovative promotional campaign Burgess conducted for Penguin on the teenage website spinebreakers.co.uk. Sara's fame is, of course, an elaborate hoax, as is the girl herself. But the (thinly disguised?)

identity of the unnamed narrator, who, we are told, wrote a book called *Lady* (249), may point inquisitive readers in the direction of the author himself. And Burgess, of course, has hit the headlines quite frequently, mainly in a flurry of press hysteria about the shocking aspects of his fiction. As such, *Sara's Face* can also be read as a satirical commentary on the ways in which Burgess has personally continued to fall foul of journalistic hype and sensational, overblown public reactions himself. The author has claimed that most of the heavily publicized controversy about his work is simply a 'paper tiger', just designed to make good copy.[28] In general he seems amused by the defamatory headlines, rather than being offended and defensive about his books. He has routinely responded to his tormentors publically, typically with urbane good humour laced with a heavy dose of comic irreverence. He claims not to take their accusations too seriously. But maybe, like Sara, he understands the rules of the journalistic game so well that he is more than well placed to ingeniously construct his public image to his advantage, courting the image of the *enfant terrible*, maybe for a whole host of reasons. It is, of course, impossible to be certain. But there is a strong possibility that Burgess's own reputation is, at least in part, a knowingly constructed story created by a resourceful and wilfully playful master storyteller.

Notes

1. Melvin Burgess, *Sara's Face* (London: Andersen Press, 2006). All further references in the chapter are to this edition.
2. Lydia Kokkola, 'Metamorphosis in Two Novels by Melvin Burgess: Denying and Disguising "Deviant" Desire', *Children's Literature in Education* 42(1) (2011): 56.
3. Robyn McCallum, 'Metafictions and Experimental Work', in Peter Hunt (ed.), *The International Companion Encyclopaedia of Children's Literature* (London: Routledge, 1996): 588.
4. *Ibid.*: 587.
5. Geoff Moss, 'Metafiction and the Poetics of Children's Literature', *Children's Literature Association Quarterly* 15(2) (1990): 50.
6. John Stephens, 'Ideology, Carnival and Interrogative Texts', in *Language, Ideology and Children's Fiction* (Essex: Longman, 1992): 120–57.
7. Patricia Waugh, *Metafiction: The Theory and Practice of Self-Conscious Fiction* (London and New York: Methuen, 1984): 4.
8. Moss, 'Metafiction and the Poetics of Children's Literature'; Dudley Jones, 'Only Make-Believe? Lies, Fictions, and Metafictions in Geraldine McCaughrean's *A Pack of Lies* and Philip Pullman's *Clockwork*', *The Lion and the Unicorn* 23(1) (1999): 86–96; Kristin Cashore, 'Humor, Simplicity,

and Experimentation in the Picture Books of Jon Agee', *Children's Literature in Education* 34(2) (2003): 147–81; Stephanie Yearwood, 'Popular Postmodernism for Young Adult Readers: *Walk Two Moons*, *Holes*, and *Monster*', *The Alan Review* 29(3) (2002): 50–3.
9. Maria Nikolajeva, 'Exit Children's Literature?', *The Lion and the Unicorn*, 22 (1998): 221.
10. Moss, 'Metafiction and the Poetics of Children's Literature': 50.
11. Yearwood, 'Popular Postmodernism for Young Adult Readers'.
12. S. Elizabeth Bird, 'Tabloidization', in Wolfgang Donsbach (ed.), *The International Encyclopaedia of Communication*, Blackwell Reference Online, 2008 (http://www.communicationencyclopedia.com/public/book?id=g9781405131995_9781405131995).
13. David P. Marshall, 'Intimately Intertwined in the Most Public Way', in Stuart Allan (ed.), *Journalism: Critical Issues* (London: Open University Press, 2005): 19–29.
14. Philip Schlesinger, 'Is There a Crisis in British Journalism?', *Media, Culture and Society* 28(2) (2006): 299–307.
15. Marshall, 'Intimately Intertwined in the Most Public Way': 23.
16. Su Holmes and Sean Redmond, 'A Journal in Celebrity Studies', *Celebrity Studies* 1(1) (2010): 1–10.
17. See also David Buckingham, 'Young People and the Media', in David Buckingham (ed.), *Reading Audiences: Young People and the Media* (Manchester: Manchester University Press, 1993): 1–23.
18. Henry Jenkins, *Transmedia Education: The 7 Principles Revisited* (2010) (available at http://www.henryjenkins.org).
19. Richard Berger and Julian McDougall, 'Doing WikiLeaks? New Paradigms and(or?) Ecologies in Media Education', *Media Education Research Journal* 1(2) (2011): 8.
20. John Fiske, *Understanding Popular Culture,* 2nd edn (London: Routledge, 2011): 83.
21. *Ibid.*: 99.
22. *Ibid.*: 83.
23. *Ibid.*: 83
24. *Ibid.*: 99.
25. William J. Hynes, 'Mapping the Characteristics of Mythic Tricksters: An Heuristic Guide', in William J. Hynes and William G. Doty (eds.), *Mythical Trickster Figures: Contours, Contexts and Criticisms* (Tuscaloosa, AL: University of Alabama Press, 1997): 45.
26. Philip Ardargh, 'Beauty and the Blubber Bunny', *The Guardian*, Saturday 15 July 2006.
27. David Self, 'Review: Sara's Face', *Books for Keeps* 159 (July 2006).
28. Melvin Burgess, 'Sympathy for the Devil', *Children's Literature in Education* 35(4) (2004): 293.

5

Dystopian Worlds and Ethical Subjectivities in *Bloodtide* and *Bloodsong*

Robyn McCallum and John Stephens

Introduction

> Sigurd took the girl in his hands and held her face so that he could see her better. Another human being—the most precious thing imaginable. She was beautiful, full of life, living and growing, knowing, remembering, rushing along with him now in the arms of the present. She was so much more than anything you could possibly make up.[1]

> The problem of the good society is to know how to treat each man and woman as an end, not only as a tool or as an instrument; not as an object alone but as a subject too.[2]

The novels of Melvin Burgess can be readily subsumed under a version of postmodern relativism, but two of his most challenging works, *Bloodtide* (1999) and *Bloodsong* (2005), in practice embody a deep concern with the questions of the nature of humanity and of ethical subjectivity in a universe that is depicted simultaneously as utterly relativist and entirely determined. An imagined world in which humans and animals are readily genetically modified and mingled poses ethical problems from both scientific and humanistic angles, as the epigraphs to this chapter suggest. Although Sigurd has been genetically augmented and designed for a purpose, he is not merely a tool but a human subject capable of emotions and feelings. His first encounter with Bryony (epigraph 1) affirms that humanity is precious beyond anything that can be 'made up', that is, invented by genetic engineering or narrative fiction. As each of the two novels in Burgess's *Volson*-saga plays out its disastrous conclusion, the central paradox is expressed in clear narrative form. What space exists in human lives for free will and agency in a world apparently shaped by capricious divinities? Can there be an ethically based behaviour if every act is predetermined by all-powerful beings which humans may not even believe in? Is free will possible? Can it be said that human beings have any real ethical choice and can be held accountable for what they do, even if 'the gods' turn out to be no more than a metaphor for human fears and desires?

Always opposing the determinist position in these novels is a Bergsonian perspective that 'the future does not exist in any sense' and that 'the life of the universe is a creative process, whereby something new and thus unpredictable appears at every moment'.[3] In *Bloodtide*, the opposition to this perspective is represented by the shape-changing cat Cherry presented to Signy, daughter of the Volson clan leader, during her husband Conor's 'halfman hunt' (Book 1, Chapter 21). Cherry—who shifts her shape between a cat, a woman, a bird and a nut—is a daughter of the god Loki (himself a great shapeshifter), a priestess of the gods, and sees her role as instrumental in bringing about what is destined. The situation constitutes a paradox of agency in the novel, which was already present in the Old Icelandic pre-texts drawn on by Burgess, in which determinism is generally mitigated by agency. In *Laxdœla Saga* Chapter 15, for example, two men trapped by pursuers on a river bank decide to entrust their lives to the swollen, icy waters: 'and because the men were strong, and a longer life was ordained for them, they got themselves across the river and onto the ice-sheet on the other side' (Ok með því at men váru hraustir, ok þeim varð lengra lífs auðit, þá komask þeir yfir ána ok upp á hǫfuðísinn ǫðrum megin[4]). This formulation has an aphoristic quality in Northern European heroic societies of the early Middle Ages: individuals are subject to fate, but their lives are also shaped by their personal capabilities. The blending of this paradox with Medieval Icelandic myths and precepts and modern conceptions of selfhood perhaps explains why Burgess's Volson novels are apparently perceived as 'difficult' and have received no more than passing mention in criticism. In this chapter we argue that Burgess adapts a medieval story of treachery and mayhem to explore the basis for ethical judgements that respond to an imagined society devoid of ethical principles. By dispersing narrative perspective amongst the narrator and several character-narrators, and by continually shifting perception between the narrator and focalizing characters, the novels both refuse a centralized perspective and place the onus on readers to negotiate the multiple perspectives represented and, by reading for ethical significance, to develop an ethical position—and hence an ethical subjectivity—of their own.

Ethics can be schematized and systematized, but ethical behaviour is premised on the possibility that an agentic subject has free choice between alternative modes of action. There are innumerable examples of characters working through ethical dilemmas in these novels, although there are also characters like the clone Styr, whose behaviour entirely lacks an ethical dimension. A simple example is evident in *Bloodtide* when Siggy (Sigmund, brother of Signy) and his two brothers, Ben and Hadrian, have been chained in no-one's land, the desolate area beyond the wall of London, as food for the mad Pig. When Siggy escapes, albeit severely wounded, he is rescued by Melanie Pig, a highly empathic half-human. While searching for him, Melanie envisages three possibilities for the broken, unconscious body she expects to find:

> If he was too badly injured, he'd make a decent dinner. If he could be nursed back to health there was the possibility of selling him back to what remained of the Volson army. Failing that, there was a good market for human slaves among the better-off halfmen.[5]

The narrative scaffolding for both novels is a regular recurrence of chapters narrated from a third-person, anonymous perspective, although often incorporating marked character focalization, as here. Because, in this case, the options are being weighed within Melanie's thought stream as free indirect thought, but not in Melanie's 'halfman' language, the place of discourse enables readers to grasp that these are not simple possibilities but constitute an ethical dilemma, and, according to the ethical assumptions attributed to the implied reader, none of these options is acceptable. The structure of the problem is very characteristic of the two novels: readers are presented with a situation which can have no ethical outcome, and if Melanie is to demonstrate that the human element of her hybrid being rises above her animal component, and hence demonstrate that she is capable of ethical subjectivity, she must eventually reject all three options and settle on the unstated, altruistic fourth option which is already present to readers: to nurse Siggy back to health and expect no personal gain. Melanie reaches this conclusion shortly afterwards, formulated now in a halfman discourse that invokes empathy through a glance at Descartes and Rousseau ('I think/feel therefore I am'): 'You gets t'knowem, see. You gets t'likeem. At's how it is … oink-oink-oink, I could never eat anythin that thinks. Now I adan uncle, e used to say, no eating anything that feels, either, but me, I'm not that fussy' (173). In addition to its centrality to the story—the outcome of the narrative, especially the overthrow of the tyrant Conor, depends on Siggy's survival and return to London—the sequence is particularly rich thematically in its depiction of the grounding of ethical subjectivity in an appreciation of alterity, a respect for the otherness of the other.

Narrative strategies and the production of ethical perspective

Fictional technique is always implicated in how a novel offers possibilities of thematic meaning, and in *Bloodtide* and *Bloodsong* this entails the possibility of ethical subjectivity. In these novels, Burgess refines a fictional technique that earlier was the basis of *Junk* (1996): there, events—often the same events—are narrated by numerous first-person narrators with the effect of creating an apparently relativist perspective and moral indeterminism.[6] In these later novels, perspective has a more overt pivot point because one of the narrative voices is an anonymous narrator who tells the story retrospectively, and hence has a hindsight knowledge of events. The characterization of the anonymous narrator shifts within and between the two novels, and as *Bloodsong* unfolds becomes increasingly embedded in the culture of the future England whose story is being told. He (it seems to be *he*) can even—just once—refer to himself as one of 'the people' of that future (the gift of the Volsons was 'to lift us above the mud' [231]); he directly addresses his audience; he is opinionated. Although he is a chronicler of events, the construction of this unidentified narrator is not an attempt to reproduce the effaced quasi-historian who narrates an Old Icelandic saga. Saga narrators notoriously stay outside the minds of their characters, so that audiences have to infer emotion and motive from action and speech. In *Volsunga Saga* Chapter 9, for example, the account of the death of King Siggeir and Signy is almost entirely a factual description of an event that is common in sagas, the killing of enemies by trapping them in a house and burning it down. In some of the great sagas—*Laxdœla Saga* and *Brennu-Njals Saga* in particular—the act constitutes an ethical dilemma: it is practical, but entails the deaths of innocent people. In the following passage, the burning itself does not involve an ethical problem but becomes the setting for Signy's resolution of her own ethical dilemma as to whether she should go on living after gaining vengeance by means of betrayal, filicide and incest:

> [Sigurd and Sinfjotli] then went back to the hall where everyone was asleep. They brought wood to the hall and set fire to the wood, and those

> inside were awakened by the smoke and the hall all ablaze above them. The king asked who had started the fire.
>
> 'Here we are, myself and Sinfjotli, my sister's son,' said Sigurd, 'and now we intend you to know that not all the Volsungs are dead.'
>
> He told his sister [Signy] to come out and receive from him every consideration, and high esteem, meaning in this way to make up for what she had suffered.
>
> 'You'll know now whether or not I have remembered King Siggeir's killing of King Volsung against him!' she answered, and I had our children killed when they seemed to me all too tardy in avenging our father, and in the shape of some sorceress I came to you in the forest and Sinfjotli is your son, and mine. His immense vigour comes from being King Volsung's grandson on his father's as well as his mother's side. Everything I have done is to bring about King Siggeir's death. I have done so much to achieve vengeance that to go on living is out of the question. I shall now gladly die with King Siggeir, reluctant though I was to marry him.'
>
> Then she kissed her brother Sigmund, and Sinfjotli, and walking into the inferno she bade them farewell and thereupon she perished there with King Siggeir and all his men.[7]

There is no suggestion that any of the characters can be attributed with a focalizing function here, although someone notices the smoke and flames. Signy explains her motives, but the process of reaching a decision is not represented. When Burgess writes a version of this episode in anonymous third person, the narrative discourse slips back and forth between narrator point of view and character focalization. Where Siggeir 'asked who had started the fire', his counterpart, Conor, upon seeing that Signy has beaten her companion, Cherry, to death, focalizes the enormity of Signy's deception and betrayal:

> At the door, Conor stood, the blood gone from his face, staring at the smashed mess [Cherry] on the floor. Suddenly, the woman he had known and loved for so many years was as fast as an animal, as strong as a machine. Where had all this been hiding for so long? […] 'You've done this … you've done all this,' he cried. […] Signy stood there before him panting, her face white, tears streaming down her face. She had shown herself to him at last but even now, Conor was more scared about the knife. (363–4)

Perception is obviously Conor's when he stares and makes an observation, and when the discourse slips into free direct thought ('Where had all this been hiding for so long?'), but less clearly so when the narrative refers to Signy's 'panting' and 'tears'. After Signey stabs Conor to death, the narrative shifts to her perception—'It seemed to Signy that in that second her heart broke'—but again switches between character focalization and narration: 'she was on her knees, grieving over the body of the man who had loved her, and whom she loved back in spite of the deformities of the years and the acts of bloody treachery. Now everything had been taken from her, the last by her own hand' (364). The marked register shift to imaginative metaphor with 'the deformities of the years' may be Signy's perception but is narrator discourse, and the dual perspective thus signalled through the character's ambivalent emotions is a means of foregrounding the larger ethical issues imbricated within this tangled tale of ambition, love and revenge. While slippage between perspectives and narrative levels has been a common mode of writing in children's and YA fiction since the end of World War II,[8] Burgess's original handling of the mode lies in the way in which he alternates it with multiple first-person narrations to undermine the perspective attributed to character-narrators, that is, those characters who are privileged by first-person narration. The ever-elusive possibility of ethical subjectivity lies somewhere in the space between these narrative positions, between the subject who speaks and the subject who is focalized. To put this another way: the difference between what *is* and what *could be* constitutes the space in which an ethical subjectivity is instantiated.

In both novels, the anonymous third-person narrator anchors the narrative process. In *Bloodtide*, he narrates 33 of the book's 76 chapters, predominantly in alternation with character-narrators. Of the latter, Signy and Siggy narrate 18 chapters each, with the remaining seven chapters divided amongst five characters. After the first few, the third-person chapters are often heavily character-focalized, and this mode greatly enhances textual perspective. It presents a more distanced angle on the mentalities of principal character-narrators; it enables access to the interiority of characters such as Cherry and Melanie, who narrate only one or two chapters, respectively; and it positions readers to make judgements about characters and events on the basis of multiple perspectives. *Bloodsong* has a similar structure, but is now preponderantly third-person narrated (36 chapters), with 16 character-narrated chapters. The third-person chapters again include substantial character focalization, and five chapters (13, 20, 24, 30 and 39) include character-narrated segments.

Within and across the two books the narrative strategies that produce this range of perspectives enable a concept of ethical subjectivity to be deduced from the narrative modes. *Bloodtide* commences with a marriage intended to unite the two gangs locked in a struggle to control the ruined city of London: Val Volson's daughter, Signy, is wedded to Conor, and the Volsons believe the two gangs can unite and wage war on the halfmen who inhabit the surrounding countryside and keep London in a virtual state of siege. When a few months later the Volsons set out to pay a ceremonial visit to Conor's territory, they are betrayed and ambushed by Conor, and the only survivor is Siggy, the youngest of the sons. Signy is hamstrung and imprisoned in a tower. This is the novel's key pivotal moment, when all power seems gathered into Conor's hand. If his behaviour is viewed in terms of the most basic principle of ethics—that the nature of the relation between self and other depends upon the rightness and wrongness of actions in relation to the other, and that the motives and ends of those actions can be assessed as good or bad—then there is no doubt that Conor has behaved unethically in seizing the opportunity to destroy his rivals, even though the Volsons have no moral superiority and are driven by the same lust for power. This point seems obvious, but ethical behaviour depends on agentic choice, and Conor readily persuades himself that he has no choice for several reasons: 'Politics is politics' (158); 'The gods wanted it' (217); and powerful enemies forced his hand to kill Signy's father, which prompts Signy to observe that 'he even believes his own lies' (218). A recurrent motif in both books, however, is that there is always a disjunction between ethics and core domains of social and material life, in particular politics (and especially between ethics and the desire for power) and science/technology (especially mind-controlling machines, cloning and species hybridization). Early in *Bloodsong*, for example, this disjunction is embodied by Regin, who is Sigurd's tutor/mentor but seeks to exploit Sigurd in his own lust for power. Thinking that Sigurd lost his own life when he killed the dragon, Regin muses, '[h]e was such a good person, it could never work. This is politics—he was bound to mess things up' (57).

Dystopian society and ethical subjectivity

Regin's desire to acquire machines that will control the emotions of whole populations is only one of the more overt links with Aldous Huxley's *Brave New World* (1932) and George Orwell's *1984* (1934), the main precursors of the dystopian genre in children's literature.[9] *Bloodsong* goes beyond reader familiarity with the genre to invoke condemnation of this desire, however, not only by setting the scene in an area turned to barren rubble by a nuclear strike as a visible reminder of the horror of weapons of mass destruction, but also by depicting Sigurd as an idealist appalled by the Orwellian prospect. Shifts of character focalization between Regin and Sigurd are an overt, almost crude, way of evoking the structure of an ethical dilemma: '[Sigurd] was a hero, a fighter. But a ruler? Someone so naïve, so young, so hopelessly idealistic—what chance would he stand in the slippery, backstabbing world of politics?' (84) and 'What had all this technology to do with his [Sigurd's] vision? Destruction and control—what sort of power was that? Where were the schools, the hospitals? Where was the hope?' (85). The ethical dilemma in this difference lies in problems of contrast between instrumental values and intrinsic values: Sigurd's only interest in Fafnir's vast possessions is in his hoard of gold, which he naively imagines can be used for the good of society, whereas Regin argues that Fafnir's hoard of technology has intrinsic value apart from its instrumental value, and thus Sigurd's resolve to destroy it is 'like burning the books, tearing down the museums, the libraries' (86). For Regin, the ethical issues of our own era concerning the moral responsibilities of science and technology are non-existent: science is value-free. An informed reader, however, will know that it is incumbent upon all domains of science to reflect on ethical principles that underlie research endeavours and to seek to articulate a normative frame for practice.

The ethical dimension is pushed a little further when Regin and Sigurd argue over the purpose of a device which 'could wipe out a city and yet leave everything intact—the machines, the buildings, even the plants [...] but every mammal would be destroyed' (81). In response to Sigurd's incomprehension at why such a weapon should exist, Regin reproduces the *mutually assured destruction* doctrine of the Cold War: 'Well, maybe it would be useful as a threat against greater powers, a terrorist weapon perhaps, something to scare them off' (81). While weapons of mass destruction had existed prior to the widescale use of chemical weapons during World War I, they primarily emerged as an international concern in the twentieth century. Nuclear disaster was a central dystopian theme for twenty years from the late 1960s, and after briefly disappearing as an issue in YA literature of the early 1990s, following the end of the Cold War,[10] reappeared in *Bloodtide* and Philip Reeve's *Mortal Engines* (2001). The idea in *Bloodtide* is part of a large suite of threats to human societies which Burgess introduces into these novels. As is widely the case in the post-disaster, dystopian genre, human beings are seen to have learned little or nothing from the cataclysm that produced the fragmented, inhumane societies therein depicted. The books thus seek to raise reader consciousness of the ongoing threats to the stability of civilization and hence for the need to inhabit society informed by an ethical subjectivity.

The evocation of contemporary ethical considerations is a powerful reminder that these fantasy novels are not merely projections of a hypothetically extrapolated future, but are our past and present. Kay Sambell observes that dystopian novels such as *Bloodtide* depict 'brutally enforced inequality, horrifying violence and the systematic dismantling of individual rights in […] future worlds',[11] although *Bloodtide* rather situates readers themselves between a dystopian past and a dystopian future and thereby suggests not that the fantasy is projecting a future possibility, but that human societies have in the past demonstrated that they are incapable of large-scale ethical practice and contemporary societies are again like this. The effect is achieved in *Bloodtide* by mapping Conor's reign of terror onto twentieth-century tyrannical regimes, particularly insofar as fascist authoritarian politics and racist ideology point fairly directly to Hitler's Third Reich and the Holocaust.

By means of this strategy, Burgess blends the dystopian genre with the young adult form of the literature of atrocity. As Elizabeth Baer argues, the Holocaust represents a special evil that is at once retrospective and could happen again, and this is perhaps the greatest reason to keep writing about it.[12] There are already ethical implications in any decision to use the Holocaust as a homology in fantasy fiction and, as Jamil Khader points out, these lie initially in the problem of 'representing acts of radical human evil' that, if not unique, are unparalleled in human history.[13] For such reasons it is strategically wise for the Holocaust to be invoked in *Bloodtide* not by specific allusions, but more broadly by combining vital parallels into an atrocity script that brings together an actual past and a fearful imagined future. The script might also be considered to encompass other 1990s atrocities, in particular the Rwandan genocide and the massacre at Srebrenica, but it ultimately hinges on Conor's hatred of 'the halfmen', hybrid beings within whom human and animal genes had been spliced, and who had subsequently evolved as identifiable ethnic groups, capable of interbreeding with each other and with 'pure' humans:

> Conor had planned genocide of the halfmen right from the beginning, but already he was suffering the madness of tyrants. His original military aims began to mutate into a philosophy of hatred, and finally into an act of faith. The halfmen were not just the enemy, they were abominations. Only the races the gods had made must walk the earth. Anyone with even the slightest trace of animal blood in them was all beast—dirty, foul, and monstrous. (222)

The gods alluded to here are the gods of the Nordic/Germanic pantheon, which Conor had appropriated from both the Volsons and the halfmen (and which the Nazis appropriated from Wagner). They are part of a script which includes an insane tyrant who eventually retreats to, and dies in, an underground bunker; an obsession with racial purity; a racial enemy, the halfmen, who are equivalent to the term *Untermensch* (or sub-humans), which in Nazi racial ideology encompassed Jews, Gypsies, Hungarians, Romanians and Slavic peoples; a secret police, known as the 'Orangers' (in place of Blackshirts), who hunted down and killed anyone classifiable as 'halfman'; ordinary people turned into spies and informants; and the execution of thousands of supposed enemies.

Victims, perpetrators and ethical significance

If the evil of the Holocaust and the motivation of its perpetrators remain always incomprehensible and largely unrepresentable, a writer must strive to offer readers a complex position in relation to what is represented. Burgess achieves this effect in *Bloodtide*, not only through his shifting narrative perspectives but also through slippages between victim and perpetrator in the relationship of Signy and Conor, which endow her behaviour with considerable moral ambiguity and his with some element of psychological complexity. The novel asserts several times that Conor's brutalization at his father's hands has rendered him void of any moral or empathic imagination. The point is made clearly, for example, when Cherry manifests before him in human form in Book 1, Chapter 31 (133–4): when she derides him and suddenly disappears (by reverting to her cat form), his irrational reaction explicitly enacts mental and moral instability, and his failure to find a meaningful response is directly attributed to his father's treatment of him, to 'the mask of iron the old man had built around his son's heart' (134). This motif is a further argument for Conor's diminished agency. As Khader argues, when atrocity narratives are contextualized historically the ambiguity of subjective agency makes it possible to explore the complex behaviour of perpetrators rather than simply attributing motives to an incomprehensible evil.[14] Although there is a tendency in *Bloodtide* to simplify the moral perspective on Conor by attributing his evil to his psychological scarring in infancy and his ever-increasing paranoid insanity, the process conforms with the perception, as summarized by Adam Morton, that '[e]vil is a special kind of self-deception' because 'evil actions result from creating barriers to knowing that one's act is wrong'.[15] Because it is obvious to readers that Conor's acts are wrong, it is equally obvious that he engages in a constant self-deception about his motives and the nature of his actions. Conor distances himself from his actions by delegating them to others, such as the nameless Orangers who torture and kill Melanie. The maiming of Signy is a prime example: ordered by

Conor himself, he quickly dissociates himself from the action and subsequently orders the execution of those who carried it out, including a senior Secret Police officer.

The complexity of Signy's feelings is abundantly represented through her roles as narrator and character-focalizer; Conor, in contrast, is never represented within these roles, but remains strictly a narrated and focalized character and therefore there is no access to his interiority. After their wedding, Signy had quickly grown to love Conor, and never quite eliminates this emotion, whereas it is suggested that Conor only ever reciprocates by desiring subjugation and possession. The reversibility of their subject positions as perpetrator and victim is developed as one of the novel's key moral strands, as Signy's desire to manipulate from her victim position and to take revenge for her family's murder and her own mutilation precludes any possibility of ethical subjectivity. And because her relationship to Conor is perceived always from her perspective, and in the context of her physical and emotional mistreatment by him, it is easy for readers to accept her self-deception that what she does is not wrong. Once Signy has borne a child, Conor finally releases her from her tower prison, and this is the first culmination of her quest for revenge. The child is not Conor's but Siggy's. To conceive this pure Volson, Signy has not only deceived Conor, but Cherry (who persuades the gods to allow herself and Signy to exchange bodies for a few hours, not knowing what Signy intends) and Siggy (who thinks he is making love with Cherry). Once the child, Vincent, is born, Signy uses Cherry to fake an abduction and take the baby away to be cloned, and deliberately creates a moral monster (in *Bloodsong* this clone, Styr, has transformed himself into the dragon Fafnir, as a further outcome of moral madness). A collateral consequence of the 'abduction' is the execution of all the guards on duty when it occurred, and of Head of Security, Margaret O'Hara, in whose house the baby was placed when he was returned.

The moral scale is firmly tipped in the episode describing Signy's release (270–1), narrated by Signy. As she is lowered from the tower, she savours the scene: 'the trees with their bare branches, the daffodils on the wet grass, the tarmac below shiny with wet rain [...] in the ringside seats, the heads of the imaginary traitors on sticks like a collection of Halloween toffee apples' (270). In Signy's perception the diverse components of the scene below her have a strange equivalence, which in turn points to her lack of moral discrimination. She goes on to reveal that 'I named them for him, the traitors' and discloses that she pretends Odin comes to her in dreams and gives her the names. Turning her gaze, inward then outward, to Margaret O'Hara, she remarks, '[s]he had the blood of tens of thousands on her hands, but now it's her blood that's soaking into the grass—hers and all her family's. I said it would be so, and there the baby was. So when I tell him that Simon Patterson, Ruddock Goodal, Randolf Carhill are traitors, of course he believes that too' (270–1). Within the frame of a narrative teleology—a structure that affirms that events are directed toward an end or shaped by a purpose—the notion that justice prevails and therefore it is apt for those with blood on their hands to die violently may be an acceptable outcome, but Burgess employs the element of randomness in Signy's mayhem to disrupt that ready assumption. The addition of 'and all her family's [blood]' and the specific names of otherwise unmentioned characters signify that Signy has devised a teleological myth ('It suits [Conor] to believe that the gods are on his side') devoid of justice and certainly devoid of ethical practice. Signy has herself become a mass murderer. At the close of *Bloodtide* (and again of *Bloodsong*), Burgess challenges any sense of a narrative teleology that reassures readers that natural justice prevails in narrative text and hence by analogy in the world. Rather, we argue, purpose lies in reading for ethical significance.

Ethics and the other-than-human

The most extended sequence in either novel with a concentrated focus on ethical subjectivity and its relation to empathic intersubjectivity is the 'halfman hunt' episode in Book 1, Chapters 18–21 of *Bloodtide*, a sequence which culminates in another situation which can have no ethical outcome. In addition to its association with *Untermensch*, the concept of halfmen also links with recent controversies about genetic engineering and especially about the possible creation of *chimeras* by means of a splicing of human genes and animal brains. Opposition to certain kinds of biotechnological research, especially stem cell research, has roots in often poorly informed public anxiety about possible changes in the nature of human being, and has become a ground for skirmishes in the culture wars of recent decades.[16] Francis Fukuyama's *Our Posthuman Future*, for example, opposes the prospect of 'the creation of hybrid creatures using human genes' (chimeras) on assumptions about what is 'natural' or 'unnatural' and on an assumption of inevitable loss of 'human dignity' if human nature is tampered with.[17]

In Greek mythology a chimera was a monstrous creature that combined parts of several different animals (for example, the head of a lion, the body of a goat and a serpent's tail), and the initial conception of halfmen in *Bloodtide* to some extent retains the notion that a chimera might have body parts that can be differentiated. The core of Burgess's representation, however, reflects the popular imagination that a chimera might entail human consciousness (cognitive and psychological characteristics and capabilities usually associated with human beings) installed in an animal, cyborg or machine body and hence constitute an affront to the very meaning of what it is to be human.[18] The prejudice against halfmen in *Bloodtide* is thus modelled on racial prejudice and the perception of halfmen as non-human or *Untermensch*. When they are first introduced they are described as 'brewed' rather than born or made, concocted in a slapdash recipe book register ('Take a man. Add a spider. Stir in a dash of wolf, a pinch of tiger' [76]); their original purpose was as servants to perform dangerous or menial work. With a glance at contemporary bioethics, the narrator here remarks, '[t]he ethics were strange, but it could be done and so it was' (77).

Such hybrids, however, are not sterile but capable of reproduction, and produced a race, '[m]ore than human, less than human, more than beasts, less than beasts' (78), to which is attributed, as to other *Untermenschen*, 'no fear of death, no love of life'. Embracing a fifty-mile circle beyond the walls of London, it is the halfmen who effectively prevent the London ganglords from spreading terror across the country. They are said to lead civilized lives, although little of this is represented; they control all trade between London and the outside world, but their *Untermensch* status in the eyes of Londoners means that '[y]ou deal with the human part of the halfman till you get bored with it, then you can hunt down the animal' (98). Excited by the prospect of hunting such ostensibly savage creatures, Signy begs Conor to take her with him on a hunt, but to her frustration only finds herself ensconced on a platform built in an old electricity pylon. When the hunt goes wrong, and a group of halfmen snatch a Land-Rover and, attempting to flee, crashes at the foot of the tower, one of them temporarily escapes the massacre by climbing up to the tower platform. The episode presents the first clear manifestation of Signy's lack of moral discrimination, in this case established through her focalization. At one point she observes the desperate attempts of the surrounded halfmen to escape:

> Almost all were down, but the big dog Signy had seen was still on his feet, trying to gather the group together, snatching at the little ones. Another hail of bullets cracked out; the creature ducked its head, shoved the few it had gathered in front of it, sank to all fours and ran. On all fours, the creatures lost any semblance they had to humans. The turn of speed they took on was horrifying, as if they had engines within them. Maybe they did. (95)

Signy sees the halfmen as 'creatures', not human, part machine. After the reference to 'the big dog' the pronouns shift from 'his' to 'it'. The shooting is expressed in highly clichéd language: 'hail of bullets cracked out'. Most significant, though, is what she sees and doesn't comprehend in the textual ambiguity of 'the little ones': these are not simply smaller creatures, but children and infants, and the 'big dog' is the family father. Signy thus watches genocide in process and fails to recognize it. Shortly afterwards, when she finds that the 'dog' has quietly climbed the tower and killed the guard left with her, she *sees* a 'creature [...] Its claws and jaws were red with blood' (96), as Burgess again astutely builds cliché into focalization ('Nature red in tooth and claw').

A switch to Signy's character-narration in the following chapter very effectively portrays the humanity of the halfman (he is a trader named Karl) in contrast with the prejudice that precludes any attribution of ethical subjectivity to Signy. In their brief conversation before he commits suicide by leaping from the tower, Karl exhibits an astute understanding of Conor's political, economic and racial policies, predicts the murder of Signey's father and brothers, and weeps for his own murdered children. Signy's response is outrage ('This thing wasn't even human!' [98]; 'These things have no feelings' [99]), and it is only her shocked utterance of what she had previously focalized—'Your family? The little ones down there...?'—that produces a spark of empathy. Even then, her impulse to reach out results in a human-to-animal response, as she scratches the back of his neck and pats him, 'like the great dog he was', although the personal pronouns now become 'he'. In evoking empathy, the text subtly positions its readers, and marks how reader empathy has been with Karl throughout the chapter, while Signy has been an object of some revulsion. Her nearest approach to full empathy comes when she answers affirmatively to Karl's question, '[h]ave I a heart?' and he then takes a kitten (Cherry) from his pocket, where he has been protecting her, and asks Signy to 'look after *this little one* for me' (101; our italics). In the next chapter, focalized by Signy, she reflects that the idea that halfmen kept pets had shocked her as much as his capacity to laugh and cry. Foolish, closed-minded Signy.

Conclusion

To conclude this chapter, we now return (belatedly and briefly) to *Bloodsong* and the representation of ethical subjectivity in the story of the thwarted love of Sigurd and Bryony, that is, in a context where the relation between self and other can be used to represent a fundamental ethical relationship within which motives and ends can be assessed as good or bad. Although their love story ends with murder and suicide, it begins as an idyll in which two young people (he fifteen, she seventeen) are the only inhabitants of an isolated world, the abandoned underground city of Crayley. In a rhetorical address to audience of a kind quite common in the narrator-dominated discourse of *Bloodsong*, the narrator depicts their love as something beautiful, but doomed:

> What is the future for these two—the boy so young, designed for greatness, so easily loved and loving? And the girl, so greedy for life? Look at the two of them, amazed at this sudden secret between them. Love is a secret society, a community of two. …
>
> And in a room half a mile away, a dead man swings by his heel and half smiles with his cold lips. If Odin wants this, surely it can work?
>
> And if he doesn't, what then? (121–2)

Crayley is a version of the Norse underworld, Hel, symbolically presided over by a self-regenerating corpse which embodies Odin in the shape of the Hanged Man from a Tarot card deck. The hanged figure recalls the Volsons' attempt to execute Odin, in guise of a stranger, at the beginning of *Bloodtide*, and the thousands of tortured victims in that novel hung from gibbets in the Hanged Man configuration.[19] Crayley is a partly sentient machine which, drawing on the science fiction 'brain in a vat' motif,[20] is directed by the corpse of Bryony's lost mother, stripped of consciousness and memory. When it thinks, it thinks like a human being, but like envatted beings in general its beliefs about its world only make sense because it is a closed system with no purpose other than self-preservation and self-perpetuation. As such, the city symbolically embodies a blind will to power that elides all ethical considerations and drives the action of Burgess's novels. *Bloodsong* goes further than *Bloodtide* in constructing a fictive world in which agency—and hence a fully ethical subjectivity—seems unattainable. The 'body in the vat' symbolizes the non-agentic being of a self-regarding entity. Sigurd, for all his capacity for loving and youthful altruism, is a genetically engineered posthuman—he has been 'designed', every gene in his body chosen for a purpose: 'the gods shaped me as the keystone for this time and place. It's no credit to me. I have less choice than anyone. I'm more a machine than a human being. Sometimes I wonder if I'm even human' (11–12). Not long after escaping Crayley alone, Sigurd is further modified by Grimhild, mother of Gunar and Gudrun, who maintains her power by cloning her family and substituting earlier versions from time to time. The Sigurd clone has no memory of Bryony or much of his early life, and behaves in an entirely unethical way when he returns to Crayley, rescues Bryony and delivers her to Gunar as a wife. When his memory suddenly returns, the aftermath presents him with a commonplace ethical dilemma not unworthy of soap opera: should he return to Bryony or remain with his wife, Gudrun? Bryony, however, has already penetrated Grimhild's laboratory and seen her collection of Sigurd clones: 'Bryony stares in disgust. Sigurd after Sigurd, mindless, unloved, unloving; not Sigurd at all, but robots of flesh, ghosts with trick blood. It is with this kind of clumsiness that Grimhild has ruined everything' (412–13). As perspective here drifts between character focalization and narratorial perspective, a position emerges that is strongly on the negative side of the ethical and moral debates about human cloning and what it means to be human that had entered YA fiction by the end of the twentieth century.[21] The perception has a strong explanatory force, and underpins Bryony's decision to cut the knot of Sigurd's dilemma once she grasps how unethically she has been treated: she invents some lies to bring about Sigurd's murder before killing herself.

Bloodtide constructs ethical dilemmas which prompt readers to posit solutions other than those reached in the text. *Bloodsong* seems less optimistic, and readers will need to work hard to discern a moral teleology perceptible from patterns of behaviour leading toward the mayhem of its ending. The task is made more difficult by the characterization of the anonymous narrator, who uses the gods to frame his story, but can also suggest they are jealous, absent, or do not exist. An effect of this instability is that readers are nudged toward a secular ethical position from which to evaluate the possibilities for human ethical subjectivity suggested by the dilemmas that confront the represented characters. Finally, the narrator is apt to remind his readers that these novels are stories whose meaning, if they have one, is not given but must be constructed through constant cognitive processing:

> Gods—what are we to them? Our lives are just poems, stories that catch them if we tell them well. When the book ends nothing has happened; no one real has lived or died. Our lives and all our pains and pleasures are images on a page. They shed tears for us, laugh at us, cheer us on, make demands of us, but they don't believe in us any more than a reader believes the pages of a book. (*Bloodsong*, 231).

Notes

1. Melvin Burgess, *Bloodsong* [2005] (London: Penguin Books, 2007): 119. All further references in the chapter are to the 2007 edition.

2. Robert S. Cohen, 'Ethics and Science', in Robert S. Cohen, John J. Stachel and Marx W. Wartofsky (eds.), *For Dirk Struik: Scientific, Historical and Political Essays in Honour of Dirk J. Struik* (Dordrecht: D. Reidel, 1974): 311.
3. Leszek Kolakowski, *Bergson* (Oxford: Oxford University Press, 1985): 2–3.
4. *Laxdœla Saga*, ed. Einar Ól. Sveinsson (Reykjavík: Hið Íslenzka Fornritafélag, 1934): 34.
5. Melvin Burgess, *Bloodtide* (London: Andersen Press, 1999): 166. All further references in the chapter are to this edition.
6. See John Stephens, '"And it's So Real": Versions of Reality in Melvin Burgess's *Junk*', in Heather Montgomery and Nicola J. Watson (eds.), *Children's Literature: Classic Texts and Contemporary Trends* (Basingstoke: Palgrave Macmillan, 2009): 321–2.
7. R. G. Finch (ed. and trans.), *The Saga of the Volsungs* (London: Thomas Nelson and Sons, 1965): 13–15.
8. Robyn McCallum offers extended analyses of numerous such texts: *Ideologies of Identity in Adolescent Fiction: The Dialogic Construction of Subjectivity* (New York and London: Garland Publishing, 1999).
9. Kay Sambell, 'Carnivalizing the Future: A New Approach to Theorizing Childhood and Adulthood in Science Fiction for Young Readers', *The Lion and the Unicorn* 28(2) (2004): 247–8.
10. See Clare Bradford, Kerry Mallan, John Stephens and Robyn McCallum, *New World Orders in Contemporary Children's Literature* (Basingstoke: Palgrave Macmillan, 2008): 13.
11. Sambell, 'Carnivalizing the Future': 247.
12. Elizabeth Roberts Baer, 'A New Algorithm in Evil: Children's Literature in a Post-Holocaust World', *The Lion and the Unicorn* 24(3) (2000): 379.
13. Jamil Khader, 'Humanizing the Nazi? The Semiotics of Vampirism, Trauma, and Post-Holocaust Ethics in Louise Murphy's *The True Story of Hansel and Gretel: A Novel of War and Survival*', *Children's Literature* 39 (2011): 126.
14. *Ibid.*: 128.
15. Adam Morton, 'Atrocity, Banality, Self-Deception', *Philosophy, Psychiatry, and Psychology* 12(3) (2005): 258.
16. See Inmaculada de Melo-Martín for an excellent summary of the issues involved: 'Chimeras and Human Dignity', *Kennedy Institute of Ethics Journal* 18(1) (2008): 331–46.
17. Francis Fukuyama, *Our Posthuman Future: Consequences of the Biotechnology Revolution* (New York: Farrar, Straus, and Giroux, 2002): 160.
18. See Elaine Ostry, '"Is He Still Human? Are You?" Young Adult Science Fiction in the Posthuman Age', *The Lion and the Unicorn* 28(2) (2004): 222–46; John Stephens, 'Performativity and the Child Who May Not Be a Child', *Papers: Explorations into Children's Literature* 16(1) (2006): 5–13; de Melo-Martín, 'Chimeras and Human Dignity'.
19. The figure of the Hanged Man is a good indication that Burgess, like many contemporary writers for young readers, assumes an audience willing to

do some research, if only to use a web search engine such as Google or Yahoo. It doesn't take long to discover that *The Hanged Man*, a trump card from the Major Arcana of the Tarot deck, is not a figure of death. As Joseph Conte succinctly sums up, the image 'is more properly regarded as a figure of suspension, not termination. It signifies a time of trial or meditation and evokes selflessness and sacrifice [...] The Hanged Man bids us to stay retribution, stop resistance, and ponder the implications of what has transpired. Only by making himself vulnerable, by sacrificing his advantage or disadvantage, does the Hanged Man gain illumination' ('Don Delillo's *Falling Man* and the Age of Terror', *Modern Fiction Studies* 57[3] [2011]: 580). This explains why the Odin hanged man in both novels is not dead, and why executions in this configuration need to be understood as cultural misappropriation of an image. The anonymous narrator often comments on the folly of embracing dubious gods.

20. David J. Chalmers, '*The Matrix* as Metaphysics' (retrieved from http://consc.net/papers/matrix.html).
21. See Hilary S. Crew, 'Not So Brave a World: The Representation of Human Cloning in Science Fiction for Young Adults', *The Lion and the Unicorn* 28(2) (2004): 203–21.

6

Transformation, Text and Genre in *The Birdman*

Mel Gibson

Introduction

Best known for challenging assumptions about what subject matter is suitable in novels for young adults, Melvin Burgess has created other kinds of texts which similarly push boundaries in books for younger readers. This chapter will focus on his picturebook, *The Birdman* (2000), illustrated by Ruth Brown.[1] The narrative is about a boy called Jarvis, who, seeing a man selling birds, wants to buy them all and set them free. In the end Jarvis buys only one, a robin. However, enchanted by the robin's song he keeps the bird rather than releasing it as he promised. A year later, when the robin is nearly dead, the bird seller returns. He transforms Jarvis into a robin and the bird into a doppelgänger of Jarvis. The next morning, the new Jarvis releases the robin, who, desperate to be transformed back into human form, seeks out the birdman, only to be refused release from his new shape. Whilst this narrative may sound very straightforward from a brief summary (the back cover of the book simply proclaims the story to be about 'the power of temptation over conscience'), the interplay of text and image, plus the ambiguity within the written text, make it much more complex and undermine such a straightforward reading.

In analysing this book, I will look at the ways in which Brown and Burgess construct a model of a reader who is active, willing to be challenged and capable of dealing with difficult subject matter. I will show how it joins other challenging picturebooks published between the late twentieth century and today, such as those by Jon Scieszka and Lane Smith, who are best known for their parodies of well-known folk and fairy tales which also highlight the need for active reader engagement. I will first turn to definitions of the picturebook, establishing why narratives perceived as more appropriate for older readers may be seen to challenge stereotypes of the medium, then move on to notions of the active reader and how he or she is theorized. I will therefore unpack stereotypical perceptions of the medium, contrasting dominant discourses regarding picturebooks with the work of theorists such as Maria Nikolajeva and Carole Scott, who see the form as complex and significant.[2] The reader constructed by Brown and Burgess in *The Birdman*, like the reader of Scieszka and Smith, is, in addition, one who can draw on a range of other texts to enhance their understandings of the narrative. As a consequence I will move on to address the ways in which intertextuality contributes to the potential meanings of the narrative, showing how views about the capabilities of reader and medium are expressed through the allusions made in both the images and text. Finally, I will demonstrate how part of the challenge of the text is because the narrative emerges from the horror genre, which is rarely associated with the medium of the picturebook in its purest form. In exploring this I will draw on Maria Lassén-Seger's analysis of *The Birdman*.[3] Discussing horror means the bleak conclusion needs consideration, as well as the moment of transformation within the text, again indicating the ways in which Burgess and Brown respond to stereotypes of the picturebook by choosing to trouble and disturb the reader.

What is a picturebook?

A typical picturebook page will contain a small amount of text alongside a single image or limited number of images and the overall book will show events unfolding in time. This medium has been used to create works for readers of all ages, on any subject, fiction or non-fiction. Such books usually employ pictures (predominantly using line and colour) and words (including the use of varied fonts and layouts) to express meaning. This use of text and image often covers a double-page spread, which, as David Lewis states, is 'the complete visual display created when a picturebook is opened out flat showing the left- and right-hand pages side by side'.[4] It may be the work of one person, or, as is the case here, a collaborative work involving several people, the author and illustrator. In talking about *The Birdman*, then, this chapter is focusing on the work of Burgess *and* Brown.

A 'commonsense' definition of the picturebook may suggest a word or two on a page with a picture which illustrates the words, like an alphabet book showing an image of an apple alongside the word 'apple'. Nikolajeva and Scott describe this kind of text as a 'symmetrical picturebook'.[5] However, this is no longer the dominant form of picturebook. *The Birdman* is much more typical in combining a narrative with images. Another possible definition of the picturebook is an illustrated book. However, in books like Burgess's *The Copper Treasure* the images may show a key moment described in the narrative but they typically do not feature an image on every page.[6] In addition, the removal of these images will not result in any difficulty in understanding the key moment. Removing the pictures from *The Birdman* would leave the reader with a great short story, but, as I will show, the illustrations add a great deal to the narrative.

As many critics have pointed out, the picturebook should in fact be understood as a rich and complex medium combining image and text and playing on the interdependence of these signifying systems. There are a number of academic analyses of how picturebooks work: Perry Nodelman's *Words about Pictures*[7] has been very influential, for instance, because as Evelyn Arizpe and Morag Styles explain, it focuses on 'the importance of design and the interconnections between word and image'.[8] Frequently, the picturebook has been seen through adult lenses as an educational tool, a way into literacy for the very young, as the alphabet book mentioned above suggests. This has had a huge impact upon what some adults think is appropriate in terms of form, demands upon the reader and subject matter. Arizpe and Styles state that picturebooks are seen simultaneously as 'art objects and the primary literature of childhood',[9] and as I have argued elsewhere,

> [t]his acknowledges the potential of the form, but also indicates its key limitation in the perception of the audience, flagging up tensions between the flexibility of the medium and assumptions about the needs and capabilities of young readers. In both cases, then, cultural constructions of childhood (especially in relation to literacy—long an ideological battleground) underpin and colour understandings of the medium.[10]

Thinking of *The Birdman* as an art object offering a complex reading experience for any age of reader, through the interdependence of image and text, moves away from the notion of the picturebook simply as a support into literacy.

Another aspect of the picturebook which makes it different from an alphabet book is that the images may offer different information than that provided in the text, something Nikolajeva and Scott describe as counterpoint: a dissonance between word and image that finds its most extreme form in contradiction.[11] A classic example of contradiction occurs in *Rosie's Walk* by Pat Hutchins, which has, in effect, two narratives.[12] The first (about a hen's simple stroll through a farmyard) is told in the words and the second (in which a fox tries to catch her and is foiled at every turn, and which hugely undermines the first) is told by the pictures. In comparison, *The Birdman* shows more consistency between image and text than *Rosie's Walk*, but the images are similarly used to show things not said in the text, for instance about the true nature of the birdman. Whilst the information in the images builds upon that of the written text in this book, the gaps in terms of explanation and information create ambiguity. There are several possible interpretations of the narrative of *The Birdman* and, further, the conclusion of the narrative contradicts assumptions about the child reader needing 'happy endings'. This suggests that *The Birdman* is indicative of a significant trend in contemporary picturebooks relating to multiple interpretations and attempting to challenge notions of what is appropriate for younger readers. It is also an addition to the corpus of texts which seeks to extend perceptions of what is possible with the picturebook medium through dealing with controversial material. Lassén-Seger, for instance, argues that it 'exposes the powerlessness of the child'.[13] In some senses it can be seen as an example of what Sandra Beckett describes as the crossover picturebook, in that it may be seen as addressing older readers as well as younger ones.[14]

Burgess and Brown's text, then, has a traditional linear narrative, but offers a high level of ambiguity, or indeterminacy regarding motives, actions or meanings. Despite the traditional linear narrative, *The Birdman* shares some of the characteristics of the postmodern picturebook as defined by Lewis.[15] Lewis sees postmodernism as being characterized by a number of features, including boundary breaking, excess, indeterminacy, fragmentation and an undermining of notions of canon. Along with Lawrence R. Sipe and Sylvia Joyce Pantaleo, and others, Lewis identifies Scieszka and Smith's *The Stinky Cheese Man and Other Fairly Stupid Tales* (1993) as a significant example of a postmodern picturebook.[16] For instance, characters in that book break fictional boundaries by questioning the text within which they reside (one enquires what the ISBN on the back cover is for). In contrast, the characters in *The Birdman* do not look out of their world into ours. *The Birdman* asks the reader to make meaning through the interplay of image and written text. However, in sharing some of the characteristics of the postmodern picturebook it adds significant additional challenges in terms of interpretation.

The reader of *The Birdman* needs to be able to read and analyse both words and images and identify tensions between them, as I suggest above. According to Lewis, reading images involves analysing the use of line, colour, action and movement, as well as the passing of time, and the size and location of separate elements within the image and symbolism. Reading written text also makes significant demands upon the reader. In effect, the act of reading can be seen as an investigative search for meaning. At the heart of the notion of the 'active' reader is the concept that reading is, as Huw Thomas has said, 'a creative act'.[17] He argues that some texts are 'more demanding than others', in terms of the reader working to make sense of them.[18] This creates a continuum ranging from closed texts which are straightforward and guide the reader very directly, offering little latitude for a range of creative responses, through to open texts that are complex and offer opportunities for a range of reader interpretations and meanings. *The Birdman*, as shall be discussed, is towards the open end of the continuum. Finally, this concept links with what Margaret Meek described as 'knowingness' in her discussion of intertextuality in children's books[19] and which Lewis developed with regard to the shared understanding between readers and authors which he sees as like '[being] a member of an exclusive club. [...The book] is something like a message sent from one, albeit privileged, member of the club (the writer/illustrator) to another (the reader)'.[20] Both parties here draw on their intertextual and shared knowledge, becoming part of a club of knowing readers who are also more competent readers of narrative and image generally.

In making such demands, *The Birdman* constructs a reader who is trusted as being capable of understanding, or working to understand, wide-ranging references and allusions, who will enjoy the way the text is open to several interpretations, and who is encouraged, through the form of the text itself, to be actively engaged in reading. Even the title offers a challenge in that the active reader may ask whether the birdman of the title is the bird seller, or Jarvis, the transformed boy. The balance between the images of the birdman and Jarvis is fairly even throughout the text, which allows a degree of indeterminacy regarding this issue. The birdman is significantly placed in the images in seven of the twelve double-page spreads that the story covers (after the first spread which sets the scene of the carnival). He is either placed high up on the page (above the other characters) or by his figure stretching across the double-page spread. On the five other pages Jarvis, or the robin, dominate the page. In the terms of Vivienne Smith, this kind of indeterminacy will help to create readers who have 'good textual health' in that they are not simply focused on the act of decoding, but instead are engaged with filling in gaps in the text and thinking divergently and widely, so finding reading enjoyable.[21]

Intertextuality and *The Birdman*

As I have argued elsewhere, most picturebooks are 'highly intertextual, with creators drawing on many sources not just from the arts, like film and painting, but also from popular media and other cultural products'.[22] The images, then, may be resonant for the reader, in indirectly referring to other texts. Smith says that texts that do this, such as Allan and Janet Ahlberg's *Each Peach Pear Plum* (1978),[23] offer rich allusive experiences which develop intertextual thinking, an appreciation of the emotional power of story and an understanding of irony, and that writers and audiences can share a common range of references.[24]

In *The Birdman* the intertextual references reside primarily in the images rather than the written text and Brown asks the reader to do a lot of interpretative work. For example, while the illustration on the first double-page spread of the book depicts a carnival and what appears to be a troupe of players (1–2), the written text reads:

> "Birds for sale!
> Song birds. Pretty birds!
> Birds for sale"
>
> The man had to shout at the top of his voice to be heard over the noise. He was dressed in a ragged coat, and hanging off every tear and tatter of it was a tiny cage made of reeds. Inside the cages were birds … stout little finches, squeaking sparrows, trilling sky-larks, scolding blackbirds, tiny wrens, fat thrushes, sleek swallows … all beating their wings and all singing and squeaking in anger at being trapped. (2)

The textual opening provides 'bare bones' of a setting, which the illustrations turn into a rich space full of colour and movement for the reader to explore. The written description also complements, but does not repeat, the chaos and carnival of the illustration, and demonstrates the way the words and pictures throughout the book work together in complex ways.

Carnival is suggested visually and intertextually by the depiction of Commedia dell'Arte characters, with the diamond shapes on one set of leggings evoking Columbine in the character of Arlecchina who wears motley similar to her counterpart Arlecchino (or Harlequin). That this figure is tumbling also evokes Harlequin, a character who can be described as quick of body, but not of wit. Further, there is also a Pierrot in the image. All but one of the figures in the foreground of this double-page spread wear masks or face-paint. Masks offer a temporary transformation, as one cannot identify the wearer of the mask, or know their social status. Historically, Venice temporarily overturned her social order in this way. Whilst the story is not specifically located geographically or temporally within the written text, the carnival and the Commedia dell'Arte references suggest, rather than specify, the past, something reinforced by the old-fashioned clothing

Jarvis wears. Indeed, the combination of the troupe, the masks, and the patterns of brickwork and shapes of the buildings suggest a sixteenth-century Italian setting.

In *The Birdman*, masks and anonymity add to the atmosphere of mystery and chaos. Other masks associated with Venice, along with those of the Commedia dell'Arte, create sinister implications. The white-beaked mask of the plague doctor is central amongst them: it is this mask which the birdman's most closely resembles. In addition, the broad brushstrokes depicting the shadows and light behind the birdman might be read as wings, a detail not obvious from first reading. However, returning to this initial double-page spread after seeing some of the images later in the book reveals that even the first page suggests a supernatural reading of that figure, as does the way that the birdman stands in shadow, when the rest of the scene is filled with light. Similarly, towards the end of the book, an image of the new Jarvis asleep in bed whilst the new robin furiously flaps its wings in a cage lends itself to varied interpretations, as the sheets pulled up around the new Jarvis resemble wings (19–20).

Masks are not the only indication of intertextuality apparent within this text. Readers might identify another allusion to the various literary and filmic versions of J. M. Barrie's Peter Pan, especially given the emphasis in both texts on the dangerous nature of windows as allowing entry into (and flight away from) family and home. The closed window excludes Peter, but protects other children. When Jarvis leaves the window open, he allows something dangerous to enter his room: the birdman—an even darker and adult version of Pan (13). This is also in accord with the final line of the book: 'and he closed the window tight' at which point the robin who is now Jarvis shuts the current robin out of the human world and of his home (23).

Yet another example of intertextuality in this text is the way that the robin can be seen as a changeling, a being who is the offspring of a fairy or other creature that has been secretly left in the place of a human child. They can also be a magically transformed piece of wood or other material.

These beings feature in many folk and fairy tales; for example Jacob and Wilhelm Grimm's 'The Woman Whose Child They Exchanged' where they appear in the third element of the tale called 'The Elves'.[25] They are also incorporated into a number of later texts including *Outside over There* (1981), a children's story by Maurice Sendak, in which goblins replace Ida's baby sister with a changeling made of ice.[26] Fairy tales, full of magical events, are an obvious influence on *The Birdman*, but also feature in other work by both Burgess and

Brown, for example Burgess's *Lady: My Life as a Bitch* (2001, to which I return later)[27] and Brown's *If at First You Do Not See* (1982).[28] The latter is a picturebook in which the text of each double-page spread appears all the way around the edge of the page. To read the text the reader has to turn each double spread through 360 degrees. As one does so, another set of images 'magically' appear. On one double-page spread, for instance, vegetables turn into an ogre. That many fairy tales are very dark in nature and not necessarily aimed at children, is also pertinent to a reading of *The Birdman*, where the disturbing nature of the narrative echoes the horrific aspects of some older versions of 'Cinderella', for instance. In the Grimm Brothers' 'Aschenputtel', for example, the stepsisters cut off their toes or heels to enable them to wear the glass slipper. They are only discovered in their deception when two pigeons sitting in the tree which grows above the grave of Aschenputtel's mother sing a warning to the prince.[29]

Although it may seem an unlikely combination with the Commedia dell'Arte and fairy-tale references, the birdman's costume of feathered hat and long ragged coat hung with feathers is also very suggestive of the filmic image of the Childcatcher from *Chitty Chitty Bang Bang* played by Sir Robert Helpmann.[30] Readers of Brown's illustrations for *The Birdman* may identify the scene in the film where the Childcatcher entices the children out of hiding, disguising his cage for children as a travelling sweetshop and wearing a sweeping long coat over his black clothing. Whilst the film, in offering moving images, makes the most of Helpmann's balletic skill, creating tension through movement, the book constantly offers images of the birdman's flowing coat which is the colour of fallen leaves, making him seem a dark, dangerous and melancholy figure amongst the bright costumes of the other members of the troupe. Both film and book emphasize the grotesque visual aspects of the character, with distended nose/beak and birdlike movements, implied or actual. Link this with the notion of the plague doctor and one might conclude that the troupe is a pestilence. The summary on the back cover speaks of conscience, but the images actually suggest entrapment. The troupe appear on all but four of the pages with the birdman and as they leave, taking the transformed Jarvis with them, the fact that he has no real choice but to join them—to choose to be caged or die—feels chilling. The excessiveness of the punishment, combined with the resonances of the Childcatcher, makes it possible to interpret this as a horrific narrative of abduction. Whilst the roles are reversed at the conclusion of *Chitty Chitty Bang Bang*, in that the Childcatcher, in an act of possible reassurance for the audience, is captured and caged by the children, the birdman, in contrast, unmasked at the end and standing in full sunlight, revealing a seemingly benign and bearded human face, is a massive figure dominating the right-hand page of the double-page spread. The size and placement of this figure, contrasting with the tiny figures of boy and bird, is suggestive of his power (24).

The Birdman draws on a range of references, including building styles, fairy tales, films, other books and theatre in both the imagery and written text. These references do not all appear by accident, but in some cases will have been chosen by artist and writer. The resonances of each of the sets of references I have outlined and the ambiguity about the representation of wings throughout the text adds to the emotional charge of the narrative. In addition, readers interpreting this text may bring their knowledge of other texts to bear in their search for meaning, leading them to make a range of possible interpretations.

Horror, endings and disturbing the reader

In the previous section I stated that *The Birdman* is a text influenced by fairy tales and that it contains disturbing elements resonant with the darker aspects of that type of tale, rather than the more familiar sanitized versions. The chilling nature of the narrative is emphasized in both the images and in the language that Burgess employs. On the second page the birds are described as '… all beating their wings', something repeated towards the end of the text when Jarvis is trapped in a cage, creating a feeling of both movement and despair (2). Burgess suggests the unpleasant nature of the birdman in his choice of words as well. For instance, the birdman 'looks slyly down' at Jarvis, threatens him when Jarvis says he might tell the police, and sneers when Jarvis says he will free the robin (3). That Jarvis is also compromised by his actions is suggested towards the end of the book, when, confronted by the birdman, Jarvis is described as lying and whining (15).

The theme, some of the intertextual references, the implied supernatural elements and the bleak conclusion might, then, lead one to step beyond the fairy tale and locate this picturebook within the horror genre. Some horror, both filmic and literary, ends with a return to equilibrium and the monster defeated, revealing it to be a genre of reassurance. Other types of horror threaten that the monster will return, but offer a temporary reprieve from its threat. *The Birdman*, in contrast, can be grouped with those horror texts which boldly offer an unhappy ending and the monster triumphant. In addition, it could also loosely be described as psychological horror due to the lack of violence, the focus on Jarvis's emotions and the potential emotional impact upon the reader through exposing them to common psychological fears (for instance of being excluded, losing a sense of self, or of being displaced or replaced). Jarvis's behaviour in not freeing the robin also suggests that this is psychological horror in that it creates discomfort in the reader by focusing on shadowy parts of the human psyche.

In discussing the horror genre in relation to children's fiction, Kimberley Reynolds argues that it is a flash-point for many adult gatekeepers, for example librarians, parents and teachers,[31] even given the tendency to incorporate an ending that restores balance. In part she indicates that this genre is associated with what some consider unsuitable knowledge in relation to child readers (that of the occult) and suggests that there are often concerns about the high levels of fear or anxiety such texts may provoke in children. Such arguments presuppose that child readers are 'blank slates' and will be influenced by what they read in a very direct way, an argument which those who believe children are active readers would refute by emphasizing young peoples' ability to interrogate a text.[32] That the perceived audience for the picturebook is often made up of some of the youngest readers throws such debate into even sharper relief. Given Burgess's intentions to stimulate discussion about issues of suitability, childhood and trusting the reader, indicated in his article 'Sympathy for the Devil' in relation to novels for young adults, his desire to stimulate similar discussion in relation to picturebooks through the creation of one that can be considered contentious, should not, perhaps, be surprising.[33]

Given such perceptions of the reader, aspects of horror in the picturebook are nearly always softened by explanation, adult intervention, or humour. Scary, but not too scary, combined with a positive outcome, is the formula. Horror stories with a comedic twist often feature in picturebooks, as is the case with Jan Pienkowski's classic *Haunted House* (1979).[34] Similarly, in her book *A Dark, Dark Tale* (1992) Ruth Brown interprets the traditional narrative of moving through a landscape into a scary house, building tension until the climax which releases it with a joke.[35] She creates deeply atmospheric and bleakly beautiful spaces and landscapes, which serve to heighten the tension further. Another example of this softening, this time explaining horror away, is Brown's *Night-time Tale* (2005), where the frightening narrative turns out to be a dream.[36] Reynolds suggests that horror for the very young often focuses on plots which reveal that childish fears are actually unfounded; for instance that dangerous strangers turn out to be perfectly ordinary and serve to reassure children.[37] None of this reassurance applies in *The Birdman*, however.

Indeed, the seemingly dangerous stranger is precisely that: dangerous. The horror is most acute on the final page where, in the background, the troupe wanders on to the next town. The way that the birdman stands, looking to his left at the robin as it flies towards him, but with his body pointing to the right, the direction the troupe are taking, suggests he too will journey on. This stance and the implication of the narrative continuing beyond the incident in the book means that the sense of the threat of the birdman is undiminished (24).

Reynolds argues that much horror fiction for children uses the horror label as a marketing ploy. These are fictions which are actually underpinned by a sense of security, an approach which typically 'backs away from uncertain endings [...] all pervasive fear and ghastly transgression'.[38] *The Birdman*, in contrast, embraces an uncertain ending, with the monster (if that is what the birdman is) simply moving on rather than being defeated. It also creates powerful feelings of disgust and uncertainty about the self and body, especially since, given their outcome, the magical transformations at the heart of the story have horrific implications in terms of mutation and degradation. These qualities can be seen as reflecting what Burgess, Brown or their publisher thinks the young reader is capable of dealing with, and also helps to confirm that picturebooks can be created that challenge and stimulate in sophisticated ways.

Lassén-Seger locates *The Birdman*, as I do here, as 'a story designed to evoke horror rather than moral indignation' and as a text which achieves a horrific end through ambiguity.[39] She focuses on the notion of Jarvis's metamorphosis as permanent, emphasizing that most narratives for children involving such transformations see the child returned to human form after punishment.[40] She offers two potential readings of the ending, depending on whether the reader sees the transformation as a dream (with Jarvis choosing to free the bird) or real, in which case the ending is 'a spine-chilling moment [when] readers [...] realise that there can be no return trip for the boy turned bird'.[41] I offer an alternative reading of the ending, below, one that is equally horrific, but based on a different view of the text. This illustrates the ambiguity of the ending and the potential the text offers readers of all ages to make their own, differing but valid, interpretations.

In addition to the birdman being seen as monstrous, Jarvis too may be seen in that light, as his purchase of the robin and his failure to free the bird is constructed as a malevolent act in need of dramatic (one might say excessive) punishment. His greed to possess beauty destroys Jarvis, but frees the robin. Potentially, then, the birdman is a hero who values birds and nature above human life; yet he cages birds. Given the transformation at the centre of the narrative it may be that the other birds were once children who were punished as Jarvis is. His replacement in his home and bed, the boy who was the robin, tells Jarvis 'Go on … you'll get used to it', ruthlessly and vengefully repeating a phrase that Jarvis as a boy said to the robin earlier in the book when he failed to release it (23). The repetition implies that the transformations are part of an ongoing sequence, a possibility which makes the narrative more, rather than less, horrific. Another disturbing question regarding the transformation of Jarvis is who he will become if he regains his humanity. If the robin was a transformed child, in becoming Jarvis, it has lost its original identity. The implication is that a return to humanity is at the expense of another child's life.

Horrific transformations

Transformation is central to another of Burgess's texts, *Lady: My Life as a Bitch*, in which a sexually active, rebellious teenager is transformed into a confused and frightened dog by a tramp with magical powers. The novel focuses on a clear question: whether one might prefer the freedom of being a dog to the restrictions of traditional expectations about human femininity, even if it meant losing one's humanity entirely. Lassén-Seger compares it with *The Birdman*, in offering a 'non-circular metamorphosis', in that both protagonists remain animals.[42] *Lady* inhabits similar territory to *The Birdman*, but heroine Sandra has to make choices about her future self and has some degree of power in relation to her decision. In contrast, the transformations of bird and boy create a narrative about entrapment, powerless and dependency. Neither has an option regarding their form (although Jarvis does make a choice in relation to freeing the robin, one depicted as incorrect).

Whilst the transformation in *Lady* is so swift that Sandra does not realize initially that the dog she is running from is herself, the double transformation in *The Birdman* is lingered over. It is an extended sequence, drawing out the central moment of punishment and horror as the birdman changes Jarvis into a robin and the robin into Jarvis across four double-page spreads (13–20). The action takes place in one night and into the next morning. The much longer temporal sequence—extending from Jarvis's purchase of the robin, the year it spends with him and the day he realizes it might die and decides to release it after all—is, in contrast, compacted into three double-page spreads (7–12). The pacing of the sequence serves to increase the tension around the transformation. The palette in this sequence is initially dominated by dark blues, black, purple and white when

Jarvis wakes to realize someone is in his room 'fumbling at the reed cage' (13). On the left is Jarvis in his bed and to the right, positioned higher on the page, is the birdman and the cage. This image, read without reference to the supernatural elements of the narrative, shows an oppressive and threatening adult male figure in a child's bedroom, evoking a very different type of horror and the issues of abuse and abduction. What is also apparent, but not mentioned in the text, are the birdman's wings. They dominate the centre of the page, boldly dividing it. As mentioned earlier, the light and shadows of the first double-page spread suggest wings, but here the use of bold white and pale blue brush strokes make their appearance much more dramatic. The whiteness also seems to form a halo around the birdman's head making his role as villain more ambiguous and offering, again, conflicting interpretations (13–14).

The following double-page spread has a similar layout in terms of the positions of the figures, but the reader looks into the image over the birdman's wings and shoulder down onto the bed. In the background there is an increasing amount of light and a pale red tinge to the background as morning begins. It is at this moment that Jarvis lies to the birdman asserting that 'it wanted to stay' (15–16). The written text emphasizes the lie and the image here simply sets the scene, making this page a pause in the action, thus increasing tension.

The next double-page spread is also dominated by the large dark figure of the birdman, but the angle has changed again, allowing the readers to see Jarvis becoming feathery and, simultaneously, the robin starting to develop a human face. The final double-page spread of the sequence is bathed in sunlight. The focus is split between the boy in the bed, with his feather-like blankets and, in the forefront, the robin trying to escape the cage. The written text reports Jarvis's realization and horror, saying the birdman is 'nowhere to be seen'. However, the images tell a different story, in that the shadow of the birdman can be seen on the wall behind the bed. Further, the shadow of the bird in the cage is a double one. The outline, in gold on white, is that of a bird, but within that there is the shadow of a human figure, leaping, arms outstretched (17–18). Horror, then, takes place in daylight and in the supposed safety of one's own room, rather than through entering into another, more dangerous space.

Finally, the new Jarvis releases the bird, and the robin witnesses his mother asking the new Jarvis about his change of heart regarding freeing the robin, completing his removal from humanity, family and home. Lassén-Seger focuses upon the text rather than image at this moment, describing how there is a shift to third-person narration meaning that 'readers no longer have access to Jarvis's point of view [so] there is no knowing for sure whether the exchange of bodies during the night actually took place, or whether it was just a bad dream'.[43] However, whilst indicating this ambiguity, she argues that the horror of the narrative rests upon 'the reader sharing Jarvis's tragedy'.[44]

In choosing to analyse the images, I would argue that they offer clues as to a different, but equally valid reading, again indicating the complexity of this text. It is on the two final double-page spreads that a link is made between the robin and Jarvis through colour, in that the red breast of the robin is reflected in the red clothing of the new Jarvis. Looking back through the book, though, the cover also indicates this link between child and bird. That the red top only appears in the final pages of the book, after Jarvis has been replaced by his bird doppelgänger makes it impossible to know which is robin and which boy in the cover image. The clothing link opens up an interpretation not apparent on first encountering the book. Whilst it initially looks benign, it may depict collusion between the birds and the birdman, and their captive bird-child.

Conclusion

Despite the assertion on the back cover that *The Birdman* is a moral tale, there is little sense here of a moral, or a clear line on meaning, something which may function as a challenge to critics and commentators if they have an understanding of childhood as a 'blank slate' and children as vulnerable and in need of protection and moral guidance. However, for other critics and commentators this text could be seen as encouraging an engagement with reading through exploring complexity and ambiguity. Here the model of the child as active reader is tied to a perspective on childhood as powerful, autonomous and skilful in interpreting text rather than simply being influenced by it. This is not a text which closes down interpretation, but an open one which encourages it.

The ways in which Brown and Burgess draw on elements of horror, intertextuality and the potential of the picturebook regarding the relationship of image and text creates a rich allusive reading experience. Given the gaps in the narrative and images in this picturebook there is a great deal of interpretative creative work possible for readers of the book, even around the bleak conclusion for the child protagonist. The reader, then, may speculate about the meanings of the ending as well as other aspects of the text.

Notes

1. Melvin Burgess and Ruth Brown, *The Birdman* (London: Andersen Press, 2000). All further references in the chapter are to this edition.
2. Maria Nikolajeva and Carole Scott, *How Picturebooks Work* (New York: Garland, 2001).
3. Maria Lassén-Seger, *Adventures into Otherness: Child Metamorphs in Late Twentieth Century Children's Literature* (Åbo: Åbo Akademi University Press, 2006).
4. David Lewis, *Reading Contemporary Picturebooks: Picturing Text* (London: RoutlegeFalmer, 2001): 168.
5. Nikolajeva and Scott, *How Picturebooks Work*: 12.
6. Melvin Burgess, *The Copper Treasure* (Dunfermline: A&C Black, 1998).
7. Perry Nodelman, *Words about Pictures: The Narrative Art of Children's Picture Books* (Athens, GA: University of Georgia Press, 1988).
8. Evelyn Arizpe and Morag Styles, *Children Reading Pictures: Interpreting Visual Texts* (London: RoutlegeFalmer, 2003): 19.
9. *Ibid.*
10. Mel Gibson, 'Picturebooks, Comics and Graphic Novels', in David Rudd (ed.), *The Routledge Companion to Children's Literature* (Abingdon: Routledge, 2010): 104.
11. Maria Nikolajeva and Carole Scott, 'The Dynamics of Picturebook Communication', *Children's Literature in Education* 31(4) (2000): 225–39.
12. Pat Hutchins, *Rosie's Walk* (London: Bodley Head, 1970).
13. Lassén-Seger, *Adventures into Otherness*: 60.
14. Sandra Beckett, *Crossover Picturebooks: A Genre for All Ages* (London: Routledge, 2012).
15. Lewis, *Reading Contemporary Picturebooks.*
16. Lawrence R. Sipe and Sylvia Joyce Pantaleo, *Postmodern Picturebooks: Play, Parody, and Self-Referentiality* (New York: Routledge, 2008); Jon Scieszka and Lane Smith, *The Stinky Cheese Man and Other Fairly Stupid Tales* (London: Puffin, 1993).
17. Huw Thomas, *Reading and Responding to Fiction: Classroom Strategies for Developing Literacy* (London: Scholastic, 1998): 138.
18. *Ibid.*: 145.
19. Margaret Meek, *How Texts Teach what Readers Learn* (Stroud: Thimble Press, 1987).
20. David Lewis, 'Ooops! Colin McNaughton and Knowingness', *Children's Literature in Education* 29(2) (1998): 60.
21. Vivienne Smith, 'Learning to Be a Reader: Promoting Good Textual Health', in Prue Goodwin (ed.), *Understanding Children's Books: A Guide for Education Professionals* (London: Sage, 2008): 33.
22. Gibson, 'Picturebooks, Comics and Graphic Novels': 100.
23. Allan Ahlberg and Janet Ahlberg, *Each Peach Pear Plum* (Harmondsworth: Viking, 1978).
24. Smith, 'Learning to Be a Reader': 33–42.

25. 'The Elves', in Jacob and Wilhelm Grimm, *Kinder- und Hausmärchen* (*Children's and Household Tales—Grimm's Fairy Tales*), 7th edn (Göttingen: Verlag der Dieterichschen Buchhandlung, 1857), no. 39.
26. Maurice Sendak, *Outside over There* (London: Bodley Head, 1981).
27. Melvin Burgess, *Lady: My Life as a Bitch* (London: Andersen Press, 2001).
28. Ruth Brown, *If at First You Do Not See* (London: Andersen Press, 1982).
29. 'Aschenputtel', in Jacob and Wilhelm Grimm, *Kinder- und Hausmärchen* (*Children's and Household Tales—Grimm's Fairy Tales*), 7th edn (Göttingen: Verlag der Dieterichschen Buchhandlung, 1857), no. 21: 119–26.
30. Cubby Broccoli, *Chitty Chitty Bang Bang* (London: Twentieth Century Fox, 1968).
31. Kimberley Reynolds, 'Introduction', in Kimberley Reynolds, Geraldine Brennan and Kevin McCarron (eds.), *Frightening Fiction: R.L Stine, Robert Westall, David Almond and Others* (London: Continuum, 2001): 1–18.
32. See, for example, Shirley J. Pressler, 'Construction of Childhood: The Building Blocks', in Derek Kassem, Lisa Murphy and Elizabeth Taylor (eds.), *Key Issues in Childhood and Youth Studies* (Abingdon: Routledge, 2009): 20.
33. Melvin Burgess, 'Sympathy for the Devil', *Children's Literature in Education* 35(4) (2004): 289–300.
34. Jan Pienkowski, *Haunted House* (London: Heinemann, 1979).
35. Ruth Brown, *A Dark, Dark Tale* (London: Andersen Press, 1992).
36. Ruth Brown, *Night-time Tale* (London: Andersen Press, 2005).
37. Reynolds, 'Introduction'.
38. *Ibid.*: 3.
39. Lassén-Seger, *Adventures into Otherness*: 233.
40. *Ibid.*: 232.
41. *Ibid.*: 235.
42. *Ibid.*: 233.
43. *Ibid.*: 234–5.
44. *Ibid.*:237.

Part III
Human and Animal Identities

7

Borderland: The Animal World of Melvin Burgess

Peter Hollindale

Introduction

Melvin Burgess's *Lady: My Life as a Bitch* (2001), though scarcely a realistic work of fiction, is regularly included amongst those novels for which Burgess is best known and (depending on one's point of view) most admired or deplored, namely socially realistic depictions of the sexual and cultural practices of contemporary teenagers. It is placed alongside *Junk* (1996), *Doing It* (2003) and *Nicholas Dane* (2010), for example, as a hard-edged depiction of a teenage world which has undergone convulsive change in recent decades. Adults often find such works disturbing. As Claire Squires observes, '[t]he debate around [*Doing It*] and around his other works, including *Junk* and [*Lady*] foregrounds how altering conceptions of the "child" (or the teenager in this case) can cause both controversy and anxiety among consumers and reviewers within the children's publishing industry'.[1]

It is generally agreed that, for better or worse, Burgess's teenage novels register profound change. Writing in the same collection as Squires, Rachel Falconer summarizes the case for the defence, and importantly includes adult readers not only as potential critics of the novels but also those who may learn from them:

> In an era in which many young people grow up surrounded by violence and crime, it is important that the books and films they read and watch should address the reality of their lives. Since these books implicitly challenge dominant cultural myths of the innocence of childhood they are likely to continue to provoke controversy amongst adult readers. But social realist fiction aimed at a primary audience of young adults may also speak powerfully to adults for the very reason that it exposes these myths as anachronistic.[2]

Falconer points to *Junk* as one such text.[3]

No one can now deny that Burgess is a prominent and controversial writer in the social realist tradition, but I shall argue that *Lady: My Life as a Bitch* has an important place in a separate and neglected thematic sequence in Burgess's work, a series of novels concerned with animals and their relationship to humankind. Several of these books are clearly accessible to much younger readers than the audience for novels such as *Junk*, and individually they may seem relatively uncontroversial, or only mildly so. When read as a sequence, however, they constitute an evolving imaginative exploration of animal life and its links with the human animal, *homo sapiens*, which is cumulatively just as radical and challenging as Burgess's social realist fictions. With one exception, their developing and progressively more bold depiction of the animal world, and the place of humans in it, follows the order of publication. Starting with Burgess's first published novel, *The Cry of the Wolf* (1990), it continues in *Tiger, Tiger* (1996), *Lady: My Life as a Bitch* (2001), and *Bloodsong* (2005). The exception is *Kite* (1997) which differs from the others not so much by being about a bird (since birds are animals just as mammals are) but by taking a simple and naturalistic narrative form which illuminates with exceptional clarity some of the ideas and assumptions which underlie the earlier books. In the following discussion I shall therefore override exact chronology and take *Kite* first. The demarcation lines between human and animal are very clear in this novel, and are largely conveyed by key words and human economic status, whereas in the earlier books they depend on a complex depiction of human and animal behaviour. Burgess himself felt that with *Kite* he had reached a point of saying everything he had to say about animals and was at risk of merely repeating himself, but the explicitness of his ideas in *Kite* provides a helpful approach to the other novels. It is also true that when Burgess did eventually resume his variations on animal fiction with *Lady* and later *Bloodsong*, his focus had switched (far more strongly than in *Tiger, Tiger*) to forms of human and animal hybridity.

Overview of the sequence

Of the first three novels in the sequence, all of which are concerned with the destruction and protection of endangered species, *Kite* is the only one where the creature at risk is a part of British native fauna at the present time and it fits most neatly into the conservationist ideology of modern wildlife protection organizations. Burgess's 'afterword', as much as the novel itself, leaves no doubt of his own commitment to wildlife conservation or his delight in the beauty of the species. The novel is deliberatively set in 1964, over thirty years before its publication, at a time when the red kite—an exceptionally beautiful carrion-eating bird of prey—was reduced to a dozen or so pairs in mid-Wales. For red kites to attempt to nest in England, as they do in the book, would have been a truly exceptional event. By the time Burgess wrote his novel and 'afterword', successful reintroductions had considerably increased their numbers and geographical range. As I write in 2012 they are relatively common not only in Wales but parts of England, especially the Chilterns. The red kite's is a success story, but the novel's political urgency concerning the practices of landowners and gamekeepers now equally applies to other birds of prey, especially the hen harrier, which is persecuted almost to extinction on grouse moors.

No other of the animal stories carries this social realist political commitment. In general, Burgess's sense of wonder, delight and protective indignation towards wild animals operates more and more through fantasy. In *The Cry of the Wolf* not only is the basic premise—the survival of small packs of wild wolves in modern England—implausible, but the story depends on the exceptional qualities of one single wolf. *Tiger, Tiger* openly rests on fantasy and magic. This stylistic development in no way displaces the tutelary protectionist theme articulated so uncompromisingly in *Kite*; but it does develop a more boldly imaginative, speculative representation of animal consciousness and of human status as perceived from the animal's perspective, and more audaciously still it has the consequence of narrowing the gap between human and animal, increasing the biological intimacy between them, and eroding established schemes of value based on human uniqueness.

In developing these themes and ideas Burgess was drawing on an intellectual tradition long established in English philosophy. Keith Thomas notes that by 1800 the world 'could no longer be regarded as having been made for man alone, and the rigid barriers between humanity and other forms of life had been much weakened', following the emergence during the eighteenth century of a form of pantheism 'when it was widely urged that all parts of creation had a right to live, and that nature itself had an intrinsic spiritual value'.[4] Burgess can be seen exploring the several elements of this tradition through his writing. In *Kite*, the threatened bird's protection is ideologically reinforced by the principle that all parts of creation have a right to live, and the wolf, and above all the tiger, powerfully signify nature's 'intrinsic spiritual value'. All three, moreover, are both beautiful and rare, the two qualities being clearly linked in Burgess's imagination. The last two books in the sequence under discussion are markedly different in emphasis. The dog which Sandra becomes in *Lady* is certainly neither beautiful nor rare, but her wonderful comedy could hardly express more vividly the weakened barriers between humanity and other forms of life. Finally, in *Bloodsong*, those barriers have effectively disappeared altogether, and humanity has become comprehensively a mongrel species. This dystopian extravaganza can be seen as the ultimate destination of ideas developed through the sequence. What might be described—to borrow a contentious American political term—as human 'exceptionalism' is all but extinguished by a range of bodily mergences with gods, other animals and machines, although the word 'humanity' retains its currency as the locus of a set of admirable behavioural characteristics.

Readers may find that *Lady* poses the question, not only 'what is it to be a teenager?' but more radically, 'what is it to be human?' Lady herself can be seen as analogous to a feral child living with animals, and in his study of feral children, *Savage Girls and Wild Boys*, Michael Newton extends the question, saying of feral children that they raise 'the deepest and most insoluble of questions—what is human nature? Does such a thing even exist? How do we differ from other animals?'[5] In the next section I shall approach his final question as it is treated by Burgess—'what part does language play in creating our humanity?'[6]

All these, however cautiously expressed, are essentially anthropocentric questions. They veer towards human exceptionalism. What sets Burgess apart, I suggest, is that he is not an anthropocentric writer. These novels raise on equal terms the questions 'what is animal nature?', 'what is it like to be an animal in a human-dominated world?', and increasingly from book to book in the sequence, 'how true, how stable and how permanent is the ostensible fact of human exceptionalism in a biodiverse world?' Sometimes playfully, but always with serious intent, Burgess opens up these questions.

Empathy and language

In another study of human and animal behaviour, *Feral Children and Clever Animals*, Douglas Keith Candland quotes a work published in 1934 by the ethologist Jacob von Uexkull, *A Stroll through the Worlds of Animals and Men*. The writer invites his reader to wander through a meadow when butterflies and other insects are on the wing, and attempt to enter their worlds:

> To do so, we must first blow, in fancy, a soap bubble around each creature to represent its own world, filled with the perceptions which it alone

> knows. When we ourselves then step into one of these bubbles, the familiar meadow is transformed. Many of its colorful features disappear, others no longer belong together but appear in new relationships. A new world comes into being.[7]

As far as he can, Burgess steps into this bubble in several of these novels. He identifies convincingly the rudimentary mental processes of a red kite, especially the conflicting impulses of desire for food and desire for self-preservation. This is the animal protagonist which has least autonomy of action, since for most of the novel it is either a helpless fledgling, or captive, or injured; only in a brief experience of apprentice flight is it able to show the 'kiteness' of its nature. Here the bird ceases to be 'Teresa', the captive chick, and becomes 'the kite', behaving as any wild bird must in first experimenting with its element of air: 'The Kite wobbled in the air. She flapped up and down, half hovering, half flying. Then she suddenly grabbed the wind properly with her wings, did two powerful flaps and disappeared beyond the trees.'[8]

In *The Cry of the Wolf* there is in the first half of the story a compelling, if inevitably speculative, entry into the secret intimacies of the wolf-pack, but this empathetic enterprise is inconsistent, and changes once the lone survivor and hero, Greycub, is left in biological solitude. There is a rare lapse into anthropomorphism as Greycub is depicted growing up at the Tilleys' farm, typified by his response to Mrs Tilley's indignation as she finds him chewing up a rabbit's head on her cushions, and throws it out of the window: 'Greycub was most offended. He looked at her in surprise as if to say, "How would you like it if I snatched your dinner off you in such a rude, unpleasant way?"'[9] After he leaves the farm, however, he is finally transformed into enhanced wolfness as the symbolic avenger of his species, a creature of potential myth.

As magical powers and fantasy drive the sequence, there is less demand on Burgess's empathetic imagination, though it remains notable how powerfully he can recreate inner being and animal consciousness through closely observed physical movement. Here is Greycub approaching a broken cottage when tracking the Hunter:

> There, he slowed right down. First, he crept downwind of it and sniffed the air. Then he crept on his belly up to his own tracks as he had approached the ruins from the other side, days before. There was no new scent alongside them. Still Greycub kept up his caution and crept by a devious hidden route right up within the ruins. (108)

The reiterated 'crept' not only registers the cautious, furtive, low-bodied animal movement but its stealthy and menacing purpose. Burgess is able to 'step into the bubble' with great skill, but his need to do so recedes as his object becomes not so much to represent the difference between humans and other animals as forms of mergence and intimate conjoining. As I shall demonstrate below, one of the major achievements of *Lady*, which is certainly the outstanding novel in the sequence, is its perfect narrative balance between humanness and 'dogness'.

There remains the insuperable problem which confronts all writers about animals—the problem of language. This is not, as is often contended by anthropocentric thinkers, an absolute distinction between humans and animals, a feature of human 'exceptionalism'. It is not true that we possess language and all other animals do not. At some level, probably more complex than we yet understand, at least some other animals certainly do. Not only our relatives the chimpanzees and great apes, but whales, dolphins, elephants and—pertinently—wolves, are among those species in whom linguistic behaviour can be shown. The difficulty is that we cannot properly understand or represent this language, although at a basic level some indicative transcriptions can be attempted, as Burgess does, for example, in *The Cry of the Wolf*. Even so, there is a point beyond which we cannot go. The dilemma is beautifully expressed in J. M. Coetzee's *The Lives of Animals*, a hybrid work, part novel, part philosophical debate, in two passages spoken by his chief character, Elizabeth Costello, a distinguished novelist and animal rights defender invited to speak to a largely unsympathetic audience at an American university. She has published a novel based on Joyce's character Marion Bloom in *Ulysses*, and uses this to assert her capacity to 'step into the bubble': '[i]f I can think my way into the existence of a being who has never existed, then I can think my way into the existence of a bat or a chimpanzee or an oyster, any being with whom I share the substrate of life'.[10] On the other hand, when she is speaking later in a literature seminar about the work of Ted Hughes, she is obliged to acknowledge the consequence of filtering exchange of feeling into human language: 'Not that animals do not care what we feel about them. But when we divert the current of feeling that flows between ourselves and the animal into words, we abstract it forever from the animal.'[11]

Because Burgess is not depicting animals enacting human roles and habits (except with intentional comedic effect, as in *Lady*, when the dog is trying to convince her family that she is their lost daughter) he is rarely exposed to the usual charges of anthropomorphism, since his other animals do not speak (Lady and the other ex-human dogs exchange sophisticated conversation, not by human speech, which is physically impossible, but by barking as the outward voice of a kind of telepathy). He is 'nevertheless trapped in the alienating prison-house of language, so can never capture the real animal',[12] and must settle for the approximations of reportage. Even when his primary animal character is privileged by fantasy, as Lila is in *Tiger, Tiger*, Burgess is careful to 'step into the bubble' of his animal supporting cast as far as language will allow him to. For example, the young tiger Will in *Tiger, Tiger* is a very minor figure compared with Lila, but his instinctive claim to leadership status as the only surviving male is emphasized by body language when possible, as he bends his face down to Lila 'so that she could lick his muzzle submissively'.[13]

The main linguistic problems occur in *The Cry of the Wolf*, and can be illustrated by contrasting examples. The first is from the scene where Greycub is released from captivity by his mother, Silver. Earlier he has heard the 'long, musical wail' of the parent wolf at a distance:

> At last, just a metre away on the other side of the wall came a small dry noise. The cub sprang up and hurled himself at the wall, whining and yelping [...] A second noise, a soft cough, and he had a vow of silence clapped on him. Instantly he crouched. That noise, which he had never heard before, was a warning to be still [...]' (59)

This seems to me excellent, and entirely convincing in its demonstration of the cub's innate knowledge of and obedience to a vocabulary of sounds outside his actual experience. The second piece, a few pages later, concerns the wolves' strategic plan to outwit the Hunter. Disbelief is not aroused by the wolves' capacity for intelligent coordinated action: there is ample evidence of their abilities. It is Burgess's attribution to the wolves of skill in handling hypothetical alternatives which fails to carry narrative conviction. Burgess has been seduced by his own linguistic skills into mental processes which cannot plausibly be *thought* without advanced verbal capability.

> Silver had hesitated a long time before giving this difficult task [of acting as decoy] to Conna [...] Luck, great good luck was needed if he was to survive. In her heart, Silver doubted whether he would [...] The only alternative was for Silver to go herself but this would mean allowing the rescue itself to be taken out of her control, and this she would not do. (61)

The trap of language is evident soon afterwards in a single sentence. The wounded Silver, cornered in a barn, is preparing to attack the Hunter in a final effort to defend herself and her cub: 'It was unheard of for a wolf to attack a human being, but this man had lost his right to live' (68). Sliding from informed impersonal narrative to Silver's mind within a few words, Burgess either intervenes to act for Silver as a moral judge by proxy, or implies her own capacity for this complex judicial verdict. Sometimes Burgess elides the voices and roles of narrator and animal interpreter, and this is when he is most obviously trapped in the prison-house of language, from which there is no escape.

Nature and supernature: kite, wolf and tiger

There are marked similarities of narrative organization in the first three books of the sequence. By identifying their common characteristics, we are placed to see the presence of ideas within this pattern which will lead in turn to the more radical visions of animal status and propensity advanced in the later books for older readers, *Lady: My Life as a Bitch* and *Bloodsong*.

Each of the first three novels has as its animal protagonist a rare, lovely and endangered species. The beauty is a constant. The rarity is variable. Although the red kite is quite rare in Britain, there are strong populations in other countries. Wild wolves are, in reality, extinct in Britain, and under threat in most of their other global habitats. The Siberian tiger is the worst case of all, reduced to a global total of at best a few hundred animals. In each novel the animals are threatened by male human predators. Harris in *Kite*, though savagely depicted by Burgess, is sadly typical of many British landowners, persecuting wildlife to protect his own financial profits. (It should in fairness be noted that many other landowners, by contrast, are ardent and intelligent conservationists.) However, the (significantly nameless) Hunter in *The Cry of the Wolf* is of a different order—an archetypal human hunter, obsessed with pointless extermination for extermination's sake. Finally, in *Tiger, Tiger*, the Chinese businessman and triad leader Lee Yung brings money, power and ruthless international predation to work in the pernicious cause of traditional Chinese medicine. The Hunter rejoices in causing extinction; Lee Yung is indifferent to it, but in *consuming* rare animals for superstitious self-betterment he goes a stage beyond even the Hunter.

Finally, in each novel there is a human boy. In *Kite* there are two. The boys all occupy a median position in the contest between human animals and others. Again the pattern is essentially the same from story to story, and is one of diminishing responsibility for harm to the animal and growing alliance with it. All the boys and all the key animals are young, confronting the threats of adult humanity. The young bird, and

Greycub, and Lila the tiger grow physically during the story, and so in maturity and understanding do the boys. Taylor the gamekeeper's son in *Kite* begins as an egg-collector and as Harris's deferential murderous errand-boy. As his attitudes change, the efforts of Taylor and his friend Alan to raise the red kite chick are sometimes comically inept, but they work, and he shows fine subversive courage in questioning Harris face to face. Like Ben Tilley in *The Cry of the Wolf*, he saves the life of his chosen animal when it is newly born and helpless. Ben's own questionable beginnings are much more limited. As a ten year old he is a juvenile hunter, hoping to shoot water voles, but his chief offence is to let slip the secret of the wolves' existence to the Hunter, an error which three years later he views with guilt and sorrow. Ben makes what (considerable) amends he can, and forms a close and trusting relationship with Greycub, of a kind no adult can. Twelve-year-old Steve Hattersly's relationship with Lila, the Siberian tiger, is different again. If his initial position is flawed at all, it is only in his pleasure at watching her in captivity, but this is nothing compared to the complex friendship which grows between himself and Lila, first activated by her own mesmeric powers, which not only allows him to save her life but changes him for ever by the unremembered supernatural sexual bond which forms between them.

The practicalities of the relationship between Taylor Mase and the young kite are as close to naturalism as the sequence comes. But *Kite*'s importance to our understanding of Burgess's ideological stance lies in its variant repetition of the word 'vermin'. At first, vermin are simply any wild creatures which threaten Harris's pheasants: 'Vermin. Rats, weasels and stoats, jays, crows, magpies and hawks: it was everywhere' (28). The book begins with Taylor obeying Harris's order to climb a churchyard tree and remove the young crows from their nest, where the vicar had hoped to offer them sanctuary. Crows, of course, are 'vermin'. When Taylor's gamekeeper father hears about the incident, he mimics and mocks his employer: 'Sanctuary? Vermin? Don't tell me God likes vermin!' (12). But Mr Mase's ridicule of his boss is the expression of a personal dislike. He does not question, as a gamekeeper, that the crows *are* 'vermin', and nor does Taylor himself.

Soon, however, the word 'vermin' is cut away from strictly animal connotations and becomes a contested verdict on humans themselves. Very early in the story Taylor and his friend Alan are waylaid by Harris's uncle, a passionate conservationist, while seeking eggs of long-eared owls. Harris Senior denounces them: 'You're vermin, the pair of you!' (18). At first Taylor resists ('Vermin was going a bit far'), but is won over by the old man to defence of kites, so that faced with Harris's determination to wipe out the bird, 'Taylor felt like vermin himself' (34). This is Harris's own chosen term for those who obstruct him. At the autumn shoot, when Taylor protests to Harris that kites cannot be shot, Harris says, 'Vermin everywhere, Mase' (102) and means Taylor. When Taylor's protest is endorsed by one of the fee-paying pheasant-shooters, Harris's reaction is, 'Bloody vermin gets everywhere' (103). The verbal climax of the story comes when Tom Mase the gamekeeper definitively reverses the term: 'You're the vermin, Mr Harris' (167). This reversal of terms, absorbing humans into the conventional animal context and hence narrowing the gap between them, is essentially what is physically enacted with increasing power in the other two stories in a challenging enhancement of animal status. The kite itself is made almost sacred. Taylor compares it to an angel, the tree where it nests is 'holy', and a gibbeted kite is twice compared to a crucifixion. Word and symbol create a porous boundary between animal and human.

In *The Cry of the Wolf*, the porous frontier is physical in nature. The Hunter stands in anonymity for one form of a human absolute. His human opposite is the (also unnamed) Breeder, who oversees Greycub's weaning. (Ben, though also a human opposite, is like the other boys in part a citizen of both worlds.) While he is growing up, Greycub is apparently an ordinary wolf. He is of his kind, but he is also the last of his kind. The relict population of English wolves has evolved into a separate sub-species. The Hunter's tireless pursuit has killed them off until only two, Greycub and his mother Silver, and finally only one, Greycub himself, are left. Greycub does not know this, of course, and spends years seeking others of his kind before settling into his lonely existence in Scotland. At the edge of extinction these last two wolves display a behavioural change. Burgess has earlier asserted that it is almost unknown for wolves to attack humans. Silver, pressured to breaking-point by the Hunter, has been planning to break this taboo when she is shot. At once Greycub, though literally still a cub, does indeed break it, by attacking the Hunter as best he can.

This behavioural conversion is directed at the Hunter only, and is then in abeyance for several years until their tracks fortuitously cross again. Finding his ultimate enemy, Greycub is transformed into something archetypal, Wolf-as-Hunter. He develops from nature to supernature (not supernatural, but a changed and magnified essence of his species) to confront the archetypal human Hunter. What follows is a duel of absolutes. As Greycub becomes a Revenger (the role of Lila also in *Tiger, Tiger*, and itself a mergence with human behaviour), Burgess systematically vindicates his solitary mission in two descriptions of the Hunter's macabre collection of dead wolves, the trophies of his genocide, in the Scottish house where Greycub finds him (Chapter 13). In each passage the word 'wolf' is reiterated like the tolling of a funeral bell: 'The room was full of dead wolves' (93). The skulls and skins are 'worse than dead'. They are 'no longer wolves' (95). Their 'wolf spirit' has been purged entirely. The narrative condones and empowers the last wolf as superwolf. Likewise, as each begins to hunt the other, the ultimate Hunter is exposed (if we still doubted it) as another animal: 'Thought was unnecessary. He became an animal of the eye' (101). Each animal is using its knowledge of the other to outthink it. Each is carried up to and beyond the extreme of its own nature, and Greycub, in the brilliant manoeuvre which brings him to the Hunter from an unforeseen direction, wins the duel by drawing into his solitary self the group hunting skills of the pack. He avenges his solitude by transcending it. The final contest is a replay of their first, in the barn, when Silver lay dead, but this time, triumphantly, it is an intimate fight between equals.

In *Tiger, Tiger*, Burgess appears at first to have crossed the boundary between realism and pure fantasy. But the literary border here is just as porous as the biological line between the human animal and others. Matthew Grenby observes in his study *Children's Literature* that 'the supernatural and the normal exist together in fantasy texts, in various proportions and combinations, but [...] there is no ratio which governs their relationship. To increase one is not to diminish the other.'[14] This is the case in *Tiger, Tiger*, where all the rare Siberian tigers except Lila are depicted naturalistically, against a background of difficult conservation politics and a human mindset of warring principle and greed, warring superstition and economic realism, which is entirely convincing. Only Lila's supernatural powers, and the boy Steve in so far as he is briefly part of them, take the book further into the spaciousness of fantasy which here and later allows Burgess to crystallize his non-fantastic view of animal and human.

Even Lila is not quite the creature of total fantasy that she appears. *Tiger, Tiger* was published in 1996. In the winter of 1997, in the remote far east of Russia, a wounded and starving Siberian tiger attacked and ate two local hunters. The hunted animal who becomes the hunter, introduced in *The Cry of the Wolf* and highly developed in *Tiger, Tiger*, is not without documentary precedent. The Siberian tiger's story is told by John Vaillant in *The Tiger: A True Story of Vengeance and Survival*. Vaillant's book is a carefully researched mixture of documentary and anthropomorphic speculation, but the factual content of his study bears eerie resemblances to Burgess's Lila, not least the probability that the Russian tiger was indeed in search of revenge, and the fact that it appeared to have a ghostlike power which made it difficult to track.[15]

Lila's supreme power of concealment is her ability to 'transform', to take on a convincing if unusual appearance as a fourteen-year-old human girl (her age reminding us that for all her powers Lila is a very young tiger). Lila cannot speak human language as herself (though she can mimic human voices) but her transformative powers in themselves take Burgess's fusion of human and animal further than the other books have done—as a magical humanized presence she illuminates human actualities. Writing about *Tiger, Tiger* among other works, Reynolds notes that 'writers of animal stories almost inevitably blur the boundary between fantasy and realism, since the genre requires them to render animals' thoughts in human language'.[16] Although I have discussed this constraint earlier, it is part of Burgess's achievement in *Tiger, Tiger* that he largely evades its limitations. Lila as Spirit Tiger is endowed with mental powers analogous to, but not identical with, those of a human, so 'thought' is a 'given' of her narrative, but it is linked as far as possible by Burgess to physical actions, and even Lila's actions when in tiger form are largely naturalistic. The other tigers are given only 'action thoughts' they would plausibly have in the wild.

Burgess's most daring step in *Tiger, Tiger* is not the fantasy transformation of Lila herself, but the reverse transformation of the boy Steve into a male Siberian tiger. Believing the other tigers dead, Lila obeys the spur to reproduce her kind in the only way open to her—to transform a human boy for one night into a male tiger who can mate with her. Burgess handles the event with great tact, absolving Steve from knowledge and memory of what happens, and showing it as totally magical in both event and setting:

> There were no memories, just feelings. Dreams of play and prey, vivid, unaccountable and full of meaning that ebbed away. There were no witnesses—only the tawny owl who hunted voles and mice in the moon shadows under stone walls and white boulders, who saw two tigers, frost in their shaggy coats, mating that night under Pen-y-Ghent. (137)

After the mating, Lila is pregnant with Steve-as-tiger's cub. Steve himself is not unchanged: 'He had grown up overnight in a way no one had ever done before. She had left inside him forever a streak of the tiger in his soul' (141). *Tiger, Tiger* here carries the progress of biological mergence to a point of magical hybridity. It is a remarkable achievement, but it obviously strains and arguably breaks the bounds of what a book for pre-teenage children can accommodate. To take it further Burgess required a change of direction and an older readership.

Metamorphosis and mutation—dog and dogman

I have tried to demonstrate that the first three books in Burgess's animal sequence, although written for young readers, are less simple than they may seem, and increasingly question human exceptionalism. Although they have comic episodes (Steve's efforts to dress the naked tiger-become-girl in human clothes anticipate Lady's attempt to resume her top and knickers before confronting her family as a dog), they are essentially serious stories embedded in a conservationist ethic. To continue his enquiry into what it is to be human, Burgess turned from rare and wild to commonplace and urban for his vision of humanity, and opted for a biological comedy which might have been countenanced by Jonathan Swift. The teenage novel *Lady: My Life as a Bitch* has proved provocative and attracted plenty of commentary, not least because of its frank and uninhibited delight in the passionate farce of human and animal sexuality.

There is some disagreement about the nature of the book and its success, but general consent that its centre of gravity is teenage sex. I do not dispute this, or doubt for a moment that it accounts for the novel's popularity with teenage readers. We see Sandra Francy, aged seventeen, first as a human teenager in full hormonal rebellion against the self-imposed restrictions of society, then metamorphosed into a dog, experiencing in actuality what David Rudd, writing about *Junk*, described as 'this rhetoric of freedom, of escaping into an alternative existence'.[17]

Critics have defined Burgess's narrative excursion in various ways. Reynolds terms it a 'comic allegory about adolescent sexuality',[18] and later in the same study as a venture into magic realism. She summarizes the magical realist text as an 'attempt to transcend the restrictions of the mundane and commonsensical. They work on the willingness to believe that there is more to the world than we can comprehend with our senses and intellects, and so subvert and override epistemological certainties.'[19] Once the sexually hedonistic and socially anarchic teenager, Sandra, has been turned into a dog (whose life her human behaviour comically resembles) the story seems bound to reach the predictable counter-revolution when she recovers human form. Instead (it seems) Sandra finally opts for a dog's life and renounces all the things that growing up as a human would entail. Reynolds, who admires the novel, locates its power in this startling venture into magical realism. In her study *Constructing Adolescence in Fantastic Realism*, Alison Waller distinguishes between the fantastic realist text and comic parody. Agreeing that teenage metamorphosis is usually 'presented as a temporary stage', and that *Lady* 'transgresses by leaving adolescent Sandra in animal shape', she sees the novel not as a work of fantastic realism but as a playful and ironic celebration of teenage irresponsibility. In leaving Sandra in her dog's life the novel resists the developmental ideology which in fantastic realist fictions would typically represent recovered and mature humanity as a desirable outcome.[20]

Roderick McGillis, whose view of the novel is by comparison lukewarm at best, briefly places it in 'Lacanian territory', and describes the book as working humorously 'in carnivalesque manner', observing that '[c]learly, the comedy in this book serves to remind us of just how important the body is to the human condition. What is less clear is how we are to take carnival in this book.' Like Reynolds and Waller, but from a different theoretical perspective, he places much importance on the ending:

> The book ends with her posterior disappearing out the window. What are we to make of this? Inside we have the human family; outside we have the dogs and the hunt and the animal delight in a life lived for the moment. Inside, we have the law of the father; outside we have, perhaps, *jouissance* of some kind. But what kind? Outside the window what waits for Sandra is the Real, a world of swirling and running and energetic chaos. Outside the window she may defecate wherever she likes, but she will also lose her memory and her capability to rationalise. She may have fun, but she will not understand why she is having fun. In other words, outside the window is a world akin to death from a human point of view.[21]

This may be true, but it is also true that—as numerous passages throughout the novel have shown us—inside the window is a world akin to death from a dog's point of view. Even in the early days after her metamorphosis Lady comments, 'I shook my head and the world of men came back to my eye—stinking cars and food in jars, and the world wrapped up like a toy for big pale monkeys. Sod them!'[22]

Because the book is on one level so indisputably a 'comic allegory about teenage sexuality', and because it appears to end in a clear choice (in favour of a dog's kind of dog's life rather than a human kind of dog's life) it attracts essentially anthropocentric commentary based on awareness of what is lost when the riches of human experience are wilfully renounced. But we need to ask, when approaching the novel from the neglected animal perspective, whether the book does indeed end with Lady's, or Sandra's, choice of life as a dog. Does it indeed end at all?

Throughout the novel Burgess has adroitly blended two temporal viewpoints, two timelines, one a kind of 'running autobiography' in which Lady as dog appears to exist in the constant present or immediate past as a dog habitually does, the other a longer retrospective (and at times prospective) viewpoint, in which Sandra, or Sandra-as-Lady, reminisces and thinks humanly. As McGillis notes, Lady as dog will lose her memory and ability to rationalize; during the novel Lady several times finds herself in memory slippage and retrieves herself. The narrator of the story, whether Sandra or Lady, has certainly not lost memory or the ability to rationalize except in instances which she *recalls and records*. For example, she asks and reflects:

> How long did I run with the pack? As you forget yourself, the past falls away behind you like a cliff crumbling at your heels. Each day I was more and more a dog, more and more myself. Before long I never even bothered to remember what I had been doing yesterday. (144)

Here the narrator is unable to fill the gap created by her former state of canine unremembering, but remembers that there *was* such a gap, remembers a past in which she did not trouble to remember the previous day. Just as 'self' has two identities in these lines ('yourself' is Sandra, 'myself' is Lady) so one memory function (the narrator's) overrides another (Lady's). So who exactly is it who 'writes' the book, and when?

There are several occasions scattered through the novel when Lady, or Sandra, as first-person narrator of the tale speaks as if she were again a human, or expected to be. On page 54, she says, '[w]hen I have children, the only thing I'll keep hidden from them are the horrible rows', and she means children, not puppies. On page 103, attacking Terry, she says, 'I was never a big dog'. On pages 134–5, she says, 'The smell of meat—when I walk past a butcher's shop it makes me whine with pleasure to this day'. *Walk*? The lines which follow are full of nostalgic reminiscence: 'Boy, we had some fun' (134–5); 'You can't even imagine the flavour of the things I did' (135). This is surely a human (who knows dogs internally) speaking to humans about the non-immediate past. She then speaks of dogs, their pleasures and the brevity of their lives, but says that 'while she's with us, she loves and is loved with passion' (135). Who exactly are 'us'?

Crucially, just before her unsuccessful attempt to reconnect with her family at the end, Sandra reflects on her limited understanding of the human state:

> Looking back, it seems naïve of me to think that being human was just about how you eat your dinner, or how often you brush your teeth, or what clothes and make-up you wear. Being human is more than that. It's about responsibility, about caring for people, about priorities, about respecting yourself. (155)

These are just the qualities that Sandra-as-teenager, and Lady-as-dog, have denounced repeatedly and scornfully as self-imposed biological flaws in the human animal—responsibility, work, worry, anxiety, the treadmill of 'Work wife kids dead' (44). It is, in some form, a *later* Sandra, or less probably a *later* Lady, who speaks here, though in full, intense and celebratory possession of the alternative truth of a dog's life. *Lady* is told by an indeterminate and dual-natured narrator, on behalf of two worlds, neither of which is decisively balanced against the other.

Lady's dog friend Fella, another metamorphosed human, much prefers his dog's life: 'Trans-species, that's what I am' (44). Lady is also accidentally trans-species, and this is a natural new stage for the biological adventure which Burgess has conducted from book to book. As human mind in dog's body, Lady (or Sandra) sees the two species on equal terms. Its ostensible final choice is an illusion, counteracted by the equivocal narrative and indeed, inevitably, by the fact of language itself. Yet language, the mark of human 'exceptionalism', is used near the end to discredit it: 'Human beings think they're it, they really do—but they're not it, I can tell you! I've tasted life from both sides and I can tell you [...]' (188). *Lady: My Life as a Bitch* is a comedy of balance, achieved by an 'open' narrative, an 'open' narrator and an 'open' ending. It ends literally, narratively and ideologically, in mid-air, with dog and human voices calling their competing invitations to a 'bitch'.

Burgess is not a misanthropic writer. Often in the sequence the word 'humanity' denotes a cluster of wholly admirable and unusual qualities. But the human species—as represented by some leading characters in these books (the boys excepted)—falls so far short of its noble biological potential that it is (in a once-famous political phrase) 'lower than vermin'.[23] Even in *Lady*, the anxious and self-damaging orthodoxy of human society is seriously challenged by the short-lived sensual zestfulness of canine life. Burgess's reductive portrait of humanity in action is set against the enhanced value and status of animals, first in beauty, then in power and in intensity of living. There is an ever-narrowing divide.

In what can be treated as a coda to the sequence, *Bloodsong*, part of Burgess's dystopian reworking of the Icelandic Volsunga Saga, the separate integrity of species has all but disappeared. Following past nuclear wars, and experiments at places such as Porton Down, 'the gene pool close to London had been scrambled',[24] and everywhere in Britain life has recombined in new mutations. The hero, Sigurd, whose life we follow between fifteen and eighteen, has a mission to pacify and restore humanity, but wonders if he is indeed human himself. 'I'm more a machine than a human being. Sometimes I wonder if I'm even human' (11–12). And indeed he is not. He is '[p]art man, part lion, part monster, part god' (290). He sets out to kill the dragon Fafnir, who was once a man and is now part monster, part machine, and who proves to be his lost brother. But Sigurd realizes that Fafnir is not the greatest monster he must defeat: 'You can kill a dragon, but a sick society was a monster with a million heads [...] Humanity, he thought,—that's a monster you can never kill; and it would be inhuman even to try' (27). Neither could better sum up the human paradox which underlies the animal sequence.

As for animals themselves, with whom humanity is now genetically mixed, here too the inherited integrity of species is heavily compromised. Sigurd's first companion and ally, an expert scientist, is a pig. His horse, Slipper, is a self-mending amalgam of animal and machine. Later he will rescue a dog-man ('a true halfman' [153]) from attack by pig-dogs, defeat an attempt on his own life by a mafia of halfman monkeymen, and form an alliance with the dog-man's powerful family who will then betray him. Even death is no longer an absolute. When Sigurd finally dies, aged eighteen, it is his third death.

The extravagant fantasy of *Bloodsong* goes beyond the bounds of recognizable human and animal which are the subject of this essay but it provides a logical continuum for the imaginative exploration of Burgess's animal sequence—a progressive demotion of human exceptionalism in a wonderfully biodiverse animal world, together with a celebration of those too scarce occasions when human beings achieve full humanity.

Notes

1. Claire Squires, 'Marketing at the Millennium', in Janet Maybin and Nicola J. Watson (eds.), *Children's Literature: Approaches and Territories* (London: Palgrave Macmillan, 2009): 188–9.

2. Rachel Falconer, 'Cross-reading and Crossover Books', in Janet Maybin and Nicola J. Watson (eds.), *Children's Literature: Approaches and Territories* (London: Palgrave Macmillan, 2009): 375.
3. Kimberley Reynolds, writing about *Lady: My Life as a Bitch*, goes further and argues that such works actively contribute to the evolution of modern teenage life. See *Radical Children's Literature: Future Visions and Authentic Transformations in Juvenile Fiction* (London: Palgrave Macmillan, 2007): 114–15.
4. Keith Thomas, *Man and the Natural World: Changing Attitudes in England, 1500–1800* [1983] (Harmondsworth: Penguin, 1984): 301.
5. Michael Newton, *Savage Girls and Wild Boys: A History of Feral Children* (London: Faber and Faber, 2002): xiii.
6. *Ibid.*
7. Jacob von Uexkull, *A Stroll through the Worlds of Animals and Men*, quoted in Douglas Keith Candland, *Feral Children and Clever Animals: Reflections on Human Nature* (New York and Oxford: Oxford University Press, 1993): 180.
8. Melvin Burgess, *Kite* [1997] (London: Puffin, 1999): 76. All further references in the chapter are to the 1999 edition.
9. Melvin Burgess, *The Cry of the Wolf* [1990] (London: Puffin, 1991): 81. All further references in the chapter are to the 1991 edition.
10. J. M. Coetzee, *The Lives of Animals* [1999] (London: Profile, 2000): 49.
11. *Ibid.*: 86.
12. David Rudd, 'Animal and Object Stories', in Matthew Grenby and Andrea Immel (eds.), *The Cambridge Companion to Children's Literature* (Cambridge: Cambridge University Press, 2009): 247.
13. Melvin Burgess, *Tiger, Tiger* [1996] (London: Puffin, 1998): 65. All further references in the chapter are to the 1998 edition.
14. Matthew Grenby, *Children's Literature* (Edinburgh: Edinburgh University Press, 2008): 150.
15. John Vaillant, *The Tiger: A True Story of Vengeance and Survival* (London: Sceptre, 2010).
16. Kimberley Reynolds, *Children's Literature: A Very Short Introduction* (Oxford: Oxford University Press, 2011): 81.
17. David Rudd, 'A Young Person's Guide to the Fictions of Junk', *Children's Literature in Education* 30(2) (1999): 123.
18. Reynolds, *Radical Children's Literature*: 114.
19. *Ibid.*: 20.
20. Alison Waller, *Constructing Adolescence in Fantastic Realism* (New York and Abingdon: Routledge, 2009): 50–1.
21. Roderick McGillis, 'Humour and the Body in Children's Literature', in Matthew Grenby and Andrea Immel (eds.), *The Cambridge Companion to Children's Literature* (Cambridge: Cambridge University Press, 2009): 266, 268.
22. Melvin Burgess, *Lady: My Life as a Bitch* [2001] (London: Penguin, 2003): 64. All further references in the chapter are to the 2003 edition.

23. In a speech on 4 July 1948, the eve of the launch of the National Health Service, the British Labour Government's Minister of Health, Aneurin Bevan, described the Tory Party as 'lower than vermin'. The controversial phrase entered political folklore, and the word 'vermin' instantly acquired emotional force, which it has never lost, in rhetorical abuse concerning human beings and animals. Burgess makes powerful explicit use of it in *Kite*, and the attitudes it collects are explored in the other animal stories.
24. Melvin Burgess, *Bloodsong* [2005] (London: Penguin, 2007): 26. All further references in the chapter are to the 2007 edition.

8

'You Know What I Mean': The Development of Relationships between Socially Isolated Characters in *An Angel for May*, *Loving April* and *The Ghost behind the Wall*

Pat Pinsent

Introduction

The critical debate about Melvin Burgess's fiction has inevitably been dominated by attention given to those novels which deal explicitly with drugs, sex and violence. As a result, other texts which also exhibit his characteristic immediacy of impact and narrative complexity, and which confront equally important but less 'sensational' issues, have sometimes been neglected. *Junk* (1996), *Lady: My Life as a Bitch* (2001) and *Doing It* (2003) are well known, even to the extent of notoriety, and have attracted much attention, both popular and academic, but relatively little has been written about some of his other books. The three shorter novels highlighted in the discussion which follows, *An Angel for May* (1992), *Loving April* (1995) and *The Ghost behind the Wall* (2000),[1] rarely feature in critical discussion, because they omit the more explicit portrayal of sex and violence for which Burgess is probably best known. Nevertheless, they exhibit the qualities for which he is justly esteemed: immediate impact; a tendency to force the reader to identify with the painful feelings of characters in traumatic situations; and a transgression of the boundaries as to what is acceptable in fiction for the young, including language that until fairly recently would have been regarded as too explicit for them. It has been generally more relevant to scrutinize the chosen texts in the light of studies involving the portrayal of elderly or disabled characters than to look at them in the context of other criticism of Burgess's work.

All these novels explore the situation of individuals isolated by age, family problems and disability, and each of them, in different ways, adds a fantasy dimension to the harsh realities realistically conveyed. They all portray young people surmounting the difficulties felt by most 'normal' members of adult society about relating to those marginalized by age or disability. In all these texts, boys on the cusp of adolescence establish, almost despite themselves, relationships with individuals peripheral to mainstream society, achieving levels of communication not thought possible by the adults around them—the quotation in my title is taken from the concluding words of *April*, suggesting that these boys are among the few people who do in fact understand these marginalized individuals. There is an interesting affinity between the relationships achieved by these boys and that depicted by Philippa Pearce in her classic *Tom's Midnight Garden* (1958) between the title character and old Mrs Bartholomew/Hatty;[2] in all instances the elderly characters are thought by other adults to be eccentric and are consequently isolated. Although it may be presumed that these three books by Burgess are initially addressed to readers younger than the audience of the texts for which he is best known, Burgess treats his audience with respect and never shirks from portraying challenging emotional relationships. Because of the affinities between *Angel* and *Ghost,* it is convenient to link the discussion of these books, before going on to look closely at *April,* which is set in the 1920s, and then to analyse the aspects which unite the three novels.

An Angel for May and *The Ghost behind the Wall*: young boys encountering elderly people

Each of these novels portrays the development of understanding between a lonely boy whose parents' marriage has broken up, and an elderly individual suffering from dementia. In both instances this communication is achieved through a form of journey: travel in time by Tam in *Angel*, and motion through the ventilation ducts of a block of flats[3] for David in *Ghost*. As might be anticipated by readers familiar with the challenging nature of Burgess's fiction for young adults, neither *Angel* nor *Ghost* is a sentimental story about a frail old person being befriended by a kind child. Rather, both are realistic portrayals of the way in which children are sometimes able to forge deeper bonds with 'difficult' elderly individuals than are the well-meaning social workers who often misunderstand both the young and the aged.

The far from ideal young protagonists are introduced at the openings of both novels: Tam in *Angel* is described as running uphill away from the house where he lives with his mother, making rude gestures and shouting 'Bloody old bag' (5), in order to vent on her his repressed anger against his absentee father. Similarly, at the beginning of *Ghost*, we meet David, 'a bit of a brute, a tough', whose anger appears to be directed against his schoolmates rather than the mother who deserted him and his father years before. Because he is small for his twelve years, they call him 'Bum Wipe, Halfboy and Shorty. He usually ignored it but once in a while he went mad and nearly killed someone' (1). Both these openings are notable for their vivid immediate impact and the use of language appropriate to the characters even though it would once have been deemed too 'strong' for young readers.

A substantial part of *Angel* is taken up by the period that Tam spends in the past during wartime, mostly in the (subsequently) ruined farmhouse, Thowt It,[4] where he meets the kindly Mr Nutter, his sharp-tongued housekeeper and later fiancée, Mrs Pickles, and May, the young girl for whom the farmer has provided a home in order to preserve her from being consigned to an institution. Tam learns how to communicate with the traumatized girl, who has been rescued from the rubble of her bombed house and is probably the offspring of an incestuous union between a retarded woman and her own father. Mr Nutter describes Tam as 'an angel for May' (91), a phrase which, as the title of the novel, takes on an almost religious significance, suggesting that Tam has been 'sent' to help May. Tam's excursions into the past are mediated by a smelly and dirty old tramp woman, whom the locals call Rosey, and her dog, Winnie. Though Rosey sometimes looks on when Tam is at Thowt It, she is never seen by Mr Nutter (though Winnie appears to flourish in both time periods). During his stay in the 1940s, Tam, as an outsider, is persecuted by men and boys in the nearby village of Cawldale, but is rescued by May. His difficulties are compounded by the fact that, unlike in many time-slip novels, time passes at the same rate in both the present and the past, which means that at one point he is missing from his mother for three days, a perhaps significant period of time, to which I shall return below.

Burgess makes very clear in *Angel* the effects of the trauma suffered by both Tam and May/Rosey. Tam has been damaged by the break up between his parents; in his refusal to acknowledge his anger that his father now has a new partner and that her children are occupying the place that he feels to be rightly his own, he irrationally wants to spend time in Bradford at his father's overcrowded flat, though he has to admit that he is better off in the country at Cawldale with his mother, nevertheless refusing to 'belong' there with her in any real sense. He is in trouble at school, and altogether angry and confused, but sees no way out of his situation (18). The process of healing, and of recognizing the needs of others, together with admitting what he owes to his mother, does not really begin until he is the recipient of the unquestioning compassion of Sam Nutter, and until he realizes he can be of value to another person. He discovers at the farm that he has a role in helping the far more badly damaged May, who is a few years younger than him.

May's upbringing—she was apparently hidden away in a cupboard to avoid being seen as a shameful proof of her father's guilt, until she was liberated by the bomb incident—has left her psychologically unable to come inside the farmhouse even at mealtimes, except for rushing in to grasp a piece of food and rushing out again. Until Tam arrives, her only 'friend' is the dog, which at the same time, to Tam's puzzlement, seems to also belong to the old tramp woman Rosey. The meeting between past and present, which Tam's timeslip makes possible, first allows him to form a relationship with May, and then permits his gradual and uncomfortable discovery that the dreadful old tramp woman Rosey, who always seems to be on the scene, is the same person as the young girl. Early in the book he throws stones at Rosey when he sees that Winnie prefers Rosey's company:

> Tam was full of hatred for that old woman who had taken the dog away from him. She was barely human, she stank […] She was useless and old and horrible […] He screamed at her […] 'Go away! […] We don't want you here.' (13–14)

His hostility to her uneasily foreshadows the way that later in the book the local boys in the past era behave towards Tam himself (56–61). But by the end of the book, once Tam has realized that Rosey is May, he is full of compassion for the dreadful life she has led: because of the death of Mr Nutter she has spent most of it in an institution before being discharged as a result of National Health Service cuts. He has learnt about her fate, and the fact that Mr Nutter was killed in a fire at Thowt It, from Mrs Pickles, who is now in a local care home. The difficulty he experiences in meeting Mrs Pickles at the home highlights the limitations of the attitudes of the well-meaning adults. None of them have any idea how to help Tam fit into life in Cawldale, but the most alienating of all is the keeper of this home: 'Mrs Cranshaw at the Beckside Home for the Aged did not like boys coming to visit her old ladies and gentlemen. She said it disturbed the old folk but the truth was, it disturbed Mrs Cranshaw.' Through Mrs Cranshaw's assumption that 'people in general, and boys in particular, never, ever, visited old people they weren't related to' (127), Burgess creates in the reader, already privy to Tam's good intentions in visiting the old woman, a feeling of hostility against the warden who treats Tam without any respect, shooing him away like an animal. By contrast, the friendly talk Tam has with Mrs Pickles suggests that he instantly makes more progress towards a relationship with her than those in charge of the home have been able to achieve in the twenty years Mrs Pickles has spent there. Burgess's hostility towards 'establishment' type adult figures is also to be found in the other books to be discussed here.

Once past Mrs Crandale, Tam learns more of May's story from Mrs Pickles, and as a consequence tries to travel back to the period before the disaster in the hope of averting it. His inability to do so leads to a feeling that he himself has an obligation to provide a place for Rosey/May, so he brings the old woman into his own house. Whatever her future will be—and Burgess certainly does not guarantee a happy ending—she now knows that someone cares for her: in answer to her sorrowful words, 'I got lost, Tam, I got lost for so long …', he replies, 'But now I've found you' (155). This emotional reunion between them inevitably recalls that between Tom and Hatty/Mrs Bartholomew in Pearce's *Tom's Midnight Garden*, although the closure of Burgess's novel is perhaps more tentative.

Not surprisingly, Tam's mother is less keen on May staying, but she does notice May's response to Tam putting his arms round her and kissing her:

> The old woman raised her arm and put her dark old hand on Tam's, and she smiled up at him. It was a real smile—not the broken remains of one that she had seen on her face before, but a real, tender, affectionate smile. It was the first time she had seen any real expression on Rosey's face […] the way the old woman was looking around her—alert, intelligent. It was as if the boy had brought her back from the dead. (157)

Although Burgess refuses to give the reader the comfort of being sure that Mrs Sams will indeed provide shelter for the old woman, the fact that she is aware that her son has, in effect, raised May from the dead—a biblical note which chimes in with the surely not entirely coincidental period, three days, of Tam's earlier visit to the past during which his mother had thought him to be dead—creates a certain degree of confidence that Tam will not be parted from May again.

Like Rosey/May, Mr Alveston in *Ghost* is not fully in possession of his mental faculties, but at least in his case the onset of Alzheimer's has come after a satisfying life and fulfilling relationships. He is, however, lonely—his children have already died (of old age!) and their children and grandchildren live in Australia. As we have seen from the beginning of the book, David is also isolated from normal friendships. Both he and his father have been badly hurt by the fact that David's mother has left them; this has caused the boy to be irrationally angry with his father, frequently telling him that he wants to go and live in America with his mother. All his father can do is 'worry and shout, worry and shout' (7). Inevitably David, like Tam in *Ghost,* behaves badly at school, and even at home looks for dangerous activities. What brings together twelve-year-old David and nonogenarian Mr Alveston seems to be their kindred bad behaviour as young boys. The ventilation ducts which lead David to the old man's flat are also a site where the eponymous ghost is generated out of the old man's memories. In a complex scene, as David and Mr Alveston look into each other's faces and the old man calls out 'Jonathon', mis-identifying David as a childhood friend (who had been led into mischief by the young Robert Alveston!), there appears the floating grey face of a boy, through which David can see the face of the old man himself (24–5). This ghost constantly leads David on in malicious behaviour, generally directed against Mr Alveston, because, as the ghost repeats, '"I hate him"' (63). Eventually this bad behaviour even disgusts David, and he tries to dissuade the ghost from trashing the old man's flat; inevitably, however, it is David who is blamed by both a social worker and Mr Alveston's cleaner, Sis Parkinson, for the vandalism.

Initially the reader is probably inclined to believe that the ghost is indeed Mr Alveston's boyhood friend, Jonathon, with whom he robbed allotments, among other misdeeds. It is not until David and his father see photos of the old man as a child that the identification with the ghost can be made: from the moment of the ghost having been generated, Mr Alveston has lost his childhood memories which have instead been infused into the ghost. The hatred that the ghost feels against the elderly Mr Alveston could perhaps be seen as a spectral representation of the way that the old man, like many elderly people, hates the debilitating age which he feels has been thrust on him. In the end it is only David who can enable Mr Alveston to regain his memories and thus free him to die as he longs to do. David achieves this by confronting the ghost with its identity as Robert Alveston—to its considerable anger—and in some way swallowing it. He manages to keep the ghost inside him and transport it to the hospital so that Mr Alveston's boyhood memories can be reunited with him. At this point of crisis, while David is a 'ghost-bearer', he is confronted with a typical instance of the inability of well-meaning adults to understand either the young protagonists or the elderly people. His attempt to visit Mr Alveston in hospital is nearly thwarted by the old man's cleaner, Sis Parkinson. A nurse pleads for them to be allowed a few minutes together: 'Sis snorted in disgust. "I wouldn't let him in here if I had my way. People are too soft on that boy [...] That child is capable of anything!"' (128). Sis's distrust of David strongly recalls Mrs Cranshaw's hostility to Tam in *Angel;* in these and other similar encounters in both books, Burgess seems to be conveying the message that often children understand the elderly better than do the generations in between.

The elderly characters created by Burgess in these two books are somewhat atypical of the majority of such portrayals in children's texts. A small research project interrogating nearly fifty recent children's books depicting relationships between the young and the old[5] revealed that in about three-quarters of these titles, the elderly people were members of the same family as the child protagonist, almost invariably grandparents. Frequently these grandparents were in the stereotypical position of taking the opportunity to tell stories about childhood to their grandchildren.[6] In neither of the books discussed here, however, for different reasons, are the elderly persons able to provide any coherent narrative about their youth. Many books portraying old people also tend to stereotype them into a limited number of roles. The project noted above led me to suggest that old people are often portrayed in one of four contrasting ways: the wise, the hyperactive, the victim and the evil old person. It is evident that the only one of these which in any way fits Rosey/May and Mr Alveston is that of the victim, but Rosey seems to have more affinity with the figure of the tramp, as analysed by David Rudd.[7] Equally, until shortly before his death, Mr Alveston's individuality defies the pathos with which his cleaner might otherwise have wanted to endow him: 'He reminded Sis of a naughty boy trapped in an old, old body' (71). Both of them defy the attempts of social services or society as a whole to cast them into the victim mould. Instead, Burgess's work implicitly conveys the simple insight embodied in *Tom's Midnight Garden*: the best point for a child to encounter an elderly person is through friendship with the child that internally they have never ceased to be.

Loving April: mutual isolation

Unlike the relationships between the young and the elderly portrayed in *Angel* and *Ghost,* the friendship in *April* reveals Tony, the main protagonist, becoming involved with a girl just a little older than he is. April's deafness not only isolates her from the village community but also leads its members to regard her as mentally defective, while some of the village boys treat her as a sexual object available for their gratification. She is in fact not only intelligent but also more than usually sensitive to nature and has the ability skilfully to navigate a small boat. More than most authors, Burgess shows here how the difficulties which disabled people have with 'normal' society generally arise from that society's treatment of them, which in turn derives from insensitive labelling, rather than from any limitations within the individuals concerned. When *April* was published in 1995, most writing about disability, for both adults and children, followed the 'medical' model which locates problems within the disabled individual; much subsequent debate has emphasized the fact that 'society disables people' by neglecting to understand them or their needs.[8] Burgess's portrayal of both the disabled girl and the society in which she functions sets him firmly on the side of more recent thinking on the subject.

The title of this novel immediately locates April in a positive context, though it does have a certain degree of ambiguity: the term 'Loving' may be a descriptor of April herself, or of Tony's feelings towards her, or indeed both of these. In the light of developments within the novel, the title could also be seen as putting into question the attitudes of the village youths who see the girl merely as a sexual object. Much of the novel is concerned with how the relationship between Tony and April develops. It starts with the hostility felt by Tony when he and his mother arrive in the village to be confronted with the spectacle of this apparently deranged girl, 'covered in mud, her hair was dried into rat's tails and she was hooting and yelling at them' (8). The shouts were in fact intended by April, whose speech is impaired, to be a friendly enquiry: 'Where are you going? Are you coming to stay?' (6). From this unpromising start, however, the relationship between them becomes one of first love:

> Inside the world they lived and moved in was a whole other world, there only for them. They carried this secret inside them like a deep well, a long, dark cavern inside that had never been there before [...] Tony loved to kiss her in the parlour [...and] when they were alone together on the river [...] April would drop her rod or the oars and just stop and kiss him ...' (117–18)

The imagery emphasizing the inner depths of their relationship is also associated with the way that Tony takes the initiative inside his own house, while April does the same outside in her own natural environment. Thus an impression of both the depth and the mutuality of their feelings is created.

Both of the positive interpretations of the title carry some degree of irony, since a contrast is made between the young people's innocent, not yet consummated, love, and the attitude of the village boys, Tad and Joe, towards April. They see her as little more than an object available for abuse, the threat of which is constantly present to her since they have in the past used her as a sexual plaything, relying on the unintelligibility of her speech to avoid exposure. Towards the end of the book they rape her, something she finds deeply shameful, at first even denying to Tony that they had gone that far. She also has (fortunately unfounded) fears that she may be pregnant, and as Tony and his mother depart the village in order to return to school, and to a totally loveless household with his father, April feels more afraid and alone than ever before. Rather than finish the book on this negative note, however, Burgess contrives a way for her to be rescued, and sent to a school for the deaf which will enable her to acquire speech and literacy. The possibility exists that in due course, after their schooldays, she and Tony will be reunited. The depth of their feelings remains, as evidenced by the understated evidence: Tony will say nothing about April when the other boys are boasting of their sexual conquests (167), and April finishes a letter to him with the words, 'You know what I mean' (169). This ending manages to avoid the clichés common to much writing about disability, as revealed by Lois Keith. She shows how in a great deal of children's fiction, disabled characters have to learn to be submissive (which April never is), and that in very many cases, the ending is 'idyllic': 'the wheelchair is literally or symbolically discarded [...] and all is well in the world'.[9] Burgess refuses to portray April as being cured of her deafness, and offers no certainty of any future union between her and Tony.

In spite of the differences between the three novels in terms of the societies portrayed and the different forms of marginalization experienced by each of the characters with whom the boys form relationships, the books have much in common. The following section examines the way in which their family situations and their search for identity have isolated the boy characters and perhaps predisposed them towards an initially unlikely sensitivity to others who are also on the edges of society. It is also interesting to observe that the means Burgess uses to make these relationships credible involves a use of symbolism often more common to fantasy than to the harsh realism with which he portrays the lives of these characters, although such symbolism is nevertheless appropriate in view of the non-realist devices he employs in two of the texts (*Angel* and *Ghost*).

Thematic and literary affinities between the novels

Parental marriage relationships

The fact that in all three of these novels the marriages of the parents of the protagonists have broken up serves as an effective backdrop, explaining to some extent the anti-social behaviour of Tam and David, together with Tony's unhappiness both while he is at his expensive school and when he is away from it. In all cases, the fact that the boys lack the warmth of a normal parental relationship accounts for some part of their loneliness and the need they experience for another person in their lives.

In *Angel* Tam's parents have split up but are still in contact, having some degree of working relationship as far as the welfare of their son is concerned. Despite Tam's anger against both of them, by the end of the book he appreciates that he has not really been so badly treated—the sufferings of May perhaps having helped him to this realization. The parental situation in *April* is worse: the cold hostility between Tony's parents is compounded by the fact that the father expects his wife to accept without question his relationship with his new mistress, together with the poverty which has been thrust upon her. It would appear that Mrs Piggot's inability to resume a previous, probably healthier, association with a previous but less classy boyfriend, David, is the outcome of the years she has spent in this loveless relationship. Her decision to go back to her husband at the end does not convey any hope that the emotional development she has experienced in the village environment will continue. The plight of a single mother is of course far more challenging in this 1920s world than in the contemporary settings of the other two novels, so that despite Tony's anger, his mother's compromise is presented as perhaps her only course of action. In *Ghost,* David's mother, having left him and his father for her American boyfriend, is inaccessible to either of them; her absence, while accounting for David's loneliness and craving for danger, is also significant in showing the reasons for his father's inability to form any relationships outside his professional commitments as an optician, or to relate properly to his own son. David therefore finds that companionship with the elderly man provides him with some of the fathering he lacks.

Identity

Burgess's interest in the question of identity is apparent in much of his writing, to the extent of being a main theme in *Sara's Face* (2006). In the three novels under consideration here, a main issue is the need for the young protagonists to establish their own identities satisfactorily in order to relate effectively to anyone else. Children who have grown up within the context of a broken marriage may well experience some difficulty in achieving a sense of their own identity, whether their fathers are actually absent as in *Angel* or finding their parental role challenging as in *April* and *Ghost.* In none of these books can the young boys find satisfactory male role models, and the people to whom they come to relate also have identity problems.

In *Angel* the main source of confusion about identity is the fact that the young girl May and the elderly woman Rosey are actually the same person. Tam's discovery of this is a reflection of how an important part of young people learning to relate to the elderly is for them to accept that old people still are, in some way, the persons they always were. The identity in *Ghost* between the spectre and the young Robert Alveston is again something that the young protagonist discovers during the course of the novel. When David is ghost-bearer he experiences a sense of dislocation of identity: 'It was the most strange feeling, not knowing if you were yourself or something completely different' (126–7). Mr Alveston himself fails to identify with the ghost, which in turn refuses any kinship with him. The old man cannot experience the peace of spirit that he needs in order to die, until he has reconciled his young, mischievous, self with the old man he has become, and indeed, has accepted himself as truly old.

On his first appearance in *April.* Tony is wearing 'his school uniform for their arrival in the village' (6) despite feeling that he has no right to claim to be a pupil at his expensive school, now that he and his mother are poor. It appears that he has depended on his father's prosperity and his own position within the school hierarchy for his sense of identity; lacking these, he does not really know who he truly is. His relationship with April involves the discovery of himself, as he comes to appreciate, and indeed to fall in love with, her qualities of natural intelligence, in spite of the fact that she is disabled and also of a lower class than he is—like the issue of single motherhood, something more important in the 1920s period of the novel than it would be today. By the end of the book, Tony's relationship with his friends has become less one of dependence, and this is displayed in the increase of his confidence both in visiting a school friend's home and in his return to school (166–7).

Symbolism

In all these novels, Burgess presents the achievement of understanding between these disparate characters not only through their conversation and introspection but also by unobtrusive use of symbolism. This generates in the reader an appreciation of the way in which the initially hostile characters begin to relate to each other, without over-explicit detail.

Given Burgess's empathy with animals, as displayed in, for instance, *The Cry of the Wolf* (1990) and *Tiger, Tiger* (1996), it is not surprising that in two of the books under consideration, *Angel* and *April,* the animals which provide part of the setting contribute a richness to the total effect of the novels, even though they do not appear to have any specific plot significance. In *Angel* Tam befriends the dog, Winnie, and plays with her; though he is nervous of strange dogs he recognizes immediately that 'this was a good dog' (7–8). This friendliness and lack of threat creates a positive note even before Tam's first visit to the past, and the communication he immediately establishes with the dog in the game of throwing and chasing a stick implies the warmth and friendliness which are missing from his own life. The dog, a 'sheepdog mongrel' (7), is named Winnie after Winston Churchill, a verbal association which generates power and confidence. Its name suggests that it should perhaps have been a bull-dog, the species most associated with the wartime Prime Minister: it may be that Burgess avoided this identification because the fighting breed might have been seen by Tam, and the reader, as less friendly. The dog is always there when Tam travels to the past, and seems to exist in both time schemes: if Rosey/May remains in Tam's house, Winnie will presumably also remain there, providing him with another friend.

Burgess's use of animal symbolism is most notable, and probably most complex, in *April.* She herself is described by her mother as a 'lovely dumb animal' (4) and images of this kind are often associated with her, as indeed is the fact of her keeping pets, particularly swans. Like the swans, April, seen from the beginning in the context of water and mud, is competent in her own environment, at ease on the water but at greater danger on the mudbanks of the tidal flow. The way in which she attempts and ultimately succeeds in capturing a female swan, Sissy, in the hope of it becoming a mate for Silas, her favourite pet, both displays her competence with wildlife and provides a mirror to the relationship between the young people. When eventually April liberates both swans, separately, it seems to portend future autonomy for both Tony and herself and also to imply that their lives will not after all be together. Additionally, her increasing boredom with her pets ('the rabbits had turned into pie, the magpies and goldfinches had flown away' [144]) seems to suggest her increasing maturity as she no longer feels the same emotional need to depend on them.

By contrast with the natural setting in these two novels, the most significant use of symbolism in *Ghost* is associated with an indoor, man-made environment, the ventilation ducts which unite the flats where both David and Mr Alveston live. The ducts serve both as an outlet for David's mischief-making (which he exercises against the occupiers of other flats in the block as well), and a space in which the ghost of Mr Alveston's childhood can exist. These dark vents can be seen as metonymic of the repressed unconscious to which Mr Alveston's youthful misdemeanours have been consigned, together with David's dysfunctional behaviour resulting from his resentment against both his parents. The lack of knowledge as to where any route may lead, and the dangerous drops which David negotiates, could be seen as characteristics of the repressed part of the human mind.

Questions of Closure

Because all these novels have a complexity which belies their relatively short length,[10] the nature of the issues involved can make the endings appear hurried, which might suggest that Burgess is providing over-optimistic solutions to the intractable problems raised. Brief consideration of other possible closures available suggest, however, that none of them would have been so effective as those which he has created.

Angel offers the potentially tragic ending of Tam abandoning Rosey/May to her wandering homeless life, but the depth of his relationship with her makes that implausible. On the other hand, if his mother had warmly hugged the old woman and explicitly stated that she could live with them from now on, the sentimentality so engendered would have been out of keeping with the book as a whole. The effect of seeing the final scene through Mrs Sams' eyes is that we side with Tam against her and cannot be totally sure that there will be a happy ending. Burgess's technique of leaving the reader to deduce what happens next is probably the most effective way of dealing with the required closure, and also credits the young reader with enough maturity to decide about which outcome seems the most likely. Similarly, in *Ghost* Burgess rejects the over-hopeful conclusion that Mr Alveston recovers and comes to live with David and his father, for it is evident from the old man's age and fragility that such a happy ending could not endure for long. On the other hand, the stasis of David's relationship with the ghost being unresolved would have been unsatisfying. The positive effect of the total experience on David and his father, as well as the old man's peaceful death, are as satisfying a resolution as seems possible in the circumstances.

The ending of *April* is perhaps the most contentious, as it happens very suddenly, just as Tony and April seem to have been separated for ever. He and his mother have gone back to live with his uncaring father and he has returned to the school he dislikes. Then he receives a letter from April where she discloses how happy she is to be in a learning environment. Her encouragement to him to write and thus keep up their relationship ends with the appreciative words, 'I haven't met anyone else like you' (169). This letter, little more than a single page in length and occurring as it does right at the end of the novel, might almost seem to be tacked on with the intention of providing some sort of sop to the reader who by this time wants the two young people to remain together, preferably in the environment of a village where everyone will have learnt to appreciate April's intelligence. While Burgess does not rule out the possibility of the two young lovers being reunited, to bring this about explicitly would have been to ignore the social barriers placed between them in 1920s England, in particular those of class and the ignorant and uncaring treatment of the disabled. But to have left April back in a hostile village would have been too harsh, so the provision of a future for her, by Mrs Piggot's former lover, David, is at least a positive solution. In the context of other fiction about disability, it is, as indicated above, also an effective rejection of over-easy optimism about a cure for April's deafness.

In spite of any questions that the details of the endings might raise, the reader is at least convinced of the positive outcome in each case. The relationships portrayed have been healing both to the young boys and to the characters with whom they are involved: May's smile, Mr Alveston's contented death, and April's fulfilment at school have all attested to that.

Conclusion

It is easy for readers to ignore Burgess's shorter novels, but closer scrutiny reveals that they possess just as much complexity and are treated with an equal degree of craftsmanship as his better known and more controversial texts. His work is notable, among other things, for its variety, and a tendency to cut across established genres.[11] In its dependence on Icelandic saga and portrayal of a futuristic Britain, *Bloodtide* is a fusion between myth/history and dystopia, while animal stories such as *The Cry of the Wolf* and *Tiger, Tiger*, in addition to being concerned with survival of species, raise questions about individuality which relate as much to humankind as to animals. A more recent novel, *Sara's Face*, is also difficult to classify, because as Kay Sambell explores in Chapter 4 in this collection, its metafictional approach to social satire coexists with psychological exploration.[12] It is scarcely surprising, therefore, that Burgess's apparently slighter works are also difficult to classify, with their combination of contemporary social issues and a use of fantasy to an extent rare in the 'gritty realism' of most other stories which confront such problems.

Like Burgess's more controversial novels, all these shorter works reveal how he is never afraid to transgress boundaries, whether those between fantasy and gritty realism, or those involving the kind of issues that until quite recently were unlikely to be treated in texts for younger readers. While the fact that May is probably the product of an incestuous relationship is only very briefly disclosed in *Angel*, rape is a far more important theme in *April,* foreshadowed by the way in which even before this event the disabled girl is regarded as sexual prey by the boys concerned. It is of course impossible to be definite about the age at which these books are likely to be read, but it seems evident, on grounds at least of length, that they are addressed to readers rather younger than the implied readers of *Junk*, *Lady* or *Doing It*. It is, however, clear that many writers today are exploring themes that would not in the past have been thought appropriate to young readers, and Burgess himself has been an important influence in this respect, as suggested by Kimberley Reynolds.[13] It is also clear that many novels of the late twentieth and early twenty-first century are intent to dispel 'the myth of childhood innocence',[14] and again, Burgess has been instrumental in this process. The novels discussed in this chapter are a part of this process, and succeed in presenting credible young characters who, with all their flaws, prove to be just the right people to deliver from their isolation the individuals marginalized by age or disability within them. The fact too that the relationships portrayed, while eschewing any over-facile optimism, are presented as integral to the process of achieving a healthy mental state for both the young boys and the people they befriend, is indicative of Burgess's overall achievement.

Notes

1. Melvin Burgess, *An Angel for May* (London: Andersen Press, 1992); *Loving April* [1995] (London: Puffin, 1996); *The Ghost behind the Wall* (London: Andersen, 2000). All further references in the chapter are to these editions and the titles of these books will subsequently be shortened in this chapter to *Angel, April* and *Ghost* respectively.
2. To some extent this is highlighted by similarity between names (Pearce's Tom, and Burgess's Tam and Tony in *Angel* and *April* respectively).

3. It is worth noting that around the same date as *Ghost* Burgess also portrays wild children roaming the ventilation system in *Bloodtide* (London: Andersen Press, 1999): 15.
4. Thowt It is 'short for Who'd-a-thowt-it Farm' (6), possibly Burgess's tongue-in-cheek defence against his readers' incredulity at the time slip.
5. See Pat Pinsent, 'The Depiction of Elderly Characters in Children's Fiction', in Pat Pinsent (ed.), *The Big Issues: Representations of Socially Marginalized Groups and Individuals in Children's Literature, Past and Present* (Roehampton: NCRCL, 2001): 142–54 and 'Crone or Alien: The Image of the Grandmother in Some Recent Picture Books and Illustrated Texts', *New Review of Children's Literature and Librarianship* 9 (2003): 142–54.
6. This framework is often used by Michael Morpurgo, for instance in *Why the Whales Came* (1985) and *Farm Boy* (1997); it is also popular in picturebooks, ranging from the storytelling in Valerie Flournoy and Jerry Pinkney's *The Patchwork Quilt* (1985), through the hyperactivity of Babette Cole's *The Trouble with Gran* (1987) to the wisdom of Grace's grandmother in Mary Hoffman and Caroline Binch's *Amazing Grace* (1991) and *Grace and Family* (1995).
7. David Rudd, 'Tramps in Twentieth Century Works for Children', in Pat Pinsent (ed.), *The Big Issues* (Roehampton: NCRCL, 2001): 84–111.
8. The earlier situation is outlined by Michael Oliver, *Understanding Disability: From Theory to Practice* (London: Palgrave Macmillan, 1996); the 'Social Model of Disability' is described in Helen Aveling (ed.), *Unseen Childhood: Disabled Characters in 20th-Century Books for Girls* (London: Bettany Press, 2009): 14.
9. Lois Keith, *Take up thy Bed and Walk: Death, Disability and Cure in Classic Fiction for Girls* (London: The Women's Press, 2001): 6.
10. Between 130 and 170 pages, as against 370 in *Bloodtide* and 330 in *Doing It*.
11. See Clare Walsh, 'Troubling the Boundary between Fiction for Adults and Fiction for Children', in Pat Pinsent (ed.), *Books and Boundaries: Writers and their Audiences* (Lichfield: Pied Piper Publishing, 2004): 142–53 for a discussion of how several of Burgess's books blur generic boundaries.
12. See also Pat Pinsent, 'The Theme of Facial Disfigurement in Some Recent Books for Young Readers', in Jenny Plastow (ed.), *The Story and the Self: Children's Literature: Some Psychoanalytic Perspectives* (Hatfield: University of Hertfordshire Press, 2008): 98–109 for a consideration of *Sara's Face* from a psychoanalytic perspective.
13. Kimberley Reynolds, *Radical Children's Literature* (Basingstoke: Palgrave Macmillan, 2007): 127.
14. Kay Sambell, 'Questioning Contemporary Views of Children and Childhood in Crisis: Burgess's *Bloodtide* as a Fantasy of the Monstrous', in Nickianne Moody and Clare Horrocks (eds.), *Children's Fantasy Fiction: Debates for the Twenty First Century* (Liverpool: Association for Research in Popular Fictions, 2005): 43.

9

Challenging the Paradigm: Examining *The Baby and Fly Pie* and *The Earth Giant* through Ecocriticism

Karen Williams

Introduction

> I think people who live in the countryside are lucky and I can't understand why so many of them come to live in London, where it's dirty and exhausting and full of people.[1]

In Melvin Burgess's 1993 novel *The Baby and Fly Pie*, the text is focalized through the first-person narrative of the central character Davey (nicknamed Fly). Fly is a 'rubbish Kid' (14) living and working alongside his sister Jane on a municipal dump in a dystopian urban setting (London). These children work for a group of women, ironically termed 'Mothers', who tightly control the children, forcing them to live in squalor and selling on for profit the items they scavenge. In their turn the Mothers are controlled by gang-masters who 'police' the streets and businesses and work with 'Death Squads' (6) to 'cleanse' the city of homeless kids and other 'undesirables'. The narrative follows Fly, Jane and their friend Sham as they flee through the city after finding a kidnapped baby hidden within the dump with a ransom of £17 million attached to it. As the narrative progresses, *Fly* becomes a novel with competing but interlinked environments at its heart: the dump, the wider city, the squatter camp, the countryside, all of which fundamentally affect both action and character. As such, a reading of this text through the lens of the critical discourse of ecocriticism can produce an enhanced appreciation of the novel and raises important questions concerning nature and culture, the animal and the human, the urban and the rural. In order to examine these questions, I will place *Fly* alongside Burgess's later novel, *The Earth Giant* (1995), which similarly interrogates the human experience of the built and the natural environments, but which also foregrounds an ecocentricity which privileges neither human nor non-human.

The extract quoted above features in a central position in the narrative when Fly and Sham have fled into the woods to escape the gangs in the squatter camp but when, for a moment at least, there is no imminent danger. These conditions are reflected in the seemingly simplistic binary opposition between rural and urban that Burgess communicates through Fly. Here the fundamentally negative characteristics of the city as 'dirty', 'exhausting' and overcrowded are emphasized whilst conversely, the country according to Fly is 'magic' and teaming with life: 'spiders hanging in their webs, berries going black, leaves and stems and flowers' (125). People living in the countryside are 'lucky'. The rural, it seems, is a fundamentally preferable environment to the urban. And yet, nature as pastoral idyll is short-lived as the boys flee back to the town for safety. In this text and in *The Earth Giant* the author constantly interrogates these ideas of urban and rural, and challenges their conventional dichotomy, often portraying the city as a 'noxious stereotype' whilst simultaneously embracing the 'urban space as an evolving, contested habitat' in its own right.[2] Equally the countryside constitutes for the protagonists both an escape from urban toxicity and a paradoxical 'alien' space filled with danger.

This ambivalent interrogation of the urban/rural dichotomy in Burgess's texts is also extended to some of the other binary oppositions that likewise form an intrinsic part of wider ecocritical discourse: concepts of human and animal, culture and nature. The connection between such elements in Burgess's texts and wider ecocritical writing is evident when one considers, for example, the work of ecocritic Lawrence Buell who is particularly adept at highlighting and interrogating similarities and differences in this diverse critical field. In his 1998 essay 'Toxic Discourse' and his later book *The Future of Environmental Criticism*, Buell, after exploring the 'project in motion' that is 'environmental criticism',[3] argues cogently for a fusing of two often seemingly opposing strands of ecocriticism: the 'preservationist' view of nature that places the natural world in the ascendancy over mankind; and the position of eco-justice revisionists that focuses on the effect of the toxification of the environment on humankind, especially on poor and disenfranchised groups. His essay discusses how these two positions can (and arguably, should) be interlinked under the umbrella term 'Toxic Discourse' to enable 'a way of imagining physical environments that fuses a social constructivist with an environmental restorative perspective' so that 'compartments begin to break down' and 'the boundaries of nature or environmental discourse now becomes much more elastic than formerly conceived'.[4] To understand the crux of Buell's argument is to become immersed in the dichotomies faced by writers in the ecocritical field. It is these tensions that, I will argue, Melvin Burgess interrogates deeply throughout *The Earth Giant* and *The Baby and Fly Pie*.

Over the last 25 years, from the point when Cheryll Glotfelty borrowed ecocriticism as a term from a 1978 essay by William Rueckert and rejuvenated it at a 1989 meeting of the Western Literary Association, the field of ecocriticism has burgeoned into a complex critical discourse. What Buell terms this 'concourse of discrepant practices'[5] now includes disciplines such as ecology, eco-feminism, postcolonial ecocriticism and eco-justice. Indeed, in the first selection of essays on ecocriticism, *The Ecocriticism Reader: Landmarks in Literary Ecology* (1996), Glotfelty carves out space for all these discourses by defining ecocriticism simply and inclusively as: 'the study of the relationship between literature and the physical environment'. This 'earth-centred approach to literary studies'[6] has thus provided the basis for a reading of literary works which foregrounds the environmental setting of a text and necessitates what Peter Barry explains as 'switch[ing] critical attention from inner to outer',[7] that is to say, treating the text's locus, not as peripheral to the work, but as critically central to it.[8] This is the approach that I will take in my exploration of Burgess's two texts, first examining the way in which nature and culture vie for ascendancy in *The Earth Giant*, then interrogating Burgess's blurring of the human/animal hierarchy in both these novels, and finally concentrating on the implications of the author's presentation of the rural and the urban particularly in *The Baby and Fly Pie*.

Nature and culture: the struggle for ascendancy

Despite the plausibility of interrogating all environmental landscapes within Glotfelty's broad definition, the early phases of ecocriticism in the 1990s tended to concentrate solely on the natural environment—the loosely 'preservationist' view discussed by Buell above.[9] It is only as ecocriticism has evolved over the last few years that what Loretta Johnson terms a 'second wave' of 'urban and ecojustice revisionism'[10] has come to the fore. Originating in Bennett and Teague's seminal text, *The Nature of Cities: Ecocriticism and Urban Environments* (1999), this urban revisionist branch of ecocriticism aims to look beyond man's relation to the natural environment and to treat the urban locus as an ecosystem in its own right. In addition, the diversification of ecocriticism into the field of environmental justice challenges the notion that the physical environment can remain isolated from the cultural influences that surround it. Instead some newer forms of ecocriticism argue for a primarily anthropocentric view where, as Dorceta E. Taylor states, 'human societies and the natural environment are intricately linked and that the health of one depends on the health of the other'.[11]

It is this diversification of views that Buell attempts to bring back together in 'Toxic Discourse' so that instead of ecocriticism constructing internally divisive binaries such as nature versus culture, urban versus rural, and animal versus human, the binaries start to dissolve into a view that acknowledges the 'necessary, like-it-or-not interdependence' of all these oppositions.[12] Writing his texts at a time squarely within the 'first wave' of nature-centred ecocritical discourse, Burgess interestingly anticipates some of the second-wave 'revisionist' writings, particularly those that focus on the urban environment and those with social considerations at their heart. In doing so Burgess often fuses together both ecocritical strands, thus manifesting in his own work Buell's call for 'interdependence'.

First-wave ecocriticism, as Buell suggests, tended to focus upon the effects of culture upon nature with the latter being celebrated and the former being decried as a threat to the natural environment. Such positive engagement with nature also dovetails into the common portrayal of the rural shared by numerous works of literature for children, particularly in the early twentieth century. In her book *The Poetics of Childhood*, Roni Natov discusses how, in novels such as Frances Hodgson Burnett's *The Secret Garden* (1911), the pastoral setting becomes a place where the characters can find safety, redemption and moral growth, something she terms the 'the healing power of the green world'.[13] In this novel, nature is beneficent, and the boy Dickon who has an intimate connection with the natural world around him, is portrayed as part of this landscape of healing—a 'child-of-nature' in the mode of Wordsworth's 'Boy of Winander'—who helps the cousins Colin and Mary to overcome their moral and physical stultification.[14] Within this Romantic legacy of a child's visionary connection to nature—a legacy with a recent iteration in the form of Mina in David Almond's *Skellig* (1998)—the character of Amy in *The Earth Giant*, has a similar role to play. Amy's ability to access a deep and intuitive understanding of nature enables her to assist another character. The novel opens with Amy and Peter, her older brother, experiencing a violent storm during which Amy senses telepathically that an ancient tree on the riverbank near their home has been uprooted. When she investigates she finds that a girl has come to life from out of the tree roots where she has been buried for many years. The girl is in fact a girl-giant who appears at first to be a vestige of an ancient tribe, but is later revealed to be from another planet and has extricated herself from the earth in order to wait to be repatriated by her people. Amy hides (the newly named) Giant in a disused cinema in order that she can wait for this event in comparative safety. In the novel, Burgess weighs Amy's innate understanding of Giant and the natural landscape against Peter's inability to communicate with the girl and his struggle with the manifestations of culture and authority—parents and ultimately the police—a conflict that leads to his betrayal of his sister and her new friend. This clash of nature and culture is at the heart of Burgess's narrative. However, the author does not portray either Amy's 'child-in-nature' role or the natural world as straightforwardly positive; nor is culture and the urban environment entirely negative. Just as occurs in *Fly*, *The Earth Giant* interestingly challenges some of the assumptions of first-wave ecocriticism and embraces the fusing of oppositions outlined by Buell.

Indeed, the novel opens with a vision of a hostile rather than a beneficent nature that threatens the manmade suburban landscape inhabited by Peter and Amy and their parents. The violent hurricane which wakes the household and which is the catalyst for the events of the novel is portrayed attempting to gain access to the family's house: '"It'll have the roof off"' Peter's dad exclaims and Peter shouts, '"it wants to come in!"'[15] This forced imposition of nature into a manmade setting is realized by the later description of a tree which has smashed the window of another house and 'gone inside', leaving its branches incongruously juxtaposed against a lampshade (10). This extract has an uncanny undertone that from the start hints at the fantasy/science fiction elements within this seemingly realistic opening and foreshadows the reader's introduction to the alien Earth Giant. This idea of a malignant nature encroaching on the constructed environment is evident in the author's own discussion of nature in his introduction to Jack London's *Call of the Wild* where he states that 'there is something magnetic in the idea that nature will come back to claim its own—covering the towns with creepers and breaking up the roads and pavements with trees, pulling the houses back into the soil'.[16] But the idea of nature impinging upon and ultimately reclaiming the world is contrary to the concept of 'environmental apocalypticism'[17] that takes a long list of manmade catastrophes like Chernobyl, Exxon Valdez and Fukishima as an urgent call to protect nature from man. Here, as Burgess's quotation suggests, it is nature not man that has the power to unsettle the constructed environment and the lives of the people in it.[18] Thus the children watch from the window of the house as objects of nature and culture mix together in a crazy maelstrom:

> The garden was being destroyed. Plants were ripped out of the ground, bushes and shrubs blown flat. The fences were wagging and flapping in the earth. Things that belonged to the ground had taken to the air. Cardboard boxes, bits of wood, twigs and even small branches the wind had torn from the trees were flying like crazy bats in and out of the light from the house. (2)

Objects like twigs and branches that were once living, are initially rendered inanimate by the natural force of the hurricane, but are then reanimated by the same power to join manmade objects as living creatures flitting like 'crazy bats'. In this way the nature/culture binary starts to dissolve. Burgess uses the same trope of the wind in *Fly* to bring artificial objects to life. In the scene in the dump when the kidnapper has died leaving the three children hiding with the kidnapped baby amongst piles of cardboard boxes, the wind at first 'play[s]' with the boxes but then the scene becomes ominous, as Fly explains: 'suddenly the boxes blew away above us. Everything went flying off into the darkness and we were hanging onto the ground, trying to get out of the way' (59). As in *The Earth Giant*, animate and inanimate are conflated and even the dead kidnapper comes 'out of his cardboard as if he were alive' (59).

In both novels it is not man but rather the natural elements of the weather that fundamentally alters the physical landscape. This is true of both the manmade construction of the dump in *Fly* and the street in *The Earth Giant* in which the Lees live—two trees have been blown down and are blocking the road—and also the natural environment in the latter text, where on Barrow Hill the grass has been flattened and trees have been uprooted. Thus all the physical environments of *The Earth Giant* become defamiliarized. When the storm finally abates and the children venture outside, they view their once familiar suburb as 'another world' (10), and later Amy perceives the half fallen trees in the plantation as 'wounded soldiers', remarking that '[t]he once familiar place was a battlefield' (25). There is a sense, then, that some kind of war between nature and culture has taken place, a kind of Armageddon as might be portrayed in an apocalyptic sci-fi narrative, or indeed in apocalyptic environmental texts where manmade damage to the environment prophesizes irreversible damage to the world. But in *The Earth Giant* it is a scenario where neither culture nor nature is in the ascendancy. Both humans and animals, as well as indistinct species like Giant, are now alien to this landscape. Burgess describes how the birds are displaced due to the trees being blown down; they 'flitted nervously about the branches of fallen trees. They were lost, their world of trees lying on the ground' (12). Similarly the need for Amy's father to venture out into the natural landscape in order to find his daughter produces an image focalized through Peter which foregrounds the same ideas of displacement: 'His father in his dark business suit and glossy shoes on the green grass looked like someone from another planet. He never went on to the meadows dressed like that' (29). In writing such elements into *The Earth Giant*, Burgess allows the reader to appreciate how reliant on our familiar environments are both human and animal alike, a strategy that, of course, serves to promote an empathetic association with the character of the giant who is the real 'alien' in the landscape. Only through Amy does Burgess portray the reverse of this coin: as other characters struggle with their changing environments, Amy becomes more comfortable and confident. This is true both in the rural environment where she feels the land is 'her land' (11), and in the urban environment where she overcomes her fears of the town at night to enable her to visit Giant. However, at the end of the novel when Amy is alone with Giant in a pastoral landscape away from both the physical and metaphorical 'built' environment of home, the human girl does not thrive but in fact grows ill. Unable to live off the land like Giant she craves not blackberries and cabbages but chocolate biscuits. Amy may have an instinctive connection to nature but she also needs culture to survive. Thus this character, who seems initially an archetypal 'child-in-nature', in fact transverses both the built and natural environments and helps to emphasize Burgess's insistence on their interconnectedness.

It is also significant that throughout this novel Burgess employs some of the tropes and images of the sci-fi and disaster movies that he evokes at the start. Thus the locale of the cinema is used not only to emphasize the contrast between dark and light which so critically affects the status of all the protagonists in the novel, but also to further critique the familiar nature/culture, animal/human binary. It is no coincidence that the Roxy cinema in which Giant hides still bears a cinematic legacy in the shape of 'the giant letters of the last film the cinema had shown—"Jurassic Park"'—and that the giant climbing up among these letters 'like an ape' to gain access to the interior evokes the iconic filmic image of King Kong climbing the Empire State Building (41).[19] Both these films have at their core the concept contained within Burgess's own remark of 'nature coming back to claim its own', in other words nature turning on man and overturning the human/animal hierarchy. As Joanne Gottlieb suggests in her essay 'Darwin's City, or Life Underground', the environment created in the novel and film *Jurassic Park* is 'so deeply technological that it can present a perfect simulacrum of a pristine natural world'.[20] Although seemingly 'real', this nature is created by culture, but it is this 'artificial' nature that eventually attacks its creator. In *The Earth Giant*, it is the manmade world symbolized by the disused cinema and the cars and telegraph poles broken down in the storm which likewise succumb to the 'nonlinear, chaotic, irrational processes' of nature[21]—the storm and the unexplained alien hiding within the earth. Even though the social constructs of authority attempt to rationalize the presence of the giant, with the policewoman who questions Peter stating, '[t]he only thing I can think is that she was wearing a mask' (102), this rational, scientific discourse is, as in *Jurassic Park,* 'fundamentally unstable' due to the ways in which fantasy elements and hints of metafiction pervade the narrative.[22] These fictive elements remind the reader how deeply complicated is the idea of nature unmediated by culture, something that has caused considerable debate in ecocritical circles.[23] Thus Peter's thought that Amy might have 'made friends with something that had escaped from one of the films they used to show' (100) becomes not just a throw-away comment, but a further problematizing by Burgess of the nature/culture binary which anticipates the complexities in ecocritical discourse that Buell indicates in his texts.

Animal/human hybridity

In *The Earth Giant*, the natural binary of day and night, light and dark is used by Burgess to explore the opposing concepts of nature and culture alongside those of the animal and the human. For example, in the terrifying scene in the cinema when Peter first encounters Giant, darkness is a key element of the narrative. Deprived of sight by the blackness of the auditorium Peter is reduced to using his sense of touch, hearing and smell. This environment is thus presented as a frightening sensory experience where Peter desperately tries to make sense of this alien locale and the unknown presence it contains. All he can hear is 'the long feet beating on the carpet, the breath of it [...] His nostrils were filled with the spicy, sweaty scent' (57). The absence of light renders Peter as an animal hunted as prey and relying on his extra-visual senses and his instincts to stay alive. Indeed it is his 'instinct' that makes 'him lie perfectly still' between the cinema seats to confuse the giant. At this point the giant is an unnamed but sinister presence, ungendered and variously imagined by Peter to be a 'wounded bird;

a giant bird; a monster', 'the beast', and 'something big' (56, 57). The imagery Burgess employs in regard to Peter positions the latter as a smaller animal threatened by one higher up the food chain. Peter is 'like an insect' caught in the beam of the torch, trapped like 'a mouse' (60). Finally as Amy wrestles the torch from the giant, the beam picks out her brother about to fall from the balcony 'like a blind beetle feeling in space' (62).

In a similar way to *The Cry of the Wolf* (1990) when Greycub the wolf becomes the hunter of his killer, or when Lila in *Tiger, Tiger* (1996) stalks the perpetrators of the massacre at the Tiger Park, Burgess complicates the animal/human binary opposition and essentially erases the hierarchical boundaries between the species. The giant was once hunted and will become so again by the manifestations of culture and authority—police, news reporters, parents—but she is equally capable of turning the tables when threatened, and of doing 'anything to anyone rather than get caught' (60). This 'deprivileging of the human subject'[24] illustrates how Burgess often writes into his works an ecocentric focus with human, plant and animal as equal constituents of the world rather than an anthropocentric narrative with humans in the ascendancy over nature.[25]

The figure of Giant in this novel is also used by Burgess as a locus of this human/animal tension. Through the separate focalization of Amy and Peter's first encounter with Giant, the reader is shown varying degrees of fear, acceptance and love of the creature reflected through her association with animals. Both Peter and Amy recognize the human/non-human ambivalence contained within this character. Amy, the girl with an innate connection to Giant, describes the giant's 'teeth [...] like bear's teeth' and her cry 'like a bird' (26). Giant's physical characteristics are perplexing. The similes here show Amy trying to define the giant, grasping for a point of reference within her experience, trying to understand. For Peter, Giant invokes more fear than curiosity. He does not try to render Giant as something familiar, but rather focuses on her 'wild' characteristics that are both repelling and bewildering in their hybridity. Thus through Peter's eyes the reader sees 'that snout, those huge jaws—an animal's jaws. Her lips twisted again into that ferocious expression' (64). He tells us 'it could almost have been a woman but it was so big and its face was so still and deformed, it was more than half an animal' (63), the ungendered pronoun denoting his refusal to accept the human characteristics of Giant. However, as both children begin to accept the character, the animal imagery moves from wild to domesticated, and thus more familiar, animals. As Peter embraces her, he describes her warmth and smell as akin to a horse and when Giant licks Amy lovingly she is portrayed as playfully puppy-like. The pronouns are feminized by both children as they draw closer to an acceptance of Giant as a hybrid creature who can show 'tears for sadness just like we do' (43). Giant becomes 'same'/familiar rather than 'other'/different and the animal/human boundary is blurred.

This same human/animal binary is also questioned in *The Baby and Fly Pie*; however, in this novel the association of child and animal has a stronger anthropocentric focus that allies the text to the viewpoint of an eco-justice narrative. In the opening sequence of the novel for example, we see kids and gulls conflated in a chaotic and repulsive representation of a toxic environment. When tons of rotten fish are tipped onto the dump, the gulls descend as quickly as the kids attempt to escape the horrifying smell, and so Fly tells the reader 'we all held our heads and ran like rats' (5). The image of rats, gulls and kids side by side on a rubbish dump feeding off human detritus is further compounded by Fly's observation that the tip is 'a city, a city for rats and cats and gulls and kids' (13). The image places children on the same axis as the animal, but unlike in *The Earth Giant* where the association functions biocentrically asserting that humans and animals *should* live in synchrony, here conversely, Burgess indicates that this is an unacceptable position. With no experience outside this way of life, Fly makes no moral judgement on it; indeed his environment has shaped him to the point where he is shockingly casual about situations such as that of another boy who 'got sold onto a fertiliser factory in Croydon [...], and the inside of his mouth turned blue' (12). Through Fly's remarks, Burgess invites the implied reader to delve beneath the surface of the narrative and to question this dystopian world that has uncomfortable overtones of our own. It is a technique that can function, as Kamala Platt states 'as an expressive agent for social change'.[26] Children living in squalor, children exploited by adults like Mother Shelley in this narrative, are very real social problems and dumping waste in centres of population has been shown to have a disproportional effect on poorer families.[27] Thus *The Baby and Fly Pie* can be read as an 'organ of environmental justice', as the epitome of Platt's concept of 'transformative poetics'.[28]

However, this is also an inherently negative view of an urban environment, one that Andrew Ross describes (in Michael Bennett and David Teague's seminal volume *The Nature of Cities*), as commonly held across environmental literature. He states, '[i]n the dominant environmental literature, the city is sick, monstrous, blighted, ecocidal, life-denying, parasitical, you name it. ...In the face of that tradition, it's easy to see why "urban ecocriticism" is considered an oxymoron.'[29] Ross does not deny the validity of a focus on texts as a catalyst to social change (indeed several essays in this volume deal with issues such as inner-city ghettos) but this critic focuses on interrogating the urban landscape as an ecosystem in its own right: 'city space as an evolving, contested habitat'.[30] In the final part of this chapter I will focus on the rural/urban binary to be found in Burgess's texts and discuss how, without denying an eco-justice viewpoint, the author once more attempts to dissolve the boundaries between these oppositions.

The beauty in the urban

At the moment in the novel where Fly, Jane and Sham flee from the dump with the kidnapped baby, Fly looks down on an urban terrain that is beautified by colour and light. He describes how '[t]he city spread out behind us—orange and white and pearly pink lights that blurred into a soggy haze in the distance. They looked pretty like that' (64). He surveys the landscape from an elevated plain reminiscent of the way in which a rural scene might be admired from the top of a hill. He sees the city as a whole, a viewpoint that only elevation can give him and that cultural theorist Michel de Certeau describes as being 'lifted out of the city's grasp'.[31] It is a positioning that allows Fly time to see beauty in the urban. And yet the next sentence stands in dramatic contrast to this description. From his position, Fly cannot only *see* the city, he can smell it: the 'smoke and traffic fumes, the Tip—all the smells of fifteen million people living in a rabbit hutch' (63). The 'pretty' view cannot eclipse the reality of the stench of an over-populated city. The image of the 'rabbit hutch' alludes to a negative harnessing of nature by man, and at the same time indicates a judgement on humans living, literally, in their own detritus. For Fly this is the 'real' city of which he is a part every day; a city where he lives, as de Certeau again describes, '"down below", below the thresholds at which visibility begins'.[32]

The first part of the 'real' city met by the reader is the seemingly 'sick, monstrous, blighted' environment discussed by Ross of the city dump; however, this locus is also presented by Burgess as a beneficent presence. Fly states 'the Tip's been good to me. It's fed me, clothed me, given me blankets to sleep on, toys to play with. All for free' (14). He describes it as 'our castle, our palace' (11). The 'Tip', thus divorced in Fly's mind from the social inequalities surrounding him, becomes a provider, a pseudo-mother, an entity that has the power to sustain life and also to provide recreation. Fly tells us: 'it [the metal scaffolding] all got bulldozed up into a tangle and left—for us to play on' (11). Equally, the huge quantity of cardboard boxes in the dump is a source of adventure within this seemingly hopeless environment. Indeed, the scene when Sham and Fly jump from a building into the huge mound of boxes is presented as though they are jumping into an ocean: the boxes are 'floating around the yard' and the boys squeal in delight as they jump from the warehouse window. Fly explains: 'it was hot, or at least warm down there. I started fighting my way down, swimming and crawling and climbing at the same time'. Like water 'it got cool as you got further from the sun' (15). Fly stops at the 'layer near the sunlight' where it is 'warm and still'. Like a swimmer floating in the ocean, or a sunbather on the shore, 'you felt that you could lie there forever' (16). Despite their poverty, the children in *Fly* display an ability to benefit from their environment and interact with it in an imaginative and playful way: Sham and Fly jump 'over and over' into the boxes (15), and with the other children have 'a wonderful party' when a surplus of food is thrown out. When Fly tells the reader 'See? It's not all bad being a rubbish kid' (8) the tragic undertones resonate deeply, but at the same time the idea of working with an environment and making the best of it is strong in this novel.

Furthermore, another key element that Burgess interrogates in his presentation of the dump is the concept of it being a part of a wider ecosystem, and indeed being an ecosystem in its own right. Not only does the dump sustain the children with food, clothes and other items, a fact not lost on Fly when they fail to find anything useful in the shantytown Santy (71), it also sustains the rats, cats, gulls and millions of micro-organisms which feed on the rubbish. This concept of symbiosis taking place in such 'compromised places'[33] is equivalent to that noted by Robert Sullivan in his text, *The Meadowlands: Wilderness Adventure on the Edge of a City* where he explains that '[t]he big difference between the garbage hills and the real hills in the Meadowlands is that the garbage hills are alive'. He goes on to refer to the 'billions of microscopic organisms thriving underground in dark, oxygen-free communities [which] multiply and even evolve so that they can more readily digest the trash at their disposal'.[34] This may not be a nature that is easy to love, but it is a valid symbiotic relationship nevertheless. Equally, it is not just micro-organisms that are in symbiosis with the dump: the Tip also gives 'the Mothers a good living' (6) and allows them to enter into their own human ecosystem where they pay the controlling gang masters to 'have their kids left alone' (7); and the gangs in turn control the streets and ensure that this ecosystem is firmly segregated from the businesses and people living in 'proper houses or offices' (67). Like the Chinese gangs that operate in Manchester in *Tiger, Tiger,* Burgess portrays here a definite human ecosystem but a morally perverse kind of symbiosis that also reflects the degraded nature of the landscape.

This is also the case in one of the other urban locales in the text 'the other city—the squatter's city' of Santy (65). Here the city location is once again the site of filth and toxicity. It is nicknamed 'Shitty City' because 'most of the toilets are just holes in the ground and they hardly ever get cleaned out' (66). The whole environment is fenced off from the wider city and patrolled by armed guards. It is an extreme dystopian example of what Andrew Light, in his discussion of the separation of inner city Los Angeles from more well-off areas, calls a fear of 'the savage enemy within the city', and illustrates a desire on the part of the authorities to 'just control this wild place and keep it separate as best we can for as long as possible'.[35] The fence and the guards that encircle Santy are of course a physical manifestation of this control. This city-within-the-city is separate but in many ways the same as its wealthier counterpart. Again, the undercurrent of social injustice which runs through the presentation of the squatter city environment runs side by side with the way in which Santy functions as a valid environment in its own right. The locale may look 'like a sort of filthy Tip with the rubbish spread out all over instead of heaped up' (79), but it functions as a town, with houses and streets, a bakery, a butcher's shop, a pub, a transport system. And ironically, even within this ultimate segregated city there are hierarchical structures in place in terms of governance (the Monroe gang) and in terms of housing. Fly describes, for example, how the standard of the housing in Santy deteriorates as they are driven further from the centre of the camp until finally they see only makeshift accommodation. However, the character of Scousie, who befriends the children, has built a more permanent house that defies this squalid environment and is an interesting mix of the organic and the manmade. Fly describes it as: 'a clever-looking thing, a sort of hangar of branches and polythene and carpet, plastered in mud and then covered again in polythene. It was made of layers like that [...]. The floor was raised high up' (80). Built to withstand an environment where rain quickly turns the camp into a mud bath, the raised platform and the daubed walls that retain heat and deaden noise ('the sound of the storm almost vanished when he pushed the door closed' [93]), allows Scousie a measure of comfort in his surroundings. Like a bird's nest skilfully crafted to optimize its environment, the house is in perfect balance with its locale. Indeed the whole of Santy could be read as a kind of 'eco' city where the only waste is the human effluvia presumably reincorporated into the ground. Unlike the 'real' city of

London with its throwaway mentality, the shopkeeper tells the children that in Santy nothing is wasted, everything is reused and reintroduced into the environment. Burgess's text thus illustrates clearly how one can interrogate the urban landscape not just as a 'compromised' version of a natural landscape but also as a fully functioning ecosystem.

Although in both novels the protagonists often voice a preference for the rural side of the binary equation, with the countryside in *The Baby and Fly Pie* contrasted strongly with the toxic urban environment, and the giant in *The Earth Giant* desperate for the open air and sun of the rural locale, these environments are often portrayed by Burgess as problematic. In both novels the lack of places to hide, the lack of people, and the fact that all the characters are 'alien' to this landscape, heightens the danger of discovery. Ross posits the idea that in 'dystopian science fiction and the disaster genre' the protagonists 'are often passively at the mercy of an urban environment that has been turned against them'.[36] As discussed above, Burgess uses some of the tropes of the apocalypse narrative and the science fiction adventure in *Fly* and *The Earth Giant*; however, especially in the former text, the narrative works contrary to this assertion with the protagonists embracing the city and working with it to gain an advantage. The city environment is harsh, but its overpopulated and anonymous nature is often vital to the survival of the protagonists in both novels.

In several places in *Fly* the characters use street knowledge to protect themselves. When Fly and Sham are on the run, Fly reports: 'We got off the bus and heard music and we headed towards that. Where there's music there's people and where's there's people there's safety [...] no one was going to notice two new faces in the crowd' (146) and when they are confronted at the fair, Fly tells the reader that he 'got clean away *among* the crowd and the noise and the lights' (137—my emphasis). He is not fleeing *from* the crowd but embracing it as a kind of camouflage. Here the characters are as much part of their 'natural' environment as any Dickon-type character is at home with a rural locale. Just as in *Cry of the Wolf* when Greycub knows his environment and his enemy so well he can outwit the hunter, so the children use the city and their knowledge of it to remain secure. Equally, Jane recognizes that part of survival is fitting in with their environment when she buys new clothes for them all: ' "Clothes, Disguise. See?" she says "You're not going to be street kids when we walk out of here"' (147). Animal-like camouflage is their greatest asset. But in the countryside at the end of the novel, their appearance spoiled by the elements, this disguise is ruined. They are exposed, no longer anonymous, and thus they are finally caught. Despite Fly's intermittent positivity towards a life in a rural environment, at the end of the novel, alone, without Jane, he literally runs away from the country to embrace the town. Fly describes how he struggles uphill until finally,

> the hill fell away before me and there it was—a town. Houses spreading out for miles, tower blocks in the distance. I knew I'd done it then, I'd got away, because every town is full of kids and we all look the same. No one was going to pick me out. No one would even notice one more lousy kid. (189)

Whilst very much short of a whole-hearted endorsement of the urban sphere, Burgess at the end of *Fly* nevertheless illustrates to the reader the validity of Buell's comment on the 'like-it-or-not interdependence' of the urban and rural environments in first and second-wave ecocriticism.

Challenging the paradigm: Burgess's 'elastic' boundaries

In my discussion of Burgess's texts in this chapter, I have highlighted how the author successfully interrogates the complexities of the binary oppositions that are often debated in ecocritical discourse. Burgess constantly plays on expectations depicting, for example, a romantic vision of the 'child-in-nature' in the character of Amy which can be equated with first-wave ecocriticism's privileging of nature over culture, and then simply undercuts this vision by showing how the child needs culture as well as nature to survive. Similarly, in *Fly*, the city seems the degraded, noxious environment of which Ross speaks of as the urban stereotype, and yet this flawed locale is shown to be as much a functioning ecosystem as any 'natural' environment, thus urging the reader to consider what Anthony Lioi terms 'a new model for ecocritical activity that does not shun compromised places'.[37] Finally, Burgess also illustrates how erasing the boundary between animal and human can provide a shared understanding between the species in *The Earth Giant*, but that in *Fly* this can verge on a dangerous lack of appreciation of social problems and inequalities, a lack that critics writing from an eco-justice standpoint would consider unacceptable. An ecocritical reading of these texts can enhance the critical experience of Burgess's writing and foreground themes that may remain in the background under a traditional critical interrogation. Written at a time when ecocriticism as an academic discipline was in its infancy, Burgess anticipates and addresses many of the issues now faced by ecocritics in reconciling the deep dichotomies of this critical discourse.

What is also interesting is that part of Buell's discussion of the way forward for ecocriticism is in rectifying the lack of attention paid by ecocritics to the genre of science fiction. He states that 'ecocriticism has been behind the curve' in responding to science fiction narratives perhaps because ecocriticism in general has a 'resistance to nature as artifice'.[38] It is perhaps fitting, then, that of all the characters in the two novels it is the figure of the alien Earth Giant herself in which there is the most potential for a demonstration of the 'elastic' boundaries called for by Buell in his narratives. Giant, hidden beneath the earth, with eyes 'dappled like the leaves of the wood in greens and browns' (26) appears entirely of nature, but in fact far transcends human knowledge of this concept, originating as she does from a different planet. Not only is she herself a blending of human and animal thus erasing the boundaries between the species, but she also conceives of the world around her in terms that fuse nature and artifice, the built and the natural environments, the animal and the human. This is evident when Giant sees a butterfly in the forest towards the end of the novel. She has never seen such a creature before and her description illustrates just how holistic and inclusive is Burgess's approach to the world. Giant focalizes her vision of the butterfly, first through colour, as would a human; it is 'black and red', and then, foregrounding her hybridity, she assigns both movement and smell to the creature as might an animal, explaining that 'it landed on the bushes and fanned its wings. [...] It was a jewel. It smelt of oranges and electricity and dust' (106). Furthermore, Burgess's choice of the origin of this scent conjoins the natural (the orange), the artificial (the electricity) and the extra-terrestrial (the dust), in one evocative image which, as Peter Hollindale suggests in his chapter in this book, successfully captures the perceptions of a creature of which humans have no real concept. The fact that the creature that describes the butterfly in this way is from outer space widens even further the scope of ecocriticism to include not just the animal and human but also the alien, not just the rural and the urban but also the extra-terrestrial. This is a 'deprivileging of the human subject' at its most 'elastic' and illustrates how a careful reading of Burgess's two texts through the lens of ecocriticism can illuminate an understanding of both these novels and the 'pluriform' nature of 'literary ecodiscourse' itself.[39]

Notes

1. Melvin Burgess, *The Baby and Fly Pie* [1993] (London: Puffin, 1995): 125. All further references in the chapter are to the 1995 edition and abbreviated to *Fly*.

2. Andrew Ross interviewed by Michael Bennett, 'The Social Claim on Urban Ecology', in Michael Bennett and David W. Teague (eds.), *The Nature of Cities: Ecocriticism and Urban Environments* (Tucson, AZ: University of Arizona Press, 1999): 19, 17.
3. Lawrence Buell, 'Preface' to *The Future of Environmental Criticism: Environmental Crisis and Literary Imagination* (Oxford: Wiley-Blackwell, 2005): ix.
4. Lawrence Buell, 'Toxic Discourse', *Critical Enquiry* 24(3) (Spring 1998): 656–7.
5. Buell, *The Future of Environmental Criticism*: 11.
6. Cheryll Glotfelty, 'Introduction: Literary Studies in an Age of Environmental Crisis', in Cheryll Glotfelty and Harold Fromm (eds.), *The Ecocriticism Reader: Landmarks in Literary Ecology* (Athens, GA: University of Georgia Press, 1996): xviii.
7. Peter Barry, *Beginning Theory: An Introduction to Literary and Critical Theory*, 3rd edn (Manchester: Manchester University Press, 2009): 250.
8. I have used the term 'locus' within this chapter to indicate the environmental setting of a particular episode within a text. I use it in most instances in preference to 'setting' in order to illustrate the critical importance of the environment to my discussion, thus combining within the term 'locus' the primary meaning of 'place/setting' and the secondary meaning of the word as a centre of great activity.
9. See, for example, Jonathan Bates' ecocritical reading of Wordsworth's poetry and its natural locale in *Romantic Ecology: Wordsworth and the Environmental Tradition* (London: Routledge, 1991).
10. Loretta Johnson, 'Greening the Library: The Fundamentals and Future of Ecocriticism', *ASLE Journal* (December 2009): 8.
11. Quoted in Kamala Platt, 'Environmental Justice and Children's Literature: Depicting, Defending and Celebrating Trees and Birds, Colors and People', in Sidney I. Dobrin and Kenneth B. Kidd (eds.), *Wild Things: Children's Culture and Ecocriticism* (Detroit, MI: Wayne State University Press, 2004): 184.
12. Buell, 'Toxic Discourse': 665.
13. Roni Natov, *The Poetics of Childhood* (London and New York: Routledge, 2003): 93.
14. See William Wordsworth, *The Prelude*, (particularly) Book V.II.
15. Melvin Burgess, *The Earth Giant* [1995] (London: Puffin, 1997): 1, 2. All further references in the chapter are to the 1997 edition.
16. Melvin Burgess, 'Introduction' to Jack London, *Call of the Wild* [1903] (London: Puffin, 2008), n.p.
17. Buell, 'Toxic Discourse': 642.
18. This idea of a 'revenge' by nature is, however, in line with ecocritical writing by postcolonial critics such as Arundhati Roy, who employs polemic rhetoric suggesting nature rising against man. In Roy's 1998 essay 'The End of Imagination' she states that in response to nuclear war, 'the very elements—the sky, the air, the land, the wind and water—will all turn against us. Their wrath will be terrible' (quoted in Graham

Huggan, *Postcolonial Ecocriticism: Literature, Animals, Environment* [Abingdon: Routledge, 2010], Kindle Edition: 51).
19. *Jurassic Park*, based on the 1990 novel by Michael Crichton and directed by Steven Spielberg, was released in 1993, two years before *The Earth Giant* was published. *King Kong* was released in 1933 with the iconic image of King Kong climbing the Empire State Building featuring on advertising posters for the film.
20. Joanne Gottleib, 'Darwin's City, Or Life Underground: Evolution, Progress, and the Shape of Things to Come', in Michael Bennett and David W. Teague (eds.), *The Nature of Cities: Ecocriticism and Urban Environments* (Tucson, AZ: University of Arizona Press, 1999): 242.
21. *Ibid.*
22. *Ibid.*
23. For an expanded discussion of the general opposition of ecocriticism to the central poststructuralist tenet that nature is a social construct see Buell, *The Future of Environmental Criticism*: 30–44.
24. Head quoted in Buell, *The Future of Environmental Criticism*: 10.
25. See Peter Hollindale's chapter in this volume for a detailed discussion of Burgess's presentation of animals specifically in *Tiger, Tiger* and *The Cry of the Wolf.* Of particular relevance is Hollindale's discussion of Burgess's ecocentric rather than anthropomorphic focus in these novels.
26. Platt, 'Environmental Justice and Children's Literature': 184.
27. See Joni Adamson, Mei Mei Evans and Rachel Stein (eds.), *Environmental Justice Reader: Politics, Poetics, Pedagogy* (Tucson, AZ: University of Arizona Press, 2002): 4 where the editors call 'to redress the disproportionate incidence of environmental contamination in communities of the poor and/or communities of color'.
28. Platt, 'Environmental Justice and Children's Literature': 185.
29. Ross and Bennett, 'The Social Claim on Urban Ecology': 16.
30. *Ibid.*: 17.
31. Michel De Certeau, *The Practice of Everyday Life* (Berkeley, CA: University of California Press, 1984): 92.
32. *Ibid.*: 93.
33. Anthony Lioi, 'Of Swamp Dragons: Mud, Megalopolis, and a Future for Ecocriticism', in Annie Merrill Ingram, Ian Marshall, Daniel J. Philippon and Adam W. Sweeting (eds.), *Coming into Contact* (Athens, GA: University of Georgia Press, 2007): 23.
34. Quoted in Lioi, 'Of Swamp Dragons': 29.
35. Andrew Light, 'Boyz in the Woods: Urban Wilderness in American Cities', in Michael Bennett and David W. Teague (eds.), *The Nature of Cities: Ecocriticism and Urban Environments* (Tucson, AZ: University of Arizona Press, 1999): 150 and 145.
36. Ross and Bennett, 'The Social Claim on Urban Ecology': 20.
37. Lioi, 'Of Swamp Dragons': 23.
38. Buell, *The Future of Environmental Criticism*: 56.
39. *Ibid.*

Part IV
Telling Stories

10

Found Fiction: An Interview with Melvin Burgess

Alison Waller and Melvin Burgess

A: Let's start with your two most recent novels for teenagers, *Nicholas Dane* and *Kill All Enemies*: stories that both deal with young people who are on the margins but that are told in very different ways. What draws you to telling those kinds of stories, and which narrative form did you find more satisfying?

M: Well I think those two books *are* linked. And as very often happens, you write one book and then you're off on something and you think 'oh, I'm going to do another one like that'. The link between them is real people's real stories—this 'found fiction' idea—that you talk to people, and there's this whole world, this whole set of fantastic stories. It's to do with drawing from life. I feel that authors don't draw from life that much. People include their aunt, or some friend of theirs, but really thinking about it, including groups of characters in relationships, and interviewing them, doesn't happen that often, which is a bit weird really.

The guys I talked to and interviewed for *Nick Dane*—you would have never otherwise have known the experiences they've had. Of course, at the time no one would have believed them if they had told their stories. So *Kill All Enemies* was linked in that sense in that it was about the fact that people could be something completely unexpected. The kids in *Kill All Enemies* are actually dreadful in school but they're heroes in another part of their life. So that's how the books grew out of one other: they were about people on the margins of society and how people who you would think are bad lots actually have really significant heroic lives in a different way.

As far as the form's concerned, I do love telling stories in multiple first person; it's such a fantastic way to tell a story. I'm very much someone who becomes involved in voices, so I love the shifting viewpoint and the three-dimensional quality that it can give you and the fact you can move the story on very quickly because it's constantly changing. *Kill All Enemies* is slightly different structurally, because the voices are quite loosely tied together. Around about the time I was thinking of the idea, I was approached by a TV company who wanted to do something for Channel Four involving teenagers, so I said 'you can come in on my next project if you like'. And it was great, because it meant that they hired a researcher for *Kill All Enemies*, so I had all that at my disposal. But it means the novel's based on a soap structure, where you have the A story, the B story and the C story. And the A story's coming up and the B story's coming down, and the C story's a bit of comedy or something. So in that sense, Billie's the A story and Chris is the C story and Rob's the B story. It's not a soap, because it's not rolling on, but you do have these three strands which are quite loosely connected together. The first third or so was written originally as a TV script, but Channel Four decided they didn't want to use it so I turned it into a book. So it's got those two elements: the first-person voice and the TV structure of episodes.

I suppose I prefer the multiple voice thing really. I feel very at home in it these days. It was nice doing third person for *Nicholas Dane*, and it was also a little tribute to Dickens, but it had its problems. By and large I prefer doing the first person. I don't know whether I'd want to stick with one form or the other forever: I've enjoyed doing them all. They really give you a different effect for each story. I must admit, there was a time when I was trying to get away from those multiple first-person voices, because it's hard, really hard, to get it right: you know? It's time-consuming. But I find myself being drawn back to it.

A: I want to return to that idea of writing a homage to Dickens with *Nicholas Dane*. Do you consider yourself as a social writer in the way that Dickens was, writing about social issues and making a difference through that writing?

M: I do like writing about social stuff and I feel that teenagers don't have much of a voice, so it's probably quite an important thing to do. It's hard though, because it's not a popular thing to do at the moment. When *Junk* was out, everyone was on the back of writing about social issues, but they're not now. So the publishers aren't terribly interested—there's this response that 'oh, it's an issue book'. So I do, but it's hard to do social issues now. It's not necessarily supported by schools and libraries anymore. Schools have become a lot more anxious about their image, with all the testing that's being done.

Everything's much less about exploring themes for the sake of it or for social reasons, and much more about passing, marks, and producing a measurable product. So it's not a good time for social writing, certainly not for young people.

A: It's interesting to think about the trends that you have initiated or followed, and the moments in recent history you have written about. *Nicholas Dane* and *Junk* are both set in the eighties. Do you think there has been some comment you've been trying to make there about Thatcher's Britain, about the way things were for young people and for society in general?

M: Probably not. *Nicholas Dane* was set at a time when it had become apparent that dodgy things and difficult abuse were happening in children's homes. And the form of children's homes in which it was happening had been set up in the sixties; so it's at the end of a period really. Whereas *Junk* simply happened because that is when it happened. It's based on real people and real events, by and large. It takes a little bit of time before you realize what actually defines a period. But I think eighties' things that have happened there are chance.

Trying to write really totally contemporary stuff is tricky for all sorts of reasons. If you try and do it completely bang up to date then by the time you've finished it's out of date anyway. It's like when people ask 'how do you get a young person's voice right?' and the answer is you don't do it too exactly, otherwise it's dated by the time it's done. It's a novel you're writing, not a magazine, so it has to last. You can't be too fashionable. There are lots of cultural references in *Kill All Enemies* and I think you can get away with it if you're writing about a specific period and a specific place. But even with *Kill All Enemies*, the people I was talking to were older, in their early twenties or late teens, talking about when they were fifteen and sixteen.

A: I hear what you're saying about the growing conservatism in schools and libraries, but I'm hoping there's also a contemporary movement for young people to feel activated in some way. It seems there has been a recent shift towards young people being engaged in politics, with a sort of protest aesthetic fashionable again in music and other media.

M: It would be nice to think that sort of thing's coming back in. It would be dreadful to think that it took a Tory government to make it happen. I was reading an article the other day saying 'they're bloody dismantling the NHS, how can they do that'. It's because they *can*, because Thatcher dismantled the Trade Union movement, which for all its flaws was a bulwark against this sort of thing, and Labour didn't put it back.

A: Do you feel as strongly about your historical characters as you do about the contemporary youth you write about, because they're still neglected or damaged by uncaring communities even if they are from a different period?

M: All my books are about underdogs really; they're about people who are afflicted or put down or haven't had proper opportunities, and I naturally gravitate towards that kind of storytelling; it's how my mind works. But I'm particularly fond of the kids in *Kill All Enemies*. I have a particular place in my heart for them, so that one is different. It was an interesting thing because it was very much based on real people I went out and talked to, so I wanted that to be very positive and show them sorting it out for themselves. I was being consciously socially minded with that one, as I was with *Nick Dane*.

A: Can you tell me something about your relationship with publishers over the years?

M: My first publisher was Andersen Press who mainly worked with picturebooks, so I was a bit of sport for them, probably because Klaus's son liked the book. Klaus Flugge was a remarkable publisher. He is great: he's a proper old-fashioned publisher so he's like your uncle and looks after you, and says [in German accent] 'we're the Andersen family and all in it together'. At the same time he's a very sharp business man. He says if you have a good publisher you don't need an agent. Well sometimes you *do* actually want an agent because sometimes Klaus's deals are five percent down…so in the end I decided to get an agent and Klaus was really annoyed with me and that was a deterioration in our relationship.

Then I was doing this memoir covering my life from thirteen to nineteen. I noticed that autobiographies tend to skirt around that bit very often just because it's such a weird period: they stop just before puberty and they come back in about fifteen or sixteen. But Klaus hated the memoir and was terrified he was going to get sued because the European Human Rights Act had brought in some really challenging issues about what you can and can't write about living people. So I departed from Andersen, which is a shame really, because I like Klaus.

Puffin were very good to me for a long time, very supportive. I think that like most children's publishers now they're really overworked. I don't think the editors have enough time to focus; they're really concentrating on their really big sellers. Literary fiction is also not very popular at the moment: children's literary fiction, that is. I mean it's swings and roundabouts—they will be interested again I hope—but at the moment they're not so bothered. It's like the stuff I'm doing with black and Asian writers in Manchester [with 'Common Word'] who always complain that they hear 'well we've already got a black writer'. It's the same with literary stuff; they say 'well we've got a literary figure, why would we need another one?'

I'm here, there, everywhere at the moment. I'm doing a horror thing for Hammer, which is an adult imprint; I'm doing something for Chicken House. So I haven't really got a home, although it's with Puffin if it's with anyone.

A: You have worked with all kinds of people, from screenwriters and TV producers to philosophers. Do you enjoy working collaboratively?

M: I really enjoy it. It's increasingly important to me to do collaborations, yeah. I mean I've done over twenty odd novels now and it's an isolating business, so it's a real relief to work with other people on projects.

I worked with Ruth Brown on a picturebook called *The Birdman*. I knew her from Andersen Press and at the time she was doing picturebooks with a number of novelists. She did one with Anne Fine, I remember. And I wanted to do a picturebook. Sometime ago I'd separated from my German wife, and she went off to Germany with my kids so I wasn't seeing them but I sent them stories. I sent Ruth a collection of these and one of them was 'The Birdman'. When I was first trying to work with her I would try and think about the design of the page and this sort of thing but she said 'er that's my job': she was very clear. So I had no idea actually what she was going to do. She wasn't interested in working close with me at all.

I'm interested now in finding ways of making novels more collaborative, but you can only go so far down that road.

A: Like the multimedia, multi-platform types of narratives you've worked on?

M: Well there isn't really a narrative, and that's problem. It becomes a conversation and as soon as the reader can start answering back, you're stuffed. Where's the script? Where's the story? It's a different thing, that's all it is.

A: You have said elsewhere that you want young people to feel there are stories and narratives that belong to them. Is there something you have read as an adult that you feel really belongs to you?

M: I always say that George Orwell has been a big influence on me. I was also an enormous fan of Peake's *Gormenghast*. I still am really. I think it's quite a unique little masterpiece. Those gothic characters which aren't human, practically, but work as characters. It is character-driven fantasy, which is a rarity. When I do fantasy I always want it to be character-driven rather than the adventure fantasy, which is what Tolkien does—none of the characters change in Tolkien. I enjoy fantasy very much. You can explore anything via fantasy, it's a very interesting genre.

My dad worked very briefly for Oxford University Press who did a whole series of myths and legends: *Folk tales from Moor and Mountain*, *Folk Tales from Czechoslovakia*, from here there and everywhere. I had the whole collection, but the one that particularly did it for me was *Tales of the Norse Gods and Heroes* by Barbara Leonie Picard, and that's where *Bloodtide* and *Bloodsong* came from, because her version of the Volsunga Saga really blew me away. I still have a real possession of those Norse myths; they really did it for me, in a profound way.

A: Maybe you have something in common with Tolkien after all…

M: But it was folktale that he did, it wasn't myth. A folktale's a nice little adventure, but mythic stuff is much more meaningful and deep. I mean there are mythic elements in Tolkien, I suppose, but the figures of the gods Odin and Loki have a much more deep and profound meaning, and the hobbits and all that are much more folktaley aren't they? Little adventures.

People do turn to the Norse myths quite often: they're very powerful. One thing nobody has done is to deal with the god cycle properly yet. So I'm kind of interested in that but I can't work out how to do it. Because the whole *Ragnarǫk* thing is all about Loki leading them astray and then saving them, but taking away from their integrity all the time until eventually it's all gone. By the time they turn on him it's too late: it's a great story.

A: Many of your novels are difficult and quite sad at times, but they still have humanity at their core and still on the whole have a certain amount of optimism and hope and love. The text that stands out for me is *The Baby and Fly Pie*, which can be read as rather pessimistic.

M: *The Baby and Fly Pie*. The idea for that novel came about after listening to a radio programme about street kids in Bogota they used to shoot. When it came out there was a lot of a discussion about it, and I remember having a public debate with one guy who said '*The Baby and Fly Pie* is a great book right up to the last page', because he really thought that every book has to end on a note of hope. Of course Jane, who is the hopeful, optimistic, striving character, she gets shot. And there were two reasons for that: the main reason was that I felt that sometimes it's just really unreasonable to say that things are going to be alright. If you were writing about life in the trenches in the First World War—or death in the trenches—you wouldn't want to say 'oh it worked out alright in the end' because it didn't—it was grim, miserable and completely fucked and that was all there is to it. So I do think that would be an immoral and an unreasonable, unfair, lying thing to do and I'm interested always in trying to write with some kind of truth and some sort of verity. And the other thing is that Jane is such an optimistic character and so idealistic and so hopeful, and if there had been a way through she would have found it. One day a 'Jane' will find it.

And sometimes the hope is in the reader. So when you come across something that is so unfair and so unjust, and you as a reader are outraged, then the hope lies in you. It doesn't have to lie in the book. I would hope after reading *Fly Pie* that your sense of justice and tragedy would be stirred: then it's worked out alright. It's not up to me to put hope in the book, but it might be up to me to leave some hope in the reader. Just the fact that everyone was saying 'that was so dark' meant that what they were really saying was 'that was so unfair'—well life *is* unfair and maybe it shouldn't be.

A: The hope you give readers quite often resides in the affection you display for your characters. However bad they might seem—however annoying young men can be, however violent young women can be—they all have something good in them at the core, it's just a case of understanding them. Do you believe in love?

M: Oh yeah! Sure I do! The redeeming power of love, is that what you're talking about? Well it's a funny word isn't it, really? And fictional love is a bit like biblical love. It's 'oh everyone loves in the end' and it makes everything alright, and I'm not sure that's entirely true. I do think that people want to be good and get on together, I do really, in my heart. There's a whole cultural thing, so it's quite easy to raise people to be violent and obnoxious and horrible, but I do feel that we are essentially communal creatures as well.

I don't know if that's love, necessarily. I mean love's great isn't it? We all want to be in love. You don't necessarily mean sexual love?

A: No. I've just noticed in a number of your books, particularly those featuring young lads, that what you seem to want to get across are their huge hearts. They might have all this other stuff going on but they've got something redeeming, which might be love towards their friends or towards their mothers in some cases.

M: Yeah ok. Yeah I do. I think that people relate to one another. We all are creatures of relationships. It's what people do. It's the first thing you do as a baby at your mum's breast; you're relating, loving if you want to put it like that. I do think that everyone really has to have those relationships and closeness with one another, and that's the redeeming thing: that we all actually want to be in one another's hearts—not in everyone's heart—but somewhere, somehow.

A: Which leads me to challenge you on *Nicholas Dane*'s Tony Creal. While you give an account outside of the novel for why he might be the way he is, inside the novel there's no explanation provided. He's not given the redeeming back-story that characters like Jonesy or even Sunshine get.

M: No you don't, with Creal. I certainly didn't think why I did that at the time. I suppose there's already this sense of time going on when Jones comes in to the story, and you suddenly realize the abuse goes way back, and who knows what's happened to him through Tony Creal.

Are there any other characters that don't have redeeming back-stories? Well there's the Chinaman in *Tiger, Tiger*, there's The Hunter in *The Cry of the Wolf*—basically he was the wolf out of Aesop's Fables, reversed. Sometimes you need a baddie. You can't explain everything. There's no real baddies in *Junk*, but as soon as you start having the multiple voice thing it's almost impossible to make someone one-dimensional. Even in *Doing It*, Miss Young had her mum there, the bigger monster, who terrified the pants off of her. I think I did want an absolute baddie in *Nicholas Dane*, although the idea was also that Creal and Jones were both versions of how Nick might have turned out—parallel narratives of the same person's history, in a way.

A: That's a good defence.

M: A good defence, but I need a defence! It's a funny book that one for me. I actually think it's not finished really. I don't know what I would have done if I'd carried on with it and started engaging with it again. In a sense it's a broken novel, because the first half is different from the second half.

A: So if *Nicholas Dane* has problems for you in its completed form, what is the novel you're most proud of?

M: It is a very difficult question. I'm very very fond of *The Cry of the Wolf*, but how much because it was my very first one, I don't know. But I kind of feel it's just perfect, just alright. I'm very fond of *Junk*, and that one has obviously had a profound effect on a lot of people. I'm proud of it as well in the sense that when I go to heaven, they might let me in just for that one. Because it's really helped a lot of people. I get so many letters from people saying it's helped them with addiction for themselves or people in their lives, or it got them into reading, or 'it saved my life when I was thirteen'. I am very proud of that. *Doing It* I'm quite proud of because I took a lot of stick for that one, and it did damage me in some ways. I still get people saying 'oh you wrote that book and I thought you were a pile of shite but I read it and it's interesting'. And I really wanted to say it's alright to be filthy and it doesn't mean you're being sexist or horrible or any of those things. And I am very proud of *Kill All Enemies*. In some ways the one I like the best is actually probably *Bloodtide*: I was really pleased with that one.

A: I know you've recently been gathering tales not only from young people from this country who have had experiences of being in care or institutions, but also tales from young people in the Congo. Can you tell me a little more about that project?

M: I was approached by Save the Children who wanted to do some stuff with children's authors to try and promote their work. They said 'do you want to go somewhere?', so I said 'yeah, fantastic!' Then they gave me a list of all these dreadful places where all these awful things were happening. It was originally going to be Angola, but it turned out to be too expensive to stay there, so they picked the Dominican Republic of Congo instead. And I was sent to meet child witches and kids being accused of witchcraft, very often by their own parents, who were being hounded out of their families. That really fascinated me because it's got a lot of things I'm interested in—the touch of magic, plus the dreadful social issue—and it also seemed so incomprehensible that you would accuse a child of witchcraft. It did my head in, really.

I went out to Kinshasa and spent a week talking to the kids. They were very often from broken families and were basically just distressed, so they were coming up with odd behaviour and being accused of witchcraft. Everyone there believes in witches, so if they don't have any other explanation that's the answer. There are all these billions of little churches which are a really revolting combination of Christianity and the fetish churches, and some of them were just exploiting the situation. It's a relatively recent situation, because it's a product of the society being under huge stress, and the children showing signs of that stress. It was absolutely fascinating and kind of heartbreaking as well.

I spoke to the children, I spoke to the church leaders, I spoke to various people running various centres, and I think the idea was that Save the Children would make some stuff about it when we got back, but nothing ever happened. It was ridiculous really. I felt really bad about it, and I want to do something. It's supposed to be saving children, not sending authors off to watch the children.

But I have got all this material. While I was there I collected folk stories. I would tell the kids 'The Three Little Pigs' or 'Red Riding Hood' and I would get them to tell me stories. So I've got a great collection of stuff. I'm still writing it up and I will do something with it at some point. I was thinking maybe some of them might make good picturebook stories, but most of them are quite bloodthirsty so I don't know about that. Of course the Grimms' fairytale tradition is also very bloody, but by the time those get to picturebooks they've all been a bit toned down. And some of these Congo stories are really very bloodthirsty.

A: How did you feel about your role as 'white ethnographer'?

M: There's a bit of me that thinks I might like to do a novel on the child witch material, but the problem is I was only there for a week and I don't want to make a fool of myself by trying to write about events in a culture that's really very alien to me. It did get a bit bizarre on occasions. After I'd done the stuff in Kinshasa I thought 'I've got to go and see somewhere else'. I did a package where I flew to Mbandaka on the Equator and they drove me to this little village. The trip consisted of being paddled up river in these dug-out canoes, stopping off to visit various villages. But it was five guys paddling: one guide, one cook; some guys helping to put up the tent, and me. One white man sat in a canoe with all these beautiful young black guys paddling away, chanting and singing songs. I thought 'what am I doing, I'm like Livingstone or something. This is ludicrous, I feel like a fool!' But I was a tourist and that's how you have to be a tourist.

A: In your Preface to *Burning Issy*, you point out that many of those accused of witchcraft in seventeenth-century England were '[m]isrepresented, misunderstood, abused'. Did your research for this novel give you a particular insight into, or understanding of, the situation in Kinshasa?

M: The research for *Issy* was a long way before I went to the Congo, so it wasn't uppermost in my mind when I was over there. It was the case that the reading I did for *Issy* left me far more informed about the European witch hunts than I was before. There were certainly parallels, in that it was mainly, if not exclusively the poor and peculiar who were accused of witchcraft—no coincidence there, I think! On the other hand, the witch hunts in Britain seemed to be very rural whereas in Congo in the present day, it all seems very urban. So there are big differences. It's fascinating to think about the explosion of superstitions that happen in a rapidly growing city like Kinshasa. As far as I know, no one has ever done any work about cityscape folk tales. But having come back, actually the European witch hunts are really more of a mystery. It was such a major blood letting at the time of the Enlightenment, and had parallels with the hunt for heretics in the Catholic countries (as far as I can tell, witch hunts were mainly a Protestant phenomenon).

A: Issy learns about her own past through reclaiming a repressed memory; and part of the purpose of retelling of the witchcraft trials is about reclaiming a history of people 'who left us no record whatsover'. How do you go about telling stories like this one about the past?

M: Telling stories from the past—well, it depends on how much information you have; and in the case of the Pendle witches, or indeed any witches from that period, the answer is very little indeed. There is some indication that Demdyke thought that she was a witch, for instance, but given the techniques employed to confess a witch, her evidence is dodgy to say the least. There is almost nothing from the witches themselves. Particularly in a novel, where we deal so much with the inner life, we can only explore it imaginatively. Exploring people and their worlds imaginatively can, oddly enough, arrive at some surprising truths—sometimes truths more insightful than if we can confront something face to face. Except, in this case, there is no way of ever checking it. All we know is that the witches were desperately poor, and that they almost certainly used the threat of curses and so on to give a bit of a boost to their begging, but beyond that we know very little.

A: Stories feature as a central structural motif in this novel. Issy tells her own tale, but it is also bound up with the story of Iohan, as well as the grand narratives of gods and devils transmitted by their society. Storytelling—in the form of memory, confession, or myth—is also quite a slippery craft in this novel.

M: Well, the whole thing is a puzzle, really, isn't it? Issy doesn't know who she is or where she comes from—this is her central task in the book, to find out who she is. In doing so she has to find out who and what Iohan is, and Tolly and the rest of them, and of course the whole problem is working out which stories are the real ones and which ones aren't—very much the problem I had in writing the thing, I suppose.

I would say that storytelling has the role of exploring doubt, faith and belief. Also—and this is true in many ways of nearly all my books—of trying to work out what is important in life.

Further Reading

Although there is a good deal of journalism dedicated to Burgess's writing, there is less by way of published scholarly work. Furthermore, as Lydia Kokkola notes, 'discussions of his novels tend to focus on their social significance rather more than their literary qualities' ('Metamorphosis in Two Novels by Melvin Burgess: Denying and Disguising "Deviant" Desire', *Children's Literature in Education* 42(1) (March 2011): 56–69 at 57). I have therefore arranged this selection of further reading into three main sections:

1. a list of primary texts and biographical references;
2. material locating Burgess's fiction in the context of young adult literature, and discussing the social debates and controversies surrounding his work;
3. a selection of critical and thematic explorations of individual novels or linked groups of texts.

Newspaper and online articles have been included to demonstrate the range of responses to Burgess's work, as well as some general secondary sources to provide context for certain critical approaches or literary fields. Some sources will appear in more than one section.

Works by Melvin Burgess

Fiction

The Cry of the Wolf (London: Andersen Press, 1990)
Burning Issy (London: Andersen Press, 1992)
An Angel for May (London: Andersen Press, 1992)
The Baby and Fly-Pie (London: Andersen Press, 1993)
Loving April (London: Andersen Press, 1995)
The Earth Giant (London: Andersen Press, 1995)
Tiger, Tiger (London: Andersen Press, 1996)
Junk (London: Andersen Press, 1996)
Kite (London: Andersen Press, 1997)
The Copper Treasure (London: A & C Black, 1998)
Bloodtide (London: Andersen Press, 1999)
Old Bag, illustrated by Trevor Parkin (Edinburgh: Barrington Stoke, 1999)
The Ghost behind the Wall (London: Andersen Press, 2000)
The Birdman, illustrated by Ruth Brown (London: Andersen Press, 2000)
Lady: My Life as a Bitch (London: Andersen Press, 2001)
Billy Elliot (London: Chicken House, 2001)
Robbers on the Road (London: A & C Black, 2002)
Doing It (London: Andersen Press, 2003)

Bloodsong (London: Andersen Press, 2005)
Sara's Face (London: Andersen Press, 2006)
Nicholas Dane (London: Andersen Press, 2009)
Kill All Enemies (London: Penguin, 2011)
Hunger (London: Hammer/Arrow, 2013)
The Hit (Frome: Chicken House, 2013)

Short stories

'Going Out', in Alan Ross (ed.), *Signals: Thirty New Stories to Celebrate Thirty Years of the 'London Magazine'* (London: Constable, 1991): 18–24.

'The Visitor', in Wendy Cooling (ed.), *On the Run: Stories of Growing Up* (London: Dolphin, 1996).

'Odin's Day', in Wendy Cooling (ed.), *Centuries of Stories: New Stories for a New Millennium* (London: Collins, 1999): 111–24.

'AD 1000', in *Just in Time: Stories to Mark the Millennium* (London: Puffin, 1999): 58–72.

'Coming Home', in Miriam Hodgson (ed.), *Family Tree* (London: Mammoth, 1999): 124–36. Reprinted in *Shining On: A Collection of Top Stories in Aid of the Teen Cancer Trust* (London: Piccadilly Press, 2006): 21–33.

'Whose Face Do You See', in Wendy Cooling (ed.), *Mirrors: Sparkling New Stories from Prize-Winning Authors* (London: Collins, 2001): 95–111.

'Nala's Nightmare (Thailand)', in Anuj Goyal (ed.), *Higher Ground* (London: Chrysalis, 2006): 139–48.

'Bunker's Lane' (extract from *Nicholas Dane*), in Richard Zimler and Raša Sekulović (eds.), *The Children's Hours: Stories of Childhood* (London: Arcadia Books, 2008): 186–95.

'Chat Up Lines', in Keith Gray (ed.), *Losing It* (London: Random House, 2010): 49–70.

'The Ill-Fitting Man', in *Brainstorms: An Expression of Depression,* Vol. 2 (London: Little Episodes, 2010): 4–6. Originally published as a 'twittertale' at https://twitter.com/MelvinBurgess.

'Backwards' and 'The Double Devil', in Michael Steward (ed.), *Outside the Asylum: The Grist Anthology of the Best Short Fiction of 2012* (Huddersfield: Grist, 2011): 89–92, 93–94. Originally published as 'twittertales' at https://twitter.com/MelvinBurgess.

Radio, TV and multimedia

'The Bald Angel': radio play (Radio 4 Afternoon Play, 15 November 1988).

'The Well': multiplatform drama (Conker Media for BBC Switch, 2009; http://www.bbc.co.uk/switch/thewell).

Adaptations

Engler, Michael and Michael Spiller (Directors), *Life as We Know It* (based on *Doing It*): television series (ABC, 2004–2005).

Grahame, Jenny, *Making Junk: From Page to Screen*, School's Pack (London: English and Media Centre, 1999).

Kahn, Iqbal (Director), *The Baby and Fly Pie*: stageplay (2005).
Milligan, Peter (Writer) and Harley Cokeliss (Director), *An Angel for May*: television play (ITV, 2002).
Purchese, Barry (Writer) and Marcus White (Director), *Junk*: television series (BBC, 1999).
Retallack, John (Director), *Junk: Adapted for the Stage* (London: A&C Black, 2009).
Romer, Marcus (Director), *Bloodtide:* stageplay (2004).

Articles

'At Home with Mr Toad', *The Times Educational Supplement*, 18 December 1997: 20 (http://www.tes.co.uk/teaching-resource/At-home-with-Mr-Toad-74383/).
'Ban Sex and Drugs? Not in my Book', *The Times Educational Supplement*, 7 July 2000 (archived as 'Rethinking Literacy' at http://www.melvinburgess.net).
'Enid's Big Adventure: Is it Insane, or a Stroke of Genius?', *The Guardian*, 15 June 2000.
'In Search of Dribblers', *The Times Educational Supplement*, 30 March 2001.
'Three Cheers for Desire, Lust and Irresponsibility', *The Guardian*, 23 March 2003.
'Sympathy for the Devil', *Children's Literature in Education* 35(4) (December 2004): 289–300.
'Then, Thank God, We Grew Up', *The Guardian*, 27 May 2006.
'Fictional Males Lose the Plot', *The Times Educational Supplement*, 12 May 2008.
'Lost your Virginity, Son? Let's Have a Party', *The Times*, 5 July 2010, Features: 44–45.
'How Do You Solve a Problem Like a Family', *Mail on Sunday*, 25 July 2010.
'"The Rioters Did What We've Been Doing for Years; When the Chance Came to Get Something for Free They Grabbed it"', *The Times*, 7 September 2011, T2 Review: 4–5.

Biography and books: selected websites and interviews

Burgess's website is a treasure-house of resources and a good starting point for a critic of his work: it includes excerpts from reviews of his novels, archives of his non-fiction writing, blog posts retelling the tales shared with him by children during his trip to the Democratic Republic of Congo with Save the Children, and news about publications and public appearances. It is also worth searching www.youtube.com for interviews and talking heads with Burgess, as he frequently appears in new videos. I have included a small selection of interviews and biographical sketches for further reference.

Burgess's website: http://melvinburgess.wordpress.com/
Burgess's Twitter page: https://twitter.com/MelvinBurgess
Author profile at the British Council: http://literature.britishcouncil.org/melvin-burgess

Author profile at Andersen Press: http://www.andersenpress.co.uk/authors/view/28997
Author profile at Puffin: http://www.puffin.co.uk/nf/Author/AuthorPage/0,,1000038764,00.html
Author profile at Penguin: http://www.penguin.co.uk/nf/Author/AuthorPage/0,,1000038764,00.html
Ballinger, C., 'Know the Author: Melvin Burgess', *Magpies* 14(2) (1999): 14–16.
Douglas, Jonathan, 'Robert Cormier Meets Melvin Burgess', *Achukabooks* (July 2000) (www.achuka.co.uk/special/cormburg.htm).
Lafferty, Fiona, 'From Rural Idylls to Class-A Drugs', *The Daily Telegraph*, 19 July 1997.
'Melvin Burgess', *Something about the Author* 198 (Detroit: Gale, 2009).
Robinson, David, 'Reality Bites', *The Scotsman*, 25 August 2001: 4.
Sennitt, Jo, 'Spotlight on Melvin Burgess', *School Librarian* 52(1) (Spring 2004): 12.
'Special Issue on Melvin Burgess' *Lecture Jeune* 139 (September 2011) (http://www.lecturejeunesse.com/index1024.php?page=revue_numeros&menu=1&num_revue=68).
Spring, Kit, 'Children's Literature: Smack, Child Abuse, Teenage Pregnancy… and Now, that Boy Who Wants to be a Ballet Dancer', *The Observer*, 15 April 2001, Review: 16.
Treneman, Ann, 'Needle-Sharp Tales for Teens: Interview with Melvin Burgess', *The Independent*, 17 July 1997: 20.

Writing for young adults and controversy

The supposed controversy surrounding Burgess's YA fiction is not the central theme of this collection, but it has generated much debate, albeit of the 'paper tiger' variety. Although Anne Fine and Rachel Johnson complain about the explicit content of *Doing It*, and Brian Alderson despairs of the "drab, anaesthetizing prose" of *Junk* and *Bloodtide*, most critics and commentators are broadly positive about Burgess's project to write honestly for young people. Articles by Jenny Daniels, David Rudd and Claire Walsh help to identify the literary quality and complexity of his YA works; and these critical analyses support Burgess's own claims to engage with 'the devil'. Carolyn Smith offers a useful overview of controversy in the history of young adult literature, while studies by Alison Waller and Roberta Seelinger Trites will support readers in locating Burgess's work in this field more generally.

Adams, Lauren, '*Go Ask Alice*: A Second Look', *Horn Book Magazine* 74(5) (September–October 1998): 587–92.
Alderson, Brian, 'Editors Absconditi', *Horn Book Magazine* 77(3) (May/June 2001): 371–6 (http://archive.hbook.com/magazine/articles/2001/may01_alderson.asp).
Brooks, Libby, 'The "Truth about Kids" Interview with Melvin Burgess', *The Guardian* (13 August 2001), Features: 6.

Brown, Chris, 'Review of *Doing It*', *School Librarian* 51(3) (Autumn 2003): 164.
Burgess, Melvin, 'Ban Sex and Drugs? Not in my Book', *Times Educational Supplement*, 7 July 2000 (archived as 'Rethinking Literacy' at http://www.melvinburgess.net).
Burgess, Melvin, 'Sympathy for the Devil', *Children's Literature in Education* 35(4) (December 2004): 289–300.
Daniels, Jenny, '"Harming Young Minds": Moral Dilemmas and Cultural Concerns', in Eve Bearne and Victor Watson (eds.), *Where Texts and Children Meet* (Psychology Press, 2000): 161–6.
Eccleshare, Julia, 'Teenage Fiction: Realism, Romances, Contemporary Problem Novels', in Peter Hunt (ed.), *International Companion Encyclopedia of Children's Literature*, 2nd edn (London and New York: Routledge, 2004): 542–55.
Fine, Anne, 'Filth, Whichever Way You Look at It', *The Guardian*, 29 March 2003, Saturday Review: 33.
Hewings, Ann and Nicola J. Watson, 'Introduction to *Junk*', in Heather Montgomery and Nicola J. Watson (eds.), *Children's Literature: Classic Texts and Contemporary Trends* (Basingstoke: Palgrave Macmillan, 2009): 313–14.
Horn, Caroline, 'Breaking the Taboos', *The Bookseller* 4778 (18 July 1997): 26–7.
Johnson, Rachel, 'Read Me a Dirty Story, Mummy', *The Spectator*, 24 July 2004.
Jones, Nicolette, '"It's Not Books that Corrupt"', *The Times*, 17 July 1997.
Moss, Stephen, 'Parents: Sex and Drugs and a Damn Good Read', *The Guardian*, 9 July 1997: T8.
Rees, Jasper, 'We're All Reading Children's Books', *The Daily Telegraph*, 17 November 2003: 1.
Richards, Chris, 'Writing for Young Adults: Melvin Burgess and Mark Haddon', in *Forever Young: Essays on Young Adult Fictions* (New York: Peter Lang, 2008): 51–64.
Richards, Chris, 'Young Adult Fictions', in *Young People, Popular Culture and Education* (London: Continuum, 2011): 116–31.
Rudd, David, 'A Young Person's Guide to the Fictions of *Junk*', *Children's Literature in Education* 30(2) (1999): 119–26.
Rosen, Michael, '*Junk* and Other Realities: The Tough World of Children's Literature', *English and Media Magazine* 37 (1997): 4–6.
Smith, Carolyn, 'Exploring the History and Controversy of Young Adult Literature', *New Review of Children's Literature and Librarianship* 8(1) (2002): 1–11.
Tilley, Carol, 'Melvin Burgess', in Bernice E. Cullinan, Bonnie Kunzel and Deborah Wooten (eds.), *The Continuum Encyclopedia of Young Adult Literature* (New York and London: Continuum, 2005): 18–19.
Turin, Joelle, 'Disturbing Books', *Bookbird* 41(3) (July 2003): 6.
Trites, Roberta Seelinger, *Disturbing the Universe: Power and Repression in Adolescent Literature* (Iowa City: University of Iowa Press, 2000).
Tucker, Nicholas, 'Angels with Dirty Minds', *The Independent*, 17 May 2003, Features: 29.

Waller, Alison, *Constructing Adolescence in Fantastic Realism* (London: Routledge, 2009).
Walsh, Clare, 'Troubling the Boundary between Fiction for Adults and Fiction for Children: A Study of Melvin Burgess', in Pat Pinsent (ed.), *Books and Boundaries: Writers and their Audiences*, Papers from the NCRCL/IBBY conference held at Roehampton Institute London on 15 November 2003 (Lichfield: Pied Piper, 2004): 142–53.

Themes

Gender and sexuality

Of particular interest to critics debating the challenging nature of Burgess's fiction is the treatment of gender and sexuality in his young adult novels. The author's positive attitude towards celebrating sex in books for young people is well documented in his journalism, and critical weight is given to this stance in work by Kim Reynolds, Ed Sullivan, and Jason Kurtz and Nicholle Schuelke. Other scholars and commentators focus on Burgess's representation of male and female characters. Michele Gill commends his warm portrayal of male friendship; on the other hand Natasha Walter worries that *Lady* offers a 'middle-aged man's fantasy of a teenage girl' and Maria Nikolajeva suggests it represents 'a male writer's contempt and fear of a wild and uncontrollable female' (135), while Chris Richards and David Mellor explore the dangers of writing towards heterosexual normativity. Claire Walsh and Lydia Kokkola provide more ambivalent readings, identifying tensions between Burgess's radical impulses and his production of conventional codes of early sexuality, masculinity and femininity. Christine Wilkie-Stibbs and Annette Wannamaker offer good theoretical introductions to gender and children's literature.

Burgess, Melvin, 'Fictional Males Lose the Plot', *Times Educational Supplement*, 12 May 2008: 23.
Burgess, Melvin, 'Three Cheers for Desire, Lust and Irresponsibility', *The Guardian*, 23 March 2003.
Burgess, Melvin, 'Lost your Virginity, Son? Let's Have a Party', *The Times*, 5 July 2010, Features: 44–5.
Gill, Michele, 'Best Mates: An Exploration of Male Adolescent Friendships in Contemporary Young Adult Fictions', *New Review of Children's Literature and Librarianship* 14(1) (2008): 1–17.
Kokkola, Lydia, 'Metamorphosis in Two Novels by Melvin Burgess: Denying and Disguising "Deviant" Desire', *Children's Literature in Education* 42(1) (March 2011): 56–69.
Kurtz, Jason and Nicholle Schuelke, 'Blume, Burgess, and Beyond: Sexuality and the Young Adult Novel', *VOYA* 34(3) (August 2011): 228–30.
Mellor, David, 'The *Doing It* Debate: Sexual Pedagogy and the Disciplining of the Child/Adult Boundary', *Sexualities* 15(3/4) (2012): 437–54.

Nikolajeva, Maria, *Power, Voice and Subjectivity in Literature for Young Readers* (New York and Abingdon: Routledge, 2010).
Reynolds, Kim, 'Baby, You're the Best: Sex and Sexuality in Contemporary Juvenile Fiction', in *Radical Children's Literature: Future Visions and Aesthetic Transformations in Juvenile Fiction* (Basingstoke: Palgrave Macmillan, 2007): 114–30.
Richards, Chris, 'Writing for Young Adults: Melvin Burgess and Mark Haddon', in *Forever Young: Essays on Young Adult Fictions* (New York: Peter Lang, 2008): 51–64.
Sullivan, Ed, 'Going All the Way: First-Time Sexual Experiences of Teens in Fiction', *VOYA: Voice of Youth Advocates* 26(6) (February 2004): 461–3.
Walsh, Clare, 'Troubling the Boundary between Fiction for Adults and Fiction for Children: A Study of Melvin Burgess', in Pat Pinsent (ed.), *Books and Boundaries: Writers and their Audiences*, Papers from the NCRCL/IBBY conference held at Roehampton Institute London on 15 November 2003 (Lichfield: Pied Piper, 2004): 142–53.
Walter, Natasha, 'Reading between the Lines', *The Independent*, 10 August 2001, Comment: 5.
Wannamaker, Annette, *Boys in Children's Literature and Popular Culture: Masculinity, Abjection, and the Fictional Child* (London: Routledge, 2012).
Wilkie-Stibbs, Christine, *The Feminine Subject in Children's Literature* (London: Routledge, 2002).

Animals

Walter Hogan, Maria Lassén-Seger and, to a lesser degree, Mark Vogel, all address a range of Burgess's animal books within wider survey studies of animals and animal-human metamorphosis. Peter Hollindale and Lydia Kokkola focus specifically on Burgess's work, with Hollindale identifying *The Cry of the Wolf* as an 'exceptionally important novel' that recasts the wolf as victim-hero, and Kokkola challenging the perception that his animal fantasies are radical in their construction of sexualized childhood. Margaret Blount's general critical text on animal stories is still a useful starting point for thinking about the genre, as is Keith Barker's more recent essay.

Barker, Keith, 'Animal Stories', in Peter Hunt (ed.), *The International Companion Encyclopedia of Children's Literature* (London: Routledge, 2004): 270–92.
Blount, Margaret, *Animal Land: The Creatures of Children's Fiction* (London: Hutchinson, 1974).
Hogan, Walter, *Animals in Young Adult Fiction* (Lanham, MD: Scarecrow Press, 2009).
Hollindale, Peter, 'Why the Wolves Are Running', *The Lion and the Unicorn* 23(1) (1999): 97–115.
Kokkola, Lydia, 'Metamorphosis in Two Novels by Melvin Burgess: Denying and Disguising "Deviant" Desire', *Children's Literature in Education* 42(1) (March 2011): 56–69.

Lassén-Seger, Maria, *Adventures into Otherness: Child Metamorphs in Late Twentieth-Century Literature* (Åbo: Åbo Akademi University Press, 2006).
Vogel, Mark, 'The Animal Within: Recognising the Fullness of Adolescent Selves', *The Alan Review* (Winter 2005): 59–64.

Family

Burgess takes a lighthearted look at the modern family in his article for the *Mail on Sunday*, while three scholarly works represented here examine the nature of family and familial roles in Burgess's Icelandic saga novels, *Bloodtide* and *Bloodsong*. The authors of 'New Social Orders' and 'Ties that Bind' set these novels in the context of changing concepts of identity and family in the twenty-first century, while Kay Sambell focuses particularly on the figure of the monstrous child. Claudia Nelson reads Burgess's *The Baby and Fly Pie* against the Victorian waif tale, *Jessica's First Prayer* (1866) by Hesba Stretton, suggesting that they express similar anxieties about the uncanny nature of homelessness, and 'unsettle our ideas about respectability, the family, and the self' (120). Ann Alston and Liz Thiel's books do not cover Burgess's work, but are a useful introduction to themes of family.

Alston, Ann, *The Family in English Children's Literature* (London: Routledge, 2008).
Bradford, Clare, Kerry Mallan, John Stephens and Robyn McCallum, 'Ties that Bind: Reconceptualising Home and Family', in *New World Orders in Contemporary Children's Literature: Utopian Transformations* (Basingstoke: Palgrave Macmillan, 2008): 130–53.
Burgess, Melvin, 'How Do You Solve a Problem Like a Family', *Mail on Sunday*, 25 July 2010.
Mallan, Kerry, Clare Bradford and John Stephens, 'New Social Orders: Reconceptualising Family and Community in Utopian Fiction', *Papers: Explorations into Children's Literature* 15(2) (September 2005): 6–20.
Nelson, Claudia, 'The Unheimlich Maneuver: Uncanny Domesticity in the Urban Waif Tale', in Kerry Mallan and Sharyn Pearce (eds.), *Youth Cultures: Texts, Images, and Identities* (Westport, CT and London: Praeger, 2003): 109–21.
Sambell, Kay, 'Questioning Contemporary Views of Children and Childhood in Crisis: Burgess's *Bloodtide* as a Fantasy of the Monstrous', in Nickianne Moody and Clare Horrocks (eds.), *Children's Fantasy Fiction: Debates for the Twenty First Century* (Liverpool: Association for Research in Popular Fictions, 2005): 39–55.
Thiel, Liz, *The Fantasy of Family: Nineteenth-Century Children's Literature and the Myth of the Domestic Ideal* (London: Routledge, 2007).

Critical readings

Burgess's novels have been the subject of some analyses that employ critical theory as a major tool or framework. These approaches can illuminate texts in new ways. Although Stephen Thomson does not explicitly identify his theoretical perspective in his early essay on *Junk*, he draws on concepts of identity and performativity that have roots in cultural theory and gender studies in order to argue that the novel produces a version of adolescence that is intrinsically performative. John Stephens also examines the constructed nature of reality in *Junk*, in this case introducing the basic tenets of literary realism, and the stylistic device of metonymy in particular, to shape his discussion. Pat Pinsent's analysis of *Sara's Face* comes from a psychoanalytic standpoint, and while Roderick McGillis's chapter on humour in children's literature does not focus exclusively on Burgess's work, it applies Bakhtin's idea of the carnivalesque and the Lacanian concept of the 'Real' to *Lady: My Life as a Bitch* to good effect.

Pinsent, Pat, 'The Theme of Facial Disfigurement in Some Recent Books for Young Readers', in Jenny Plastow (ed.), *The Story and the Self: Children's Literature: Some Psychoanalytic Perspectives* (Hatfield: University of Hertfordshire Press, 2008): 98–109.

McGillis, Roderick, 'Humour and the Body in Children's Literature', in Matthew Grenby and Andrea Immel (eds.), *The Cambridge Companion to Children's Literature* (Cambridge: Cambridge University Press, 2009): 258–70.

Stephens, John, '"And it's So Real": Versions of Reality in Melvin Burgess's *Junk*', in Heather Montgomery and Nicola J. Watson (eds.), *Children's Literature: Classic Texts and Contemporary Trends* (Basingstoke: Palgrave Macmillan and the Open University, 2009): 320–9.

Thomson, Stephen, 'The Real Adolescent: Performance and Negativity in Melvyn Burgess's *Junk*', *The Lion and the Unicorn* 23(1) (January 1999): 22–9.

Index

Note: 'n.' after a page reference refers to a note on that page.

Printed in China